HM
141
.M56
1961

301.155 M766p
The path to leadership [by] Field-M

Y0-ASV-712

3 1569 00190 413 2

COLLIER LIBRARY
FLORENCE STATE COLLEGE
FLORENCE, ALABAMA

WITHDRAWN
FROM
LIBRARY

THE PATH TO LEADERSHIP

THE PATH TO LEADERSHIP

FIELD-MARSHAL THE VISCOUNT
MONTGOMERY
OF ALAMEIN, K.G.

Bernard Law Montgomery

G. P. PUTNAM'S SONS
NEW YORK

© 1961 by Bernard Law, Viscount Montgomery of Alamein

FIRST AMERICAN EDITION

All rights reserved. This book, and parts thereof, must not be reproduced in any form without permission.

Library of Congress Catalog
Card Number: 61-9230

MANUFACTURED IN THE UNITED STATES OF AMERICA

Contents

	INTRODUCTION	page 7
1	LEADERSHIP—WHAT IS IT?	9
2	MILITARY COMMAND—SOME REFLECTIONS	20
3	MILITARY COMMAND—SOME EXAMPLES	28
4	POLITICAL LEADERSHIP—ALFRED AND CROMWELL	53
5	ABRAHAM LINCOLN	73
6	JAWARHALAL NEHRU	83
7	GENERAL DE GAULLE	95
8	CHURCHILL AND ALANBROOKE	112
9	A GREAT CIVIL SERVANT—SIR JAMES GRIGG	133
10	A CAPTAIN OF INDUSTRY—NUFFIELD	143
11	LEADERSHIP OF YOUTH	158
12	LEADERSHIP IN THE WEST	183
13	COMMUNIST LEADERSHIP	201
14	A BACKWARD LOOK—MOSES	227
15	CONCLUSIONS	233
16	THE EPILOGUE	253

Introduction

FOR reasons which will become obvious to the reader, I have entitled this book *The Path to Leadership*. My practical experience of leadership has been almost entirely military; and here it has been extensive, covering as it does fifty years of unbroken service on the active list of the British Army.

But leadership extends into far wider fields than the purely military—national, political and industrial, for example, and in these I have no first-hand experience. But I have known and closely observed many of the chief actors in these wider spheres, and I consider that I am entitled to draw on my experience, knowledge and observation, in order to try to discover the principles on which leadership should be based.

We are met at the outset with one great difficulty. The words "leader" and "leadership" are used to cover a wide range, if not variety, of meaning. Often by "leaders" we mean no more than those whom fate, luck and sometimes intrigue have placed at the head of a particular branch of affairs—without reference to the quality of the leadership which they exercise, or its influence on others for good or ill.

My purpose goes far beyond this. *It is to seek to discover what it is which makes a man capable of exercising his position at the head of affairs for the good of his fellows.*

I hope, therefore, that in what I have written I have avoided ambiguity in my use of the words, and in particular have never allowed it to obscure my objective, which is, I repeat, to discover what it is which enables men to influence or even control other men for their own good, and for the good of their children and children's children.

In my first chapter I discuss this broad objective in a some-

INTRODUCTION

what general way. In subsequent chapters I examine the leadership exercised by various persons whom the world has, rightly or wrongly, designated as leaders. And finally in the last chapters I consider what general principles have emerged—if any.

I doubt if such a book as this has ever been written before; if one has, it did not come my way. The subject is, of course, difficult to handle, so much so that when I suggested to a friend that I might attempt it he replied, "I will give you the same advice often given to a man contemplating matrimony: don't."

Difficult or not, I decided to have a shot at it. Here is the result. Possibly somebody else will now take up the challenge and produce some better thoughts on the subject; if so, good luck to him.

No index will be found at the end. My experience tells me that on receiving a book many turn at once to their own name in the index, look up what has been written about them, and then put the book down—having no further interest. That is not the way to read this book!

Certain of my friends have helped me, reading the drafts and suggesting improvements. They are not mentioned by name for fear of causing embarrassment, but to them all I extend my grateful thanks.

Finally, I apologise if I have caused anger or offence to anybody.

Montgomery of Alamein

F.M.

Isington Mill,
Alton, Hampshire.

CHAPTER ONE

LEADERSHIP—WHAT IS IT?

When we human beings, be we men or women, are gathered together in large masses, or even in small groups, we need leadership. The question then arises—what kind of leadership is needed, how is it best exercised among these different masses or groups? In fact, what *is* leadership?

Expressed in its simplest terms, a leader is one who can get people to follow him. Such a person can, of course, be good or bad.

We must be clear what is the opposite of leadership. It is "misleadership," for want of a better word. There are many brave and strong-minded people whom one wouldn't follow on any account—because one doesn't know what they stand for, or where they are going. Leadership which is evil, while it may succeed temporarily, always carries with it the seeds of its own destruction. Good examples of evil leadership would be Hitler and Mussolini. Misleadership is something false coming through a strong personality, and the stronger the personality the worse the ultimate crash. But both kinds, good and evil, would need to have courage, and the will to exercise their leadership—and thus commend themselves to others. We can say at once that leadership should properly be exercised by people in authority. What matters is how they lead. When they have no power to enforce their will, then much will depend on their personality, on what they are.

In no case will good results be obtained unless the leader is a man who can be looked up to, whose personal judgment is trusted, and who can inspire and warm the hearts of those he leads—gaining their trust and confidence, and explaining what is needed in language which can be understood. It would seem, therefore, that *the beginning of leadership is a battle for the hearts and minds of men*, and this I firmly believe is the essence of the whole matter.

The first approach to leadership should be intellectual, and a definition is needed. My own experience teaches me that the following definition is about right:

> The capacity and the will to rally men and women to a common purpose, and the character which will inspire confidence.

It is no use having the capacity if you haven't got the will to use it.

It involves a close study of human nature; it is "men" that are the factors of reality and importance. The greatest of all Leaders known to history once said:

> " I will make you fishers of men."

What Christ meant was that He would teach His disciples how to win the hearts of men, implying that leadership has to be taught. Some will say that leaders are born, not made, and that you can't make a leader by teaching, or training. I don't agree with this entirely. While it is true that some men have within themselves the instincts and qualities of leadership in a much greater degree than others, and some men will never have the character to make leaders, I believe that leadership can be developed by training. In the military sphere, I reckon that soldiers will be more likely to follow a leader in whose military knowledge they have confidence, rather than a man with much greater personality but with not the same obvious knowledge of his job. To the junior leader himself the mere fact of responsibility brings courage; the mere fact that by his position as the recognised head of a group of men he is responsible for their lives and comfort, gives him less time to think of his own fears and so brings him a greater degree of resolution than if he were not the leader. I know I found this to be the case myself in 1914, when as a young lieutenant I commanded a platoon and had to lead them in charges against entrenched Germans, or undertake patrol activities in no-man's-land. By the training I had received from my superiors in peacetime, I gained confidence in my ability to deal with any situation likely to confront a young officer of my rank in war; this increased my morale and my powers of leading my platoon, and later my company.

In other words, it is almost true to say that leaders are "made" —rather than born. Many men who are not natural leaders may have some small spark of the qualities which are needed; this spark must be looked for, and then developed and brought on by training. But except in the armed forces this training is not given. In civilian circles it seems to be considered that leadership descends on men like dew from heaven; it does not. There are principles of leadership just as there are principles of war, and these have to be studied; let us look at some of the more important.

Leadership is based on truth and character. A leader must himself be the servant of a truth, and he must make that truth the focus of a common purpose. He must then have the force of character necessary to inspire others to follow him with confidence. Both are necessary, truth and character—with will-power in the character.

What is "character"? Put simply, it is knowing what you want to do and having the determination to do it—and in a way which will inspire confidence in those around you or for whom you are responsible.

Then the leader must have infectious optimism, and the determination to persevere in the face of difficulties. He must also radiate confidence, relying on moral and spiritual principles and resources to work out rightly even when he himself is not too certain of the material outcome. He must have a sound judgment in which others will have confidence, and a good knowledge of human nature. He must be able to see his problems truly and whole. Self-control is a vital component of his make-up.

He must be a good picker of men, a good selector of subordinates—in fact, a good judge of character. Some think that pre-eminence in sport is necessary in a leader; it may help in developing leadership but is in no way a necessity; there is no need to be a gladiator in sport to be a leader.

When all is said and done, the true leader must be able to dominate, and finally to master, the events which surround him; once he lets events get the better of him, those under him will lose confidence and he will cease to be of value as a leader.

I suggest that the final test of a leader is the feeling you have when you leave his presence after a conference or interview. Have you a feeling of uplift and confidence? Are you clear as to what is to be done, and what is your part of the task? Are you determined to pull your weight in achieving the object? Or is your feeling the reverse?

To-day, leadership is being challenged in a good many fields —national, political, industrial—and by a good many groups, youth among them. But few of us can say where the trouble lies. Must you be a genius to find the answer? Surely not! The fundamental elements of leadership will be found in the man, in his sincerity and his selflessness, and whether he has the right answer.

Has religion anything to do with it? There are many notable leaders to-day who are of different religious faiths, and some of none. But all are motivated by some inward conviction which appeals to their followers—for example, Nehru of India, Tito of Yugoslavia, Nasser of Egypt, Ben Gurion of Israel. And to go back in history, there are Mohammed and Buddha—pretty successful leaders in their own particular spheres if the number of their followers is any criterion. I firmly believe that in all branches of life in a Western democracy, with our long Christian tradition, a leader will not appeal to many unless he possesses the Christian virtues.

Can we define the Christian virtues? Many books have been written on the subject and it will be difficult for a soldier to contribute any more—but I must try. The great theologians of the Church seem to have based their thinking on the pagan classification of:

"The Four Cardinal Virtues"

because all other virtues hinge on those four. Their four cardinal virtues were:

1. *Prudence.*—The habit of referring all matters to divine guidance. On this virtue will hinge wisdom, impartiality and tact.
2. *Justice.*—The habit of giving to everybody, including God and man himself, their due. On this will hinge the duties of religion, obedience, and gratitude—also integrity, and goodwill to others.
3. *Temperance.*—Self-control, for the highest development of man's nature, and also for personal and social ends. On this hinges purity, humility and patience.
4. *Fortitude.*—The Spirit which resists, endures, and triumphs over the trials and temptations of life. On this will hinge moral courage, industry, and self-discipline.

The theologians appear to have filled these virtues with a Christian content, changing their emphasis somewhat—probably because they held that the Christian Gospel helps all men to realise that which is universally within them, and also because these four cardinal virtues are psychologically correct and deal with the intellect, the desires, and the will.

There is also the trio of St. Paul—faith, hope, and charity—which are the "Theological Virtues." The more "Christian" a man is, the more will his inner dispositions be controlled by these theological virtues.

Fundamentally it amounts to this—get your major purpose clear, take off your plate all which hinders that purpose and hold hard to all which helps it, and then go ahead with a clear conscience, courage, sincerity and selflessness.

I hope this short analysis will help to give the reader my ideas on a very difficult subject—but one which we must get right before we pass on.

Who are the great leaders of all time? They were the founders of the great religions—Christ, Mohammed, Buddha. I note two outstanding qualities in these three leaders.

First. Their power of concentration.

It is interesting to recall that all three disappeared for a certain definite period in their lives—presumably to prepare for what was to follow. The ministry of Our Lord did not begin until He was about the age of 30, and little is known of His life during His years of childhood and youth. But we know that for long periods He was often alone, in the wilderness and elsewhere.

Mohammed (about A.D. 600) went into religious retirement, during which time he is reported to have communed much with the angel Gabriel.

Buddha (about the 4th century B.C.) sat for six years under a Bo tree, a sort of wild fig, during which period of concentration he received the enlightenment he needed to found his religion.

I would like to pause for a moment on this matter of "concentration." The capacity to concentrate is essential in a leader; the constant exercise of this ability makes him a disciplined human being. It enables him to simplify a problem, to discover the essentials on which all action must be based and the details which are unimportant—in fact, to separate the gold from the dross.

Secondly. I note their arrival at a decision.

The capacity for decision is a pre-requisite in a leader. In their case a decision was necessary before emerging to begin their crusades. Two of them, Christ and Mohammed, came to a decision to serve a Universal Being and lay down a way of life for all humanity. I am not so sure in this matter about Buddha; I think his was a religion without God, although modern Buddhists are much influenced by Christian thought.

When all is said and done, the work of these three has certainly lasted; therefore they must head any list of great leaders, and it is not easy to add to the list. We might attempt it later on, when we have had a look at certain leaders of the past—and perhaps even of the present.

Was the private life of these three part-cause of their influence and success? Must a leader's private life be above reproach?

My own opinion is that in this particular matter, and indeed in all other respects, the most powerful factor is the sincerity of the man, his example and influence—particularly in respect to the Christian virtues—whether he be in the upper or lower classes of our society. I do not see how anybody can set out to be a leader if his private life is not above reproach. In such cases those he leads will cease to respect him, they will withdraw their confidence, and when that happens his leadership will quickly lose its effectiveness.

Did these three take, or follow, one consistent line? Many will say that "consistency" is a necessary qualification for sound leadership. But there are some who would add that consistency is not always possible, and that life is, as Heraclitus said, a strife of opposites, and of opposites which cannot always be reconciled —in this world at any rate. For example, there is a law of love which is binding on every Christian, and by this law all warfare must stand condemned as evil—as says the Christian pacifist. But love may also involve defending your house, as said the Christ.

The Bible serves to show that the matter is not quite so simple as some seem to think. Of whom did Christ say: " I have not found so great faith, no, not in Israel."?

And who, looking up at the Cross, said: " Truly this was the son of God."?

In both cases, a Roman soldier.

And who saved St. Paul from the mob? Roman soldiers, and with what results!

It has always seemed to me that those soldiers of the New Testament, simple men, and men whose trade was war, stand as symbols of the difficulties with which the Christian is beset in this world of politics and war. His basic difficulty is that he lives in an imperfect and disordered world. There is the *ideal* of love, whose demands are unconditional. There is also the *fact* of human corruption; this might be termed the law of human limitations, or in old-fashioned and sometimes misunderstood language, the law of original sin. So we have to work within the situation created by human nature as we find it. That means, for example, that justice cannot prevail without the sanction of force. It also means that the violent have to be dealt with. I reckon that the consistent Christian pacifist ought to retire from civil society altogether. If he rejects the use of force, can he fairly claim police protection?

It is all very difficult. And one has to do some quiet thinking before discarding an undeviating consistency as an essential attribute of a leader—since consistency may lie in pursuing the same end by diametrically opposite roads, sometimes fighting and sometimes not. But I consider that consistency in the great moral issues, and in the Christian virtues, is vital to his success in the free world.

Have great leaders outstanding qualities and virtues? Some qualities are obvious and straightforward. For example, a thorough knowledge of his job, of his profession, is an absolute pre-requisite; and then a never-ending study to keep himself up-to-date. Not only must he be a master of his trade; he must also be always learning. As William Cowper said:

"Knowledge is proud that he has learn'd so much;
Wisdom is humble that he knows no more."

Some qualities are exceedingly tricky, but important. One such would be a knowledge of his own language, and in this respect I fear I have sometimes erred. Let me explain.

Many of my contacts in Europe have been anxious to find out what sort of person was General de Gaulle—amongst them President Tito and Mr. Khrushchev, and it is of these two that my story will deal. Both said to me—"Tell me about de Gaulle. What is he like these days?"

Now I know President de Gaulle fairly well; I like him and I admire him, but more about that anon. I first began to know him during Hitler's war when he was, at times, somewhat difficult. To-day he is a very different man. So my reply to both Tito and Khrushchev was the same—" He has mellowed." My difficulties then began, because it is exceedingly difficult to explain to a foreigner what is meant by this very English expression. With both I failed to explain what the word meant. With Tito I was so unwise as to take for an example a bottle of wine, which, I said, matured, or mellowed, with age. He looked at me with a twinkle in his eye and said—" What do you know about wine; you don't drink it." I gave it up, defeated.

With Khrushchev, I attempted no explanation. When the interpreter had failed to translate the meaning, a dictionary was demanded. The correct page was found, and Khrushchev, having examined the word, said—" Yes, I see, it means a little drunk." I quickly changed the conversation! And when I got back to England I looked the word up in the *Concise Oxford Dictionary* and saw that one definition of the term mellow is "partly intoxicated." I decided not to use the word again in international conversation!

What we want to find is a good leader. But how shall we recognise him? He must definitely have the confidence of those he leads. Leadership is a major problem in our age and, indeed, in every age. If we can contribute towards its right solution, we shall certainly have achieved something. But we must tackle the problem fearlessly, and say what we believe to be the truth; any other approach will be of no avail.

Before we proceed further I would like to summarise some of my thoughts on the subject.

The first characteristic of the leader we seek must be a deep, great, and genuine sincerity. The sincerity I mean is that type of which the man himself is not conscious—it is there naturally—he just cannot help being sincere.

Added to sincerity must be selflessness, by which I mean absolute devotion to the cause he serves with no thought of personal reward or aggrandisement.

Then comes the ability to dominate, and finally to master, the events which encompass him. Once he fails in this respect, his leadership will become suspect—since he will lose the respect and confidence of those he leads.

Overall then, it is "captaincy" which counts, or leadership in the higher sense, together with the power of decision; this latter quality, decision, cannot be exaggerated. I would add to this, a bit of luck—which is seized with both hands and turned to boldness.

But the leader must also have a genuine interest in, and a real knowledge of, humanity—which will always be the raw material of his trade. He must understand that bottled-up in men are great emotional forces and these must have an outlet in a way which is positive and constructive, and which will warm their hearts and excite their imagination. If this can be done, and the forces can be harnessed and directed towards a common purpose, the greatest achievements become possible. But if the approach to this human problem is cold and impersonal, little can be achieved. Here is the basic lesson of leadership, whether it is in the military or civilian sphere; after all, the soldier and the worker are the same man. I agree there is a difference in application, in that the worker has to be "persuaded" and cannot be ordered to do something he doesn't want to do.

Of course it is always a good thing to persuade the soldier that what you want him to do is right, but in the upshot he can be ordered and he has to obey. But in spite of the difference, the lesson is comparable.

The more I ponder over this problem, the more I become convinced that the fundamental elements are—"the man," his sincerity and selflessness, his ability to grasp the conditions of a problem, and then to make the right decision.

I once heard that some general reported during an awkward situation in a battle:

"We will do all that is possible at once; the impossible will take a little longer."

I think the story was told by Field-Marshal Slim, but I am not sure.

It is not "impossible" to find the answer to the persistent

LEADERSHIP—WHAT IS IT?

problem of leadership, but it will take a little time. Let me repeat again, at the risk of being wearisome—it is "the man" which matters, his capacity for the right decision, and his knowledge of human nature.

We will have to consider certain types, and will begin with military command.

CHAPTER TWO

MILITARY COMMAND—
SOME REFLECTIONS

MY AIM in this short chapter is to give the reader a brief introduction to the subject of military command before considering certain examples of how it has been exercised in the past. A point to note is that whereas the title of the book indicates "leadership," in the military sphere I have decided to refer to it as "command." This has been done in order to emphasise the different way in which the handling of men is carried out in the two spheres—the general can give orders, the political leader can only persuade.

I have written so much in my *Memoirs* about my own doctrine of command that it is not necessary to go over the ground again. But as we are going to have a look at certain commanders in the next chapter, a few reflections on the subject first will be worthwhile.

It is clear that military command is much easier when the final decision, political *and* military, lies in one hand—that of the military commander himself. There are many examples from the distant past—Hannibal, the great Carthaginian; Cæsar, dictator of Rome; Jenghiz Khan, Emperor of the Mongols.

In later periods there are other good examples. There is Gustavus Adolphus, born in 1594. He became King of Sweden when he was 17 years old. Under him the Swedish Army proved itself superior to all other armies in Europe. He was ruthless in weeding out inefficient generals and promoting younger officers; he considered that merit was more likely to win battles than seniority. He ensured that the morale and loyalty of his soldiers did not have to stand undue strains from inferior equipment, hunger, or lack of pay. Others may have been more brilliant in strategic and tactical conceptions, but Gustavus Adolphus was certainly one of the greatest creators of an army that we know.

Then there is Charles XII, who became King of Sweden in 1697, at the age of 15. But he can hardly go down to history as one of the great captains. I can find no evidence that he saw clearly what he wanted to achieve; he overestimated the military value of his allies and underestimated the great powers of resistance of the Russians. He was completely ignorant of international politics. He had, indeed, great physical courage, but he lacked wisdom and intelligence; he finished up as a prisoner of the Turks. I suppose he was the last king who actually fought in the front line with his soldiers, and who was killed in battle at the head of his army—receiving a bullet in his head from a sniper during his campaign against Norway in 1718. I have often wondered what they think of him in Sweden. My own assessment would be that he had little regard for the lives of his soldiers, and brought his country to the brink of ruin.

And, of course, there is Napoleon. He disobeyed one of the first rules of war—which is "Don't march on Moscow." We will refer to him again later on in this chapter.

But to-day, kings and emperors do not take command in the field, and we find that the relationship between a general and his army in the past has little resemblance to the present times. The great military geniuses of those days forged their own instruments, and then cut their way to victory unhampered by political control. It is very different to-day. I suppose that in Britain the change came with the death of Cromwell in September 1658. That great military commander imposed a dictatorship upon England and, by the time the New Model Army was disbanded, the people had had enough of large standing armies. From that time to the present day the British nation has preferred to face embarking on war unprepared, rather than hand power over to a soldier in peacetime. Maybe they are right. To-day, in the free world the higher direction of war is in political hands, with Parliament holding the purse strings. The Service Chief, be he soldier, sailor or airman, has got to learn the techniques of politics—which are appeal, persuasion, manœuvre (which in politics is much the same as intrigue) and finally compromise. He has got to learn the foibles and phobias of his political chief, in whom lies the overall and final responsibility—which is right and proper.

All very difficult you may say! And it certainly is. It has greatly added to the complications of war. The soldier and the politician have got to learn to understand each other; this is essential for the conduct of modern war. Too often each is liable to disregard or underrate the other's difficulties.

Military command has always required technical skill, and spiritual power and quality; both are essential. The great commanders in history have been those who had a profound knowledge of the mechanics of war and the stage-management of battle, and who were able to focus and call forth the spirit and qualities of their soldiers. Their military leadership has been exercised on two levels:

(a) the known high command;
(b) the unknown subordinates.

There are the known commanders—the Jenghiz Khans, Marlboroughs, Wellingtons, Nelsons, Napoleons—with a thorough knowledge of the mechanics of war and of human nature. There are the unknown junior leaders—the good regimental officers and N.C.O.s, who lead their men forward, or hold their positions to the last in order that success may come elsewhere, and who often fall unknown. It is these latter who in the end win the battle by their initiative and courage—sometimes in spite of the generals.

In fact, the two are complementary—the great known commander-in-chief, and the insignificant unknown. Where would either be without the other?

When the known commander had a sound knowledge of the

conduct of war, a genuine interest in humanity, initiative and imagination, and the will to win, with perhaps a bit of luck which he seized with both hands and turned to boldness—he succeeded. In cases where he had not these things, he failed.

Oliver Cromwell is an interesting case. When the civil war began he was in command of a troop of 60 men, and fought in command of that troop at Edgehill in 1642. By January 1644 he was a Lieutenant-General and, with Fairfax, the outstanding commander in the Parliamentary army. After the Battle of Worcester in 1651 he became the first man in England. I doubt if he was a likeable man. But he was a great soldier and circumstances forced him to the front as a national leader. He then had five years of power and supreme eminence, during which he did not show up so well. He died in 1658.

Then there is Marlborough, born in 1650. He went to my school—St. Paul's School in London. He was a military geniu. and had great diplomatic skill. He was responsible for the rise of the British Army to become one of the foremost armies in Europe. He had studied the human side of the military art and cared greatly for the welfare of his troops. In battle he had always a firm grip on the situation, remaining calm and confident throughout. One of the outstanding military commanders. He died in 1722.

And about a hundred years later there is Wellington—a superb commander in the field. He was born in 1769, the same year as Napoleon, though the two never actually met in battle until Waterloo—by which time Napoleon was a shadow of his former self. Wellington was a thoroughly practical soldier, and one who at the same time made a serious study of the science of war. He died in 1852.

I suppose that Marlborough and Wellington were two of the finest soldiers ever produced by our nation, and, indeed, possibly by any nation. So much has been written about them both that it would be an impertinence for me to say any more.

I do not propose to bring into discussion in this book the military commanders of Hitler's war who are alive to-day, whether I served under them or not. But I am going to make one exception—Alanbrooke. If we refer back to the qualities which I outlined in Chapter One as being fundamental to a leader—the "man," his sincerity and selflessness, his ability to grasp the conditions of a problem and then reach a decision—I reckon that Alanbrooke had them all. Nevertheless, I doubt if he would have been such a highly successful commander in the field as he was a national Chief of Staff—because I don't think he would have got himself over to the soldiers in the right way. He was superb as a military counterpart to Churchill—as Chairman of the British Chiefs of Staff. We will discuss these two, Churchill and Alanbrooke, in a later chapter.

I would like to say a word here about Haig, in whom I have always been interested. Perhaps this is because we both held the same job i.e. C.-in-C. of the British Armies in North-West Europe. Perhaps also it is because we were both faced with a similar problem.

The only military leader in the field who believed that the German war could be finished in 1918 was Haig. He considered that in order to avoid the war going on any longer, it was essential to take risks in the summer of 1918 which would have been unthinkable in earlier stages of the war. And this could safely be done, because the Germans were by then nearly finished. He persuaded Foch to agree, and it was done.

I worked on exactly the same general philosophy in August, 1944, when I urged that we must finish off the war that year—adding that the Germans were on their last legs. But I was unable to persuade the Americans to take the risk—which, in any case, was practically nil. So it was *not* done, and the war went on into 1945—thus increasing our post-war political problems, and tragically wasting a great many valuable young lives. The fundamental trouble here was that United States military leadership was directed purely in terms of winning the war, and post-war political considerations were not allowed to influence military decisions while the war was going on. So far as I am aware no political directive was issued to Eisenhower by his political chiefs or by the Combined Chiefs of Staff—British and U.S.A. But military victory alone is never enough; war must have a political objective, it must result in a more peaceful world. If it does not, we merely substitute one enemy for another— which is what happened after Hitler's war ended. Military command has now made this same mistake in two world wars— the Kaiser's war and Hitler's war. Future commanders must realise the basic truth that unless there is a marriage of military and political factors in war, the result is merely useless slaughter —particularly in the atomic age.

It is interesting to note that great military commanders have, on the whole, been few. It required a war to produce them, and some proved their greatness after only a very short apprenticeship. Over the ages it has been one of the phenomena of military history that events have invariably produced the man. Age has little to do with it; the opportunity came sooner to some, later to others. Some were ready when the opportunity came, seized it with both hands and turned it to good account—others did not. Some were luckier than others, while some never had the chance to prove their ability. Napoleon was only 27 when he conquered Northern Italy in 1796. Wolfe was 32 when he captured Quebec. At the other end of the scale, Marlborough was 54 when he fought the Battle of Blenheim; Abercrombie conducted a short but brilliant campaign in Egypt at the age of 68. Lord Roberts, born in 1832, was 68 when he was sent to take command of the British forces in the South African war in 1900.

To me, it is intensely interesting to reflect that if in years to come some schoolboy, or even grown man, is asked to name the greatest French commander in Hitler's war, he will reply "General de Gaulle"—who, in fact, commanded nothing more in battle than an armoured division, and that only for a short time!

Let us pause for a moment on Napoleon, one of the greatest generals of all time. What was it which enabled him, at the age of 27, to take command of an independent army in the field and wage war successfully. He was a genius who made tremendous use of the initial instruction he received as an officer of artillery, and he was early able to put into practice the military theories which were then beginning to emerge. At the age of 20 he became involved in the French Revolution and in 1794, when only 25, he was a general. In October 1795 he subdued a violent mob in Paris; by his quick grasp of the situation, his rapid issue of orders, and his ruthless shooting down of the insurgents, he saved the Republic. The next year, 1796, he was given command of the French Army in Italy, the Republic now being greatly indebted to him.

Napoleon is an example of a man to whom opportunity came early; he had prepared himself for it, he was ready, and he seized the opportunity with both hands. He gained the position he did, not so much by a study of rules and strategy as by a profound knowledge of human nature in war. In 1796, when only a young man, he inspired a ragged, mutinous, and half-starved army, he gave it energy and momentum and made it fight, he dominated and controlled generals older and more experienced than himself—thus proving his knowledge of psychology. It was said by Machiavelli that fortune is the arbiter of one-half of our actions, leaving us to direct the other half ourselves. Napoleon had no difficulty with that other half, and Europe was soon to ring with his name. But it must be recorded that he was driven forward by a selfish and evil ambition, and not in pursuit of a great ideal—like Cromwell. And in the end, he fell—possibly because of his selfish ambition.

I would like to make one last point. In former days Commanders-in-Chief and senior officers encouraged, and indeed led, their men from the front—and not like the Duke of Plaza Toro, from behind. There are many instances in the days of Wellington and before, in the American Civil War, in the Crimea, in the South African War—when we read of generals exercising true moral leadership from in front, being up with the soldiers and being seen by them, even in the heat of battle. Then, as methods of inter-communication improved, a change came and generals began to direct operations from a headquarters well in rear. One well-known military historian has written that this " Plaza Toroing it in rear" did not help us to win our battles during the Kaiser's war, when it was rare for a senior commander to be seen in the forward area during a battle—a brigadier possibly, but not a general! I would agree with this stricture. But I consider that things improved in this respect in Hitler's war. However, there is no doubt that modern war, with all its immense complications, can result in generals losing touch with their soldiers. This has to be constantly remembered, and guarded against. Military command is, fundamentally, a great human problem and no good results will follow unless there is mutual confidence and sympathy between the known commander and the regimental officers and men—the former being seen frequently in the forward area by the soldiery. It follows that the technique of command to-day demands that the general who is in overall control of the battle must direct operations with a very small staff from a Tactical Headquarters well forward in the battle area—and not " Plaza Toro-it" behind with his large staff, the bulk of whom have of necessity to be well to the rear.

And when talking about staffs, we should all remember that in 1864 General Ulysses Grant commanded five armies operating in an area half the size of Europe—and his headquarters staff consisted of fourteen officers!

Let us now pass on and select for brief examination certain generals whose careers suit my purpose.

CHAPTER THREE

MILITARY COMMAND—
SOME EXAMPLES

THE SOLDIER has to learn his trade from a theoretical study for the most part, interspersed with a few periods of practical experience in the field—during which he bases his action, certainly initially, on what he has been taught and learnt. When he joins the army he is given a number of text books and manuals in which he finds the principles of war set out in a readable form, with rules for their application. It all seems quite simple; he learns later that it is not so simple as it appears at first sight, and the books don't teach him much about the principles of command. He is apt to think that the principles set out in the books are the results of recent war experiences. Here he is very wrong; they are as old as time.

It was Napoleon who advised his officers to read and re-read the campaigns of the great captains. And in Machiavelli's *The Prince* we read:

> "To exercise the intellect a man should read histories, and study there the actions of illustrious men, to see how they have borne themselves in war, to examine the causes of their victories and defeat."

No better advice was ever given to a student of war. Let us now follow that advice and take a quick look at a few of the commanders of the past, and see if we can discover the secret of their success—or why they failed.

Commanders of the twentieth century will suit my purpose best, because my own experience in command will give better value to a critical analysis of their actions. But we should discuss two of earlier periods—Jenghiz Khan of the twelfth century whose campaigns are a superb example of the principle of mobility, and Von Moltke of the nineteenth century who was the first to work on the principle of "the nation in arms." I will deal only briefly with these two, sufficient to illustrate the parallels between them and commanders of the twentieth century, and to show that over the ages military commanders have based their operations on the same principles of war as we use to-day—in fact, to prove the statement I have made that these principles are as old as time.

Jenghiz Khan

The years which followed the collapse of the Roman Empire produced no military leadership of any distinction. There was, indeed, a great deal of fighting and much bloodshed. I suppose the Crusades were probably the greatest military effort of those days; these may have been noble in purpose, but insofar as generalship was concerned they produced no lessons.

Deprived of intelligent leadership, fighting men took to armour; mobility was forgotten, fire-power was considered of small value, and surprise took a back seat.

Then in A.D. 1162 Jenghiz Khan was born, the son of a minor king or chief of Mongolian herdsmen. His father died when he was only thirteen, and from that early age the boy chief found it necessary to fight for supremacy—and he succeeded. For the next forty years he was continually fighting tribal wars, although there is no record of any great victories. But he was learning his trade and moving towards the ruthless efficiency which he was later to display.

In 1213, when he was fifty-one, he achieved his first major success—overthrowing the Chinese Empire. The Chinese had gone in for fixed defences, sacrificing mobility and skill in the field as had the European nations. To defend the home country they placed their faith in the Great Wall. Jenghiz Khan breached the Wall in three places and his forces then overran the Chinese Empire. He spent the next six years reorganising the Mongol

Army, and the resulting combination of Chinese learning and Mongolian brutality produced a fighting machine the like of which had not been seen before.

The Golden Horde, as the Mongolian forces were called, consisted entirely of horsed cavalry. The armament was the lance, the sword, the bow, and catapults for assault. The fire-power was intense and accurate, and a missile bombardment always preceded a Mongol attack. The mobility of this force was incredible.

A major factor in the successes was the intelligence system; fifth column tactics were used and the enemy morale was weakened by propaganda and the use of traitors. Terror was also used to weaken morale. It is estimated that in his invasion of China, Jenghiz Khan was responsible for the deaths of some 18 million people. From that time, the fear which the Mongol name inspired played a full part in paralysing the defence.

Jenghiz Khan may well go down to history as the most brutal of all leaders, although there has been a certain rivalry for this distinction during more recent days. But it could be said that his brutality was logical, being directed against the enemy will to fight as well as raising the enthusiasm of his own cruel and savage hordes. This quality of brutality, therefore, has to be added to the other qualities which he possessed.

A study of his campaigns reveals that he had a thorough knowledge of the same principles of war which we use to-day—surprise, mobility, concentration, security, offensive action, attention to morale. To these were added a steadfast maintenance of his objective. He was always careful to ensure that what was strategically desirable was tactically possible with the forces at his disposal. He consistently refused to be drawn into adventures which he reckoned were beyond the capacity of his army.

I place this Mongol general, Jenghiz Khan, in the front rank of great soldiers—a military commander of the highest class. His campaigns are models in the art of war. His conquests extended from India in the East to Poland and Hungary in the West. He died in 1227. After his death his generals continued to conduct brilliant campaigns in the West, conquering Central Russia up to and including Moscow. In 1241 came the successful invasion of Poland and Hungary. The Mongolian armies were then recalled to deal with internal troubles in the home country; if this had not happened the occupation of the plain of Europe might have been permanent. What lesson are we to learn from all this? Surely it is that Asiatic forces are not to be despised; from the vast areas of Asia there may again come an invading force with which the Western world must be ready to deal.

Von Moltke

I am now going to skip some six hundred years. This period saw many remarkable figures pass across the military stage—Robert Bruce, Edward III, Henry V, Turenne, Marlborough, Napoleon, Nelson, Wellington, Robert E. Lee.

These great commanders are so well known, and so much has been written about them, that there is really little more which can usefully be said.

In olden times, and even up to the days of Marlborough and Wellington, Britain sent a "team" overseas to fight her wars. The nation as such was not organised or geared for war, and the mass of the people probably knew little of what was going on.

Prussia was the first nation to understand the concept of "the nation in arms." Let us therefore take a bound forward to that period—the period when the Germans professionalised war.

Von Moltke, Chief of the General Staff of Prussia from 1857 for the next thirty years, played no small part in the business—under, of course, Bismarck his political chief.

Bismarck considered that the destiny of Prussia, and the creation of a German Empire, could be fulfilled only by war. For this purpose it would be necessary to create a military state. Aided by Roon, his Minister of War and by Von Moltke, his Chief of the General Staff, he set about this task.

Moltke was a master of organisation. He had profited much from past experience and he realised that, if you contemplate war, you must ensure that the man-power of the nation is geared to the needs of war, and that the national transport system is suitable for the vast movements which will be necessary. By 1870 he had so organised the German mobilisation that, within a couple of weeks of receiving the order, one million fully equipped troops were deployed for battle on the French frontiers.

Moltke was fifty-seven when he became Chief of the Prussian General Staff in 1857. He had never commanded even a regiment; he was a staff officer. His picture reveals classical features, with a high forehead; he looks very much the student, the thinker—which indeed he was.

Moltke gave a new conception to war. He exploited the railway in order to give greater tactical and strategical mobility. Napoleon, because of a lack of roads and poor Intelligence, had been forced to bring masses of men to the decisive point for a concentrated blow—interior lines, in fact. Moltke, with the new means of transportation and communication (the railway), developed a new method—a scattered deployment on exterior lines. This method had a further advantage. Because of railways, troops could be moved rapidly from west to east, or vice versa, thus giving strategical flexibility in case of a war on two fronts. In fact, Moltke once declared that the proper organisation and development of the railways system was more important than the building of frontier fortifications. There is no doubt whatever that he was right.

This development of the transportation system led to the need for an improved system of command. Larger armies could be maintained in the field and they moved and fought on wider fronts than formerly. A looser control became necessary. Napoleon had demanded absolute obedience from his marshals, and had little use for individuality; as a result, when they were on their own they generally failed. Moltke trained his generals to think and act on their own, basing their operations on a broad directive. He gradually gave his generals and staff officers a " line of country" on which to work. There thus came into being the German General Staff which later came to be regarded as a very sinister organisation—planning aggressive war, and indulging in intrigue of all kinds. But whatever may be said about the German

General Staff, it was the pioneer of military staff work as we know it to-day—enjoying great prestige. It was eventually destroyed by Hitler, and perhaps rightly so.

The generalship of Moltke during the 1870 war against France was very different from that of the other commanders we have studied. He directed operations from a headquarters well in rear. His strategy was remarkable for its thoroughness in planning and in detailed preparation, rather than for imagination or skilful manœuvre. He knew the French were unprepared for war, but not to the extent that became revealed. We read that the French conscripts, without uniform or arms, flooded the mobilisation centres and fortresses; that the French staff had drawn up no adequate movement programme; and finally, that one French regiment actually detrained in a border town which had just been occupied by the Germans!

Against all this Moltke advanced his columns slowly towards the French frontier, on a wide front but ensuring that they were mutually supporting. He seems to have had no master plan. His intention was to advance steadily and in good battle order, and to give battle when he met the French; he was confident that his deployment on exterior lines would give him superiority in the battle, and victory—which it did. His plan was not inspiring, but it was justified by events—which has not always been the case in more imaginative conceptions.

What was Von Moltke's contribution to the technique of military command? With him we certainly come to the threshold of that organisation of the national resources which makes for the "nation at war." He brought about strategic mobility by improving railway systems. He invented a new system of command. All this must be agreed. He forged the weapon. But it is not clear that he could wield it against a skilful opponent—and nobody could call Napoleon III a skilful opponent!

Can we place him in the front rank of great soldiers? I doubt it. He was a great national Chief of Staff, an organiser, a thinker, but hardly a genius in battle.

THE PATH TO LEADERSHIP

TWENTIETH-CENTURY MILITARY LEADERS

THE FIRST WORLD WAR—1914-18

Now that we have reached the era of the "nation in arms," I propose to bound forward some fifty years—to the Kaiser's war in 1914-18, generally known as World War I.

There are many commanders we could discuss. I will select two from the Western front in France, where I served from August 1914 onwards—except for an interval in England recovering from a bad wound. Both are now dead.

French

Though I served under his command from the earliest days of August 1914, I never met him—and, indeed, never saw him. What follows is the result of what I heard from others, at the time or since, and from my study of his period as C.-in-C. French was a cavalry soldier. He had gained a great reputation in the South African War, and when I joined the army in 1908 he was regarded as the best fighting commander we had. He later rose to be Chief of the Imperial General Staff, but resigned in May 1914, having become entangled in the Irish question. But he was recalled to active duty in August 1914 to command the British Expeditionary Force which was to go to France and fight side by side with the French Army.

He wasn't clever; but he was a natural soldier, gifted with a certain imagination. He certainly needed all the soldierly qualities he could muster during his period as Commander-in-Chief of the British Army in France—which didn't last very long, only from August 1914 to the end of 1915. He was then sixty-two, having been born in 1852.

Why did he fail? To find the answer it will be necessary to take a quick look at what went on during those eighteen months of his command.

When he arrived in France with the B.E.F. in August 1914

he did not know very much about the French plans, nor did anybody in London; those plans were wrapt in secrecy. But he knew that the French mobilisation was faulty. That nation has always relied on the *levée en masse* system for mobilising its army. In August 1914 over one million reservists responded at once to the call and these crowded into the depots to find a shortage of equipment, of arms, and of officers.

The French doctrine was to attack always: " *Vive la France! En avant!* "

This they did, beginning on the 20th August in the area to the south of Metz. The infantry uniform was blue and red; the artillery officers wore black and gold; and the cavalry in some cases wore armour. The Germans had invaded; but the French attacked before the situation was clear, and before it was known that conditions were favourable for offensive action. The French casualties were appalling; in these unjustified offensives along the French frontier they quickly suffered more than 300,000 casualties. The colour scheme of the French uniform was not likely to save life. Meanwhile the overwhelming strength of the German turning movement through Belgium hit the left of the Franco-British line of battle. This left, which included the British Army, was also to be launched to the attack. The British Army escaped disaster only by the wise decision of Sir John French to retreat in conjunction with the French Fifth Army on his right (commanded by General Lanrezac), and by the dogged resistance and skilful rifle fire of the British infantry.

All these things concerning the French Army were known to Sir John French. I do not know what effect the action of the French Army had on his thinking, and whether he still had confidence in General Joffre—who was the C.-in-C. of the French armies, and responsible for the strategy on the Western front. But on the 2nd September 1914 he wrote to Joffre offering to throw the whole British Army into the battle if the French would turn and engage the Germans in battle on the Marne. Joffre declined the invitation. Later, the battle on the Marne did indeed take place but not on Joffre's initiative; he had to be pushed into it by General Gallieni, Military Governor of Paris.

Then followed the extension of the battle front to the North Sea, sometimes called " The Race to the Sea," and the agony of the fighting by the British Army in Belgium—including the First Battle of Ypres in the autumn and winter of 1914.

By the end of 1914 a deadlock existed between the mighty forces; the trench lines ran from Switzerland to the North Sea and stagnation gripped the battle front. Winter descended on the tired soldiers and exhaustion congealed the armies—German, French, Belgium and British—into trench warfare. Barbed wire and machine-guns dominated the battlefield and the generals on both sides tried in vain to smash through the opposing front; but they knew not the answer, and merely lost more lives. During 1915 Sir John French loyally tried to support Joffre, who was responsible for the strategy on the Western front—as I have already said. This loyalty led him into unsound ventures, such as the offensive at Neuve Chapelle in March 1915 where 20,000 British casualties were sustained for no appreciable result. The battle of Loos in September 1915 followed. This was French's final defeat; it was grossly mismanaged and the British Army suffered 95,000 casualties.

The war of exhaustion was eating up British lives at a rate which alarmed the Government in London. French was removed from his command in December 1915 and given command of the forces at home. He was succeeded in command by Sir Douglas Haig.

Joffre lasted a year longer. In December 1916 he was promoted Marshal of France and removed from his command.

Was French a great commander? My answer would be " No." One has to examine the facts, the situation, and the circumstances—in order to decide the build-up in the matter of generalship. He did not get the right answer. He was the victim of circumstances which proved to be beyond his capacity to handle; and the result was failure. His loyalty to Joffre may have been magnificent; but it was not war.

One should add that it was his fate to be a very senior general at the beginning of the 1914-18 war. We British always start our wars with a series of appalling disasters; this is because the armed forces are neglected in peace, and when war breaks out we have neither the trained man-power nor the equipment necessary for the task. It takes us a year or two to get going and during that period the Commanders-in-Chief in the field get removed, because Prime Ministers like generals who win battles—which after all is what they are meant for. The lesson is: don't be too senior at the beginning of a war! I was a major-general at the beginning of Hitler's war in 1939; in the danger zone undoubtedly, but I survived! As a general rule, it would probably be safer to be a good young colonel in the early stages of a war, since nobody would know you—neither politicians nor Press.

Haig

Like French, Haig was a cavalry soldier. In 1914 he commanded the Aldershot Command, and from there took the 1st Corps to France in August of that year. He was then fifty-three. I never met him.

He was what was called in those days a " Westerner." That is, he believed passionately that the Western front in Europe was the decisive front; there, and only there, could the war be won or lost; all our resources in man-power and equipment must be sent to the battle in the West, and any " Eastern " strategy was out of the question. He could, of course, point to the Gallipoli campaign as an example of the uselessness of an Eastern strategy. This began on the 25th April 1915, and ended on the 8th January 1916 with the evacuation of all the troops engaged—the total casualties being very severe. My own view is that the Gallipoli venture was a brilliant conception; if it had been properly handled from the start, it would probably have succeeded. But it wasn't and so it failed. The " Westerners " then came into their own; headed by the C.I.G.S. (Sir William Robertson) and Haig, they proceeded with the war of exhaustion—of armies and of nations. There was to be no more strategy, and very little tactics. It was to be a gigantic test of endurance.

In July 1916 came the battle on the Somme, which went on until November. The British casualties are given as over 400,000 —of which 60,000 were incurred on the first day, including some 20,000 killed.

In the spring of 1917 the French Army suffered very heavy losses in an offensive under Nivelle; there were some dangerous mutinies and a serious loss of morale. Petain, who had succeeded Joffre in command of the French armies, demanded increased activity from the British Army in order to relieve pressure on the French. Haig responded, but with some reluctance. Then followed the Third Battle of Ypres, beginning in July 1917 and continuing well into the winter—culminating in the capture of the Passchendaele Ridge. It was a very wet autumn, with almost continuous rain; the ground became a quagmire, and men fought, and died, in the mud—many being drowned in the shell holes. The total British casualties were in the neighbourhood of 250,000. Many British soldiers recall the word "Passchendaele" with horror—even to-day.

Then came the one imaginative battle in this tremendous test of endurance—the Battle of Cambrai. The best account of this battle is that written by Liddell Hart in Vol. 1 of his brilliant book *The Tanks*, published in 1959. It was the first time that tanks were used in mass. The battle opened with a great success on the 20th November 1917; it finished on a dismal note some ten days later, due to faulty direction by the High Command. Great opportunities had been missed. None the less, the Battle of Cambrai was a landmark in British warfare.

The toll of casualties in 1917 began to have its effect on the Prime Minister, Mr. Lloyd George. His mistrust of Haig, which began after the losses on the Somme and gathered momentum after Passchendaele, now began to deepen. Haig was losing the confidence of his political chief; this mistrust was a grave handicap to him in his conduct of operations.

Thus the year 1917 closed on a dismal note for Haig. But many will say that during 1918 it was his fortitude, tenacity, and generalship which brought the war to an end in November 1918 with the collapse of the Germans. After the defeat of the three tremendous German offensives in 1918—the 21st March on the Somme, the 9th April on the Lys, and the 27th May on the Chemin des Dames, in all of which battles I took part as a major —Haig was convinced that the war could, indeed must, be won that year, if we played our cards properly.

But to win in 1918 demanded a decision to be bold, and to take risks. A most interesting book called *Command Decisions* was published in the United States in 1959; the book is a study undertaken by a corps of military historians. My attention was drawn to it by John North in connection with the Arnhem operation in September 1944—the decision of the historians being that Arnhem was a daring strategic manœuvre which was wholly justified. But the interesting point for us to note is that the historians compare the situation which existed after the great victory in Normandy in August 1944 with that which existed in France in the summer of 1918. Haig was the only military commander who believed that the First World War could be finished and won in 1918, and, in *Command Decisions* page 341, we read that he wrote the following in August 1918:

"Risks which a month ago would have been criminal to incur ought now to be incurred as a duty."

Foch, who was then Supreme Commander on the Western Front, was not so sure. But Haig persuaded him to be bold, and he was justified—the end coming on the 11th November 1918.

This was a great achievement on Haig's part, and as John North wrote in 1959:

"he may well have saved the world from another year of war in which the casualties, civilian and military alike, from disease and war's destruction generally, must certainly have dwarfed the Passchendaele figures."

Few will disagree with this statement; indeed it is an understatement. I would add here that exactly twenty-six years later the same situation arose. We are suffering now from the lack of boldness displayed after the great victory in Normandy in August 1944—as has been outlined in Chapter Two.

I find it very difficult to decide the place to be given in history to Haig as a great captain.

He certainly made mistakes; and under his command the British Army suffered the most appalling casualties. I would say he lacked imagination. But he was a man of sterling character, brave, and with great determination. He never crumpled in adversity. He was single-minded, and his confidence was unshakable. He had his own methods of making war and he pursued them relentlessly. His methods resulted in victory, but one has the feeling that perhaps it could all have been done better some other way.

The soldiers certainly believed in him. Some may think this curious, because he was a shy man. My own view would be that he never really got himself over to the rank and file—finding it difficult to speak to the soldiery, and the following story illustrates this point.

Haig normally inspected troops in complete silence, never speaking to anybody. It is related that one of his staff once told him that it would make a good impression if he spoke to one or two men. Accordingly, on his next inspection he said to a man: " Where did you start this war? " The man replied: " I didn't start this war, I think the Kaiser did."

I understand he decided after this encounter that his previous policy of silence was right! But in spite of all he managed to convey to those below him something of his own fortitude and courage.

In the Kaiser's war we have discussed two well-known British military figures—French and Haig. Two French figures pass across the stage—Joffre and Foch. The first two in each case were discarded—French and Joffre. Haig and Foch lasted to the end.

Let me close this period with a quotation by Sir Winston Churchill in Vol. II of *The World Crisis*:

" These chapters will recount the fall from dazzling situations of many eminent men; and it is perhaps worth our while at this point to place the reader on his guard against uncharitable or unworthy judgements. All made their contribution and fell. Only those who succeeded, know by what obscure twists and turns of chance they escaped a similar lot."

Let us leave it at that.

We may well have to recall these words from time to time as we proceed.

THE SECOND WORLD WAR—1939-45

We have now reached the period during which I myself was to rise to high command, and eventually to the post of professional head of the British Army. I do not propose to discuss the qualities and capabilities of any of the commanders of Hitler's war who are alive to-day—whether I served with or under them, or not. Instead, I select for examination two soldiers who are now dead—Gort and Wavell. I do not select these two because they cannot answer back, but because they both serve to illustrate my purpose; both were Commanders-in-Chief in a theatre of war. It would be difficult to select two more different characters, as we shall see.

Gort

I had known Gort since 1920—but had never been very close to him, and I doubt if anybody had. In those early days I used to respect his opinion greatly, and often sought it. But as time goes on, one gains in knowledge by reading and experience—and then I began to have doubts. I was always looking forward. I would ponder over the writings of the military thinkers of the day who were constantly analysing the past and applying its lessons to the future. Gort seemed to me to lack vision; he loved detail and couldn't see the wood for the trees. He had made a deep study of the strategy and tactics of the 1914-18 war. Even when he was Commander-in-Chief of the B.E.F. in France in 1939-40, he would discuss at length the battles of 1914, and the handling of operations by Haig from 1916 onwards—of whom he was a great admirer. He was a student of Foch, whose *clichés* he would often quote; a favourite one was: " My flanks are turned; my centre gives way; I attack! "

This didn't interest me greatly. I wanted to hear from my C.-in-C. some wise thoughts on the coming battles with the Germans, and how we should conduct operations in 1940—not in 1914.

At the end of 1937 Hore-Belisha had selected Gort to be Chief of the Imperial General Staff. The senior officers of the Army knew he was unfitted for that post. He was not clever and he lacked imagination. He was a first-class regimental officer, and he had not commanded anything larger than a brigade.

I had twice stayed in his house. The first time was in Delhi in 1935, when he was Director of Military Training in India; his son, a delightful schoolboy, was with him at that time. The second time was at Camberley in 1937 when he was Commandant of the Staff College; his very charming daughter was at home with him. It was difficult in those days to get him to talk about anything except the past. He never at any time gave me the impression that he was a happy person. His marriage had ended sadly; and later on, about 1941, he lost his son.

As C.I.G.S. he did not get on well with his Secretary of State for War, Mr. Hore-Belisha. I did not know much about it before Hitler's war began. But it always seemed to me that in 1939 Hore-Belisha took the opportunity to get rid of Gort by making him C.-in-C. of the Expeditionary Force. Here again, he was unfitted for the job—and we senior officers all knew it. I was then a major-general, in command of the 3rd Division.

When Gort assumed command of the British Expeditionary Force in September 1939 he was fifty-three. His two Corps Commanders were Dill and Brooke (now Lord Alanbrooke). Dill was senior to him in the Army, and both were far superior to him in overall military knowledge and in the technique of high command. This made things difficult for him. However,

MILITARY COMMAND—SOME EXAMPLES

he pursued his way calmly and it didn't seem to worry him. But the trouble was that a very complete unrealism existed in that first winter of the war, and it was beyond Gort's capacity to bring some realism into our affairs. He took no steps to inform his political and military masters in London of the true situation in France; he never complained, and this helped to create a feeling in London that all was well on the Western front. All was far from well. And Gort's mind wasn't engaged in tackling the major problems. He was always thinking on the lower level—about the soldiers, the details of their equipment, their dress and how the helmet and gas mask should be carried, and so on. His great subject was "fighting patrols," and in the training of the soldiers in all forms of inquisitiveness. All these things were really the province of battalion commanders and their brigadiers—and not the business of a Commander-in-Chief.

Then came the German onslaught on the 10th May 1940. When the crisis burst on the French and British armies, and developed in ever-increasing fury, Gort did his best to make up for past unrealism. But it was too late; much of what should have been done had not been done. None the less, Gort's own special qualities now began to shine forth. He was quick to see that there was only one end to it—the French would crack, and he must get as much as possible of the British Army back to England, to live to fight another day.

I always think he rose to his greatest heights on the 20th May 1940. On this day, the Chief of the Imperial General Staff (Ironside) arrived at G.H.Q. with orders from the Cabinet in London that the B.E.F. was to retreat southwards into France, and there join hands with the French Army. This was a purely paper plan and, by that time, was utterly impracticable. Gort refused to carry it out, and very rightly. He did, however, stage a small counter-attack south of Arras which had a remarkable effect in imposing caution on the German forces in that area—which, curiously enough, were commanded by Rommel. The next day, the 21st May, planning was begun at G.H.Q. for the evacuation via Dunkirk. He got over a quarter of a million men back to England; but we left behind in France and Belgium practically the whole equipment of the army, to which the priority of the factories in Britain had so far been given.

Gort was not employed again in command of troops in the field. We all felt sorry for him. He was a man of upright and sterling character, with magnificent qualities of courage and integrity. Later he was employed as Governor of Gibraltar, and then sent to Malta in the same capacity. In both cases he threw himself with restless energy into the organisation of the defence, tasks which suited him down to the ground.

Finally, in 1944 he went as High Commissioner to Palestine. He was by now a very sick man, and he died of cancer soon afterwards.

I think the truth is that Gort was the scapegoat of political intrigue. Hore-Belisha fastened on him and used him for his own purposes, building him up in the Press, and, finally, appointing him Commander-in-Chief in order to get rid of him from the War Office and thus solve his own political problems. If Gort had been given command of a division, and had been left free to make his own way quietly up the military ladder, he would in due course have risen to command a Corps—but no higher, in my personal opinion. Instead, this very fine officer was pushed quickly up to dazzling heights over the heads of others far more capable than he, and was finally discarded—a very unhappy man.

But when all is said and done, it must never be forgotten that in the supreme crisis of his military life, in May 1940, he acted with courage and decision—doing the right thing for Britain. If he had failed at that moment, disaster might well have overtaken British arms. He did not fail.

Wavell

When Hitler's war began in 1939, Wavell was fifty-six. He was a very different person from Gort. He began his military service in the Black Watch. He was highly intellectual, very well read, and something of a poet. I had served under him when I was a major, and again as a brigadier; I got to know him well and had a great respect for his intellect, integrity, and soldierly qualities. He was, of course, far senior to me, but he never let that come between us in our conversation—and eventually we became firm friends. In his early military life and, indeed, up to the summer of 1939 when war loomed ahead and he was rushed out to Cairo to take command in the Middle East, he was regarded as one of the best soldiers in the British Army and a fine trainer of troops—one who was destined for great things. But in the event he was removed from his command in July 1941 and relegated to India as C.-in-C. in that country—replacing Auchinleck, who was sent to Cairo. In fact, the two exchanged jobs. But Auchinleck himself was later to fall from grace; he was removed from command in the Middle East in August 1942, after little more than a year in the job, and was sent back to India. The two, who had exchanged jobs in 1941, found themselves both in India in 1942. Such is fate!

In the summer of 1943, Auchinleck again relieved Wavell as C.-in-C. in India—Wavell becoming Viceroy of India in October 1943.

From second-lieutenant in the Black Watch to Commander-in-Chief in the Middle East in wartime, and finally Viceroy of India! Is not that enough? Not under the circumstances. Wavell was a soldier and, as such, he was relieved of his command when engaged in active operations against the enemy. For a soldier that takes some getting over. He felt it keenly, but took the blow wondrously well, and was prepared to continue serving in any capacity where it was considered he could still be useful.

He was a tremendous thinker, with a clear brain and great strategic insight. He wrote well. In 1939 he gave the Lees Knowles Lectures at Cambridge, the subject being "Generals and Generalship." The lectures were the best treatise on that subject which I have ever read (they were published in 1941). I think the best book he wrote was *Allenby—A Study in Greatness*, published in September 1940.

Why did this brilliant soldier fail? I think there were two main reasons.

First, he was not sufficiently ruthless with those below him whom he reckoned were not fit for their jobs.

Conversations on this subject took place while we were walking on the deck of the *Queen Mary* in 1949, returning from New York. When I gave my view and said I reckoned he had acted wrongly in incidents we discussed, he remained silent while we completed two rounds of the promenade deck—more than half a mile, I suppose. He then turned to me and said—" Perhaps I was wrong!"

I enjoyed that voyage greatly—chiefly because of his company. He was a delightful companion and I had a great affection for him. Besides our walks on the deck we played much bridge in the evenings; he was a good player, but slow; he liked to think things out, as he did in his military life.

Secondly, he never seemed able to establish good relations with his political masters. These will always press the soldier in wartime to undertake bold ventures for which the military resources do not exist—and which are often extremely hazardous. But it is imperative that the Service chief should give his definite opinion on the military side of hazardous ventures—is there a good chance of success, or will they most certainly fail? Having given his opinion, if the venture is none the less ordered by the political chief, it must be carried out. But against this, no political chief will order an operation if the combined weight of military opinion is against it.

The Greek adventure in the spring of 1941 is an interesting case in point. The Secretary of State for War (Eden) and the C.I.G.S. (Dill) both visited the Middle East in February 1941, and both advised that we should send forces to Greece to help repel the Germans if they invaded the country—which they did on the 6th April. From the military angle British intervention in Greece had no possible chance of success; it could result only in a first-class disaster. That is exactly what happened; and it was followed by a second disaster in Crete in May 1941.

When it was decided to intervene in Greece, Wavell did not raise his voice against such action. Being the good soldier he was, he must have known it could not succeed. He did not say so. Indeed, he gave the impression that he reckoned there were reasonable prospects of success. To provide forces for Greece he had to weaken the front in the desert south of Benghazi, and he left there comparatively unequipped and untrained troops, contrary to the strongly worded advice of General O'Connor, the victorious commander of the Western Desert Force—thinking that any German offensive to rescue the Italians would not be possible for at least two months. But Hitler decided to send Rommel to Africa, with two Panzer Divisions. Rommel attacked on the 31st March, one week before the Germans invaded Greece. By the middle of April our forces in Cyrenaica had been driven back to the Egyptian frontier, and Tobruk was besieged. By the 1st May the Germans had pushed us out of Greece, and done the same in Crete by the 1st June.

The Government in London had by now lost confidence in Wavell. He was relieved of his command on the 5th July, 1941. I have always considered that the intervention in Greece was a major error. In the event it led to the most frightful losses in men and equipment in Greece, in Crete, and in Cyrenaica.

I think the judgement of history will be that Wavell was too apt to agree to hazardous operations which were urged on him by his political chief. The question of "resignation" does not arise in wartime. All that is necessary is to say to your Government that if they order a certain operation to be done, they must understand it will fail. The political chief is then faced with an awkward decision. Unfortunately, in the case of Greece the C.I.G.S. had agreed the operation was "on." Even so, little could have been done if Wavell and his brother C.s-in-C. in the Middle East had said "No." I am under the impression that later the C.I.G.S. (Dill) realised a mistake had been made.

It is a curious story. By the first week in February 1941 the forces under Wavell's command had destroyed the Italian forces in Abyssinia and in Africa. He became known throughout the British Army as the one great victorious general of the day; his name was a household word in Britain. Five months later, in the first week in July 1941, he was removed from his command —the Government having lost confidence in him.

The Churchill Coalition Government who had removed him, appointed him Viceroy of India in the autumn of 1943; very serious difficulty was being found in filling this job. The Attlee Labour Government lost confidence in him and recalled him in March 1947.

When he had climbed the heights, he never stayed there very long; his life became a series of crashes. I suppose he wasn't tough enough in resisting ventures which he knew in his heart to be unsound. And he wasn't good at arguing with politicians —which often has to be done.

It is interesting to reflect that Wavell's only major victories were against the Italians in Africa—in Abyssinia, and in Egypt and Cyrenaica. He never fought the Germans until his forces were attacked by Rommel and his Panzer divisions south of Benghazi in the spring of 1941, and were defeated. Is it possible that he underestimated the Germans when he took on the Greek adventure?

When he left the Middle East and went to India as C.-in-C., he was later placed in charge of all operations in South-East Asia. I have heard it said that he underestimated the Japanese, rating them as a second-class enemy—whereas it is clear from what I have read since that they were as formidable an enemy as the British Army has ever had to face, and I think this would be agreed by the American Army too.

At any rate, Wavell had to face little but disaster in South-East Asia while he was in command—the fall of Singapore in February 1942, the defeats of the First Burma campaign in March and April 1942, and many other deadly blows to British rule in Asia.

I believe it was Wolfe who said: " War is an option of difficulties." And Clausewitz wrote: " War is the province of chance. In no sphere of human activity is such a margin to be left for this intruder."

These sayings were certainly true for Wavell. He was beset

with difficulties during his years as a Commander-in-Chief, and also when Viceroy of India. I have never ceased to admire his courage and integrity, and I had the greatest affection for him. His death from cancer after he had withdrawn from active employment caused me deep distress and I lost a valued friend.

SUMMARY

Where do we stand in this matter of military command? We have had a brief look at certain commanders and have examined their methods, observing the reasons for success or failure. Some will say that I have dealt with this particular subject in a series of short and disjointed narratives—what is called "episodic." I do not think it could have been handled clearly in any other way. The point that now matters is this—has anything emerged from the study? Have I been able to say anything important about military command which may be new to at least some of my readers—of course, not to all. Maybe I have made it clear that some well-known military figures of recent times do not measure up to my standards. There is no harm in that so long as it has been done in a manner which does not cause offence—which I hope has not happened.

It will be noted that I have dealt only with soldiers; it seemed best to restrict the analysis to fields in which I can speak with some knowledge, but the lessons will be comparable in the other Services. Let me now try to sum up, in outline, the results of my investigations.

I have shown that the principles of war are the same to-day as they were in the days of Jenghiz Khan, but the complications of modern war have made it more difficult to apply them. War is now a highly professional business. The man who aspires to rise to high command has got to make an intense study of the military art, and equip his mind professionally with all he needs —so that he will be ready when the moment arises, when the opportunity comes his way.

He must be a man of decision and action; calmness in the

crisis and decision in action must be his watchwords; indecision and hesitation are faults to be avoided by any soldier, but in a commander-in-chief they are criminal.

He must be a good judge of men, a good picker of subordinates. Then he must be tough, and ruthless in dealing with inefficiency in battle—when men's lives are at stake. The good general is not merely one who wins battles; they must be won with a minimum loss of life.

And he must be prepared to take a chance when the situation favours boldness. He will lose part of the fruits of victory if he is never prepared to soar from the known to seize the unknown.

There are, of course, many other qualities we could enumerate; let us add just one more. He must be absolutely straight and speak the military truth to his political masters, hoping that they will be straight with him. None the less, he must understand that the higher conduct of war lies in political hands; he should bend over backwards to try and get on terms with his political chiefs, and they with him—however difficult, or indeed impossible, it may appear to both sides. Intrigue on the part of soldiers or politicians in war, or in peacetime, is indefensible.

My own experience in military command has been extensive. I have drawn my sword in battle and led my platoon against the German positions—in 1914. Beginning with the command of that sub-unit of thirty men, I have, in succession, commanded every echelon up to and including a Group of Armies totalling two million men—in North-West Europe in 1944. Therefore, it will not be out of place to include some of the results of my experience in the realm of high command—since my analysis in this chapter has been in that particular field.

When studying commanders of bygone days and comparing them with the present, we must remember that times have changed. It can almost be said that Marlborough and Wellington won their campaigns single-handed; to-day a commander-in-chief in the field is the captain of a team, and a large team at that.

High command is now far more complicated than formerly and a C.-in-C. must have a good staff—and a superb Chief of

Staff to co-ordinate its activities. *He must know his soldiers and be recognised by them.* I do not believe the leadership displayed on the Western front in the 1914-18 war would have succeeded in Hitler's war; it will be clear from what I have written in this chapter that I never saw French or Haig, although I served in France throughout the 1914-18 war—except for a year in England recovering from wounds.

No modern C.-in-C. can have any success if he fails to understand the human approach to war. *He must be a student of human nature, with a thorough realisation of the fact that battles are won primarily in the hearts of men—and that when dealing with men, and women too, justice is vital.*

I hold that a C.-in-C. of great armies in the field must have an inner conviction which, though founded closely on reason, transcends reason. It is this which will enable him at a certain moment in the battle—the right moment—to take a short cut which will take him to his objective more swiftly and more surely than equally careful but less inspired commanders.

One could put it another way. There are three types of commanders in the higher ranks:

1. Those who have faith and inspiration, but lack the infinite capacity for taking pains and preparing for foreseeable contingencies—which is the foundation of success in war. These fail.
2. Those who possess the last-named quality to a degree amounting to genius. Wellington is the perfect example of this type.
3. Those who, possessing this quality, are inspired by a faith and conviction which enables them, when they have done everything possible in the way of preparation and when the situation favours boldness, to throw their bonnet over the moon. There are moments in war when, to win all, one has to act thus. Nelson was the perfect example of this—when he broke the line at St. Vincent, when he went straight in to the attack at the Nile under the fire of the shore

batteries and with night falling, and at the crucial moment at Trafalgar.

No commander ever took greater care than Nelson to prepare against foreseeable contingencies, but nobody was ever so well able to recognise the moment when, everything having been done which reason can dictate, something must be left to chance or faith.

One can sum it all up in this way. To exercise high command in war successfully a C.-in-C. has to have an infinite capacity for taking pains and for careful preparation; he must also have an inner conviction, which, at times, will transcend reason. Having fought, possibly over a prolonged period, for the advantage and gained it, there then comes the moment for boldness. When that moment comes, will he throw his bonnet over the mill and soar from the known to seize the unknown? In the answer to that question lies the supreme test of generalship in high command.

CHAPTER FOUR

POLITICAL LEADERSHIP— ALFRED AND CROMWELL

IT IS DIFFICULT for a soldier to tackle this subject, but it must be done if our study is to have full value. My inclination is to begin by examining how leadership in the political sphere contrasts with military command.

I suppose that politics is, in the end, the wielding of power over men, and I gather from Machiavelli that there are no principles in the matter; the power must be exercised without scruple. I also gather from Acton that power has a demoralising effect, tending towards corruption. Of course, Machiavelli was writing about the nation-states of his day, when dictatorship was the rule; these have given way to the present-day international groupings, with all the immense complications of democracy and nationalism; his dictum would hardly apply in the modern democratic world.

It often seems to me that the political leader of to-day is so anxious for power that he tends to neglect principles. Christ, the greatest Leader of all time, gave His followers a set of principles and an unforgettable example. That is what is needed in national leadership to-day and what we seem to lack. The clash between power and principle needs to be viewed in a better perspective by the national leaders of the free world.

The difference between military and political leadership can be expressed very simply—the military leader can command those he leads, whereas the political leader has to use the methods of appeal and persuasion. Both types must have a well-balanced judgment and must know instinctively when to be bold and when to be cautious; both must be able to judge the true value of the mass of good and bad tidings which will flow in upon them in times of stress; courage and mental robustness are vital to both.

I once asked a friend, a general to be exact, and one with a very good knowledge of Whitehall and of those who work there, what he reckoned were the fundamental qualities for success in political leadership. Without any hesitation, he replied: "Tremendous vitality and colossal conceit." He looked at me with a twinkle in his eyes; I reckon he thought the two qualities applied equally to me! I agree the vitality; it is essential for a leader in any sphere to keep going all the time. I suggested to him that by "conceit" he really meant confidence.

Successful military commanders have always been confident that they could achieve their object. They got this confidence from their ability to view a problem in its simplest form, to discover the few essentials necessary to the successful solution of the problem and on which all action must be based, and to decide how those few essentials could be achieved; they never allowed a mass of detail to submerge the essentials to success. Their confidence inspired the soldiers, making them feel stronger than the enemy—thus producing the will to conquer. This power to move men's spirits, to inspire their enthusiasm, to convince them that what was asked of them was possible, could only be done— and was only done—by personal contact with their men. For myself, I used to talk to the soldiers, addressing them in large gatherings and telling them what we were going to do, my plans for doing it, and their part in the whole affair. Once the soldiers knew what was required of them, and why, and when, they never failed to do their stuff.

I do not see this particular aspect of leadership practised by political leaders in the free world, though it appears in the Communist world in certain countries. I do not see the same interest in human relationships, the same realisation that it is "men" who are the factors of importance, the same moving of men's spirits—except perhaps when an election is to take place, and then it is attempted more by bribery than in any other way.

How does the political leader address those he wants to follow him? I do not know because I have never been to a political meeting; but he wants people to vote for him because it will give him "power." The military commander is not dependent on votes to obtain the power he needs. He knows that bottled-up in men are great emotional forces and that these must be given an outlet in a way which is positive and constructive, and which will warm their hearts and excite their imagination. He therefore sets out to win the hearts of those he leads—because there lies his power.

A further difference is that the politician procrastinates in order to ensure that what he does is politically acceptable to his supporters, and his plans seem to the soldier to be immensely complicated; the soldier is trained on the principles of simplicity, decision and action.

I suppose each is right when operating in his own particular sphere. But the inclination of the political leader to avoid decision is anathema to the soldier; it leads inevitably to ever-increasing complications, and results in simplicity (which is an important factor in the military art) disappearing out of the window.

However that may be, it is interesting to note that most of the best British generals had political experience. Cromwell was a member of Parliament before he took to soldiering.

Marlborough had far more experience of political intrigue than of military service when he began his career in high command; and when at the height of his power he directed the foreign policy of Britain from his headquarters in the field. But then, as I have already said, he was a genius.

Wellington had been a member of the Irish Parliament, and of the British, and actually became Prime Minister—but not for long.

Of course, the politician has certain advantages over the soldier; he is always on active service so to speak, whereas the soldier's opportunities in peace to practise his trade are few, and even then are artificial. It would be true to say that we soldiers are too apt to disregard or underrate the difficulties of the political leader in peacetime; we become impatient at his slowness to implement some political measure which had been agreed was essential. We forget that the politician has to prepare public opinion, anticipate objections from the Opposition, examine the financial implications, and so on. And the soldier has the enormous advantage of never having to explain in public the reasons for his actions.

Even so, much which passes for political leadership in the world to-day is difficult for a soldier to understand. It often seems to me that since the conception of a universal Christendom was lost, and became replaced by nationalism, nations have lost the ideal of unity and the response to leadership—particularly when political leaders have no real means of coercion. But when a leader cannot coerce, success will depend on the man himself, on his character and personality.

I suppose there is a difference between a politician and a statesman—as there is between a politician and a soldier. Did not somebody once say that a politician has his eye on the next election, and a statesman on the next generation? The good soldier, when in high command, always thinks two battles ahead —planning to win not only battles, but wars. Perhaps there is a lesson here for the party politician.

This is only a brief introduction to a very big subject. I now want to take a quick look at two men, very different in character, each of whom became the political and national leader of our own nation—the first over one thousand years ago and the second about three hundred.

ALFRED THE GREAT AND CROMWELL

I place these two together because each governed England for a period during his life—Alfred for twenty-eight years and Cromwell for five. Both died when comparatively young, Alfred at the age of fifty and Cromwell fifty-nine.

Alfred can be described as one of the great men of all time and possibly the greatest king England has ever had. Furthermore, his kingdom did not perish with his death; his work endured, being carried on by his son Edward the Elder and his grandson Athelstan, and between them they gave England a unity it had never known before.

Oliver Cromwell was a man of a crisis, who was born to rule. But he strove to impose the will of a minority on the people of England, and he failed to create a dedicated and united nation—as Alfred had done. Much of what he achieved perished with him, but not all as we shall see. He was not revered after his death in 1658, as was Alfred. Indeed, in December 1660 his body was dug up and hung in chains at Tyburn, and his head was set up on a pole on the roof of Westminster Hall to be despised by all.

Let us see what we can learn from their lives.

Alfred the Great

As you drive down the hill into Winchester, coming from Alton, you see at its foot the statue of Alfred, King of England, facing the main road through the town and looking towards the castle. It is well placed and impossible for the traveller to miss; it is intended to remind him of one of the greatest kings in English history. So stands Alfred, sword in hand, watching over his ancient capital. His sword is held upright in his right hand, shoulder high, the cross at the top of the hilt being visible for all to see. It reminds me of the moment in the Coronation Service, when the Sword of State is taken from the altar in Westminster Abbey and handed to the Sovereign with these words:

"With this sword do justice, stop the growth of iniquity."

Alfred did just that. His statue has always had an interest for me and I never pass it by without pausing to look, and to revere.

He was born in 849 at Wantage, three hundred years after the Saxons first settled in Wessex. When he was a young boy his father, King Ethelwulf, took him on a pilgrimage to Rome; and it may well have been that that journey across Europe, and the sights of the great city of Rome with its ruins of learning, produced the inspiration which later gave him the urge to teach himself and his subjects the arts of learning and of order. It was in Rome that he had his first lessons in reading. When still only a boy he had to abandon his books and become an active soldier, fighting beside his two elder brothers against the Danes who were ravaging the land.

At this early age he at once won the hearts of the rough soldiers of the Wessex army, who were mostly peasants and farmers. It would now have been easy for him to take part in intrigues against his brothers, each of whom in turn was king, and to seek the kingship for himself. But his greatness of spirit, and his complete selflessness, at once made him do the opposite—he loyally supported his brothers and devoted all his energies to serving his country and his king. In 871, when he was only twenty-one years old and second-in-command to the last of his brothers, it was his initiative and presence of mind which was mainly responsible for the heavy defeat, at Ashdown in Berkshire, of the Danish Army which had invaded Wessex. Later in that same year his brother died and Alfred became king, at the age of twenty-two.

But he took over a difficult situation; he was hopelessly outnumbered, and his country was not organised for all-out war against the Danes—whose sea power gave them a great advantage. For the next five years he was continually leading his unhappy people in battle against the Danes, and refusing to submit to the cruel and heathen foe. It was during these years of struggle that he saw the need for an English fleet with which to attack the invaders and upset their plans before they could land on the English coast. He seemed to know instinctively that if he could gain time and keep up the morale of his people, he would win in the end.

After the victory at Ashdown he had a breathing space, owing to the activities of the Danes in northern and central England. He took full advantage of this, re-organising his peasant levies and working on his plans for a fleet. He had some success in 876 and managed to expel the Danish Army from his realm. But in the following year the Danes returned in overwhelming strength and heavily defeated Alfred and the Wessex army. He himself was forced to flee in order to escape capture, and he went into hiding in the isle of Athelney, in Somerset; it was here that the legend was born of the burnt cakes in the shepherd's cottage.

From his hideout in Somerset he began at once to re-organise his scattered army, sending messengers to his men to assemble at a rendezvous in the vale of Knoyle. Here they were joined by Alfred some weeks after Easter 878. The whole force then moved northwards and met the united Danish forces on the downs north of Warminster, inflicting on them a decisive defeat. The Danes then laid down their arms and agreed to make peace.

Alfred now displayed all the Christian virtues on which his life was based. Instead of putting his cruel and treacherous enemies to the sword, he fed them and helped them in their troubles. The Danish king accepted baptism, Alfred becoming his godfather.

We now come to a turning point in English history. Alfred saw very clearly that if he followed up his victory by driving the Danes out of England, they would return at some later date and seek revenge. So he offered them a home in England and persuaded them to settle on the land, to give up the sword and to take to peaceful pursuits—thus paving the way to the civilisation of the Norsemen and to their conversion to Christianity. This was possibly the greatest act of statesmanship ever performed by an English king. He realised that unless there is a clear-cut political object in military plans, war merely results in useless slaughter. It would seem he was over a thousand years ahead of his time; we could well have done with some of his thinking during the first half of the twentieth century!

But Alfred was under no illusions about the future. There were other Danish armies which could land on the English coast and ravage his realm. So while he offered friendship to the defeated he prepared for a renewal of the attacks from their countrymen overseas. How wise he was! He re-organised his own army and built a fleet of war-galleys. And when in due course the Viking army descended again upon England to raid and to plunder, it was finally defeated and driven ignominiously from the realm. Thus Alfred, by his wisdom and military skill, saved England and gave new hope to Christendom.

It may well be that Alfred's true claim to greatness lay not in war but in peace.

As a soldier we can place him with sureness in the front rank of military chiefs—a great leader, with a stout heart and tremendous fortitude, and with a sound knowledge of organisation for war on a national scale. Throughout history soldiers have always followed a successful general. But here was one who suffered many defeats; yet in spite of all, the rough peasants of England gave him their confidence, and followed him—to death, if necessary. In adversity the spirit of the man himself, his character, his vitality, his personality—all combined to give him victory in the end.

But as a national leader in peacetime he is outstanding. After two generations of warfare his country was in ruins—the farms destroyed, the countryside laid waste, monasteries burnt, and the people in a state of ignorance and squalor. Now became apparent the dividend from his journey to Rome when a boy—he set himself to teach his people and restore the kingdom. But first he learnt himself before starting to teach others. In the early days of my military life a well-known general, a Corps Commander on the Western front in the Kaiser's war in 1914-18, would constantly repeat the following slogan:

"Teach the teachers what to teach,
Before they teach the Tommies."

How right he was! And this is exactly what Alfred did. He learnt how to design and build houses, and then taught the art to craftsmen. He learnt to read. And then he personally translated into the language of his country the books of Christian and classical knowledge which were needed for the monastries and to give his people a taste for learning and wisdom.

What a man! Overall he was a real Christian, practising all the Christian virtues as we know them to-day. His achievements are unforgettable. Having saved his own country he made no attempt to conquer others. He did unto others as he would they should do unto him, defeating enemies and not making them. He ruled by force of character and example. He died in 899 at the age of fifty. His early death was probably due to his being worn out by a life of almost continuous struggle and danger. He left no bitterness to be avenged after his death. His kingdom endured, and his work. And it has been said of him by a famous historian:

" More than any other man he was the first maker of England."

I put him in the front rank of leadership, military and national —very unsusual in the same man. He gave England a noble leadership, the kind for which we are searching.

Oliver Cromwell

We now come to a very different man. On guard outside the House of Commons in London stands the statue of Oliver Cromwell. It seems a curious place for the statue of a man who found it impossible to govern through Parliament, dismissing three and finally becoming a dictator. He stands there, holding the Bible and his sword—both of which he wielded to some purpose.

Not far away, and overlooking the threshold of Westminster Abbey, stands the statue of Abraham Lincoln—a firm believer in representative government and institutions, and on the right of the majority to rule. I wonder what he thought of Cromwell, who saw no virtue in a ballot-box majority—the fundamental essence of democracy.

And the statue of Smuts is not far away; I often wish I had discussed Cromwell with him.

Oliver Cromwell was born at Huntingdon on the 25th April, 1599, and little is known about his childhood and youth. But we read that he often visited his uncle's house at Hinchingbrooke and it is thought by some that he may well have met there the young

Prince Charles who was one year younger, and for whose execution he was later to be primarily responsible. Being a country lad, he loved horses and soon became a good rider to hounds. This knowledge of horses was to stand him in good stead later on, as we shall see.

He was educated at the local grammar school and in April 1616, when he was nearly seventeen, he went to Sidney Sussex College, Cambridge. But he stayed there only one year and took no degree; this was because his father died in June 1617, and he returned to Huntingdon to wind up the estate and manage the property. Having completed that business he went to London to study law so that he could run his own business affairs without recourse to a legal adviser. It is possible that while in London he was a witness of the execution in Palace Yard of Sir Walter Raleigh in October 1618; but of this there is no proof and we do not know what influence, if any, the execution of Raleigh had on his mind.

While in London he met, and married in August 1620, the daughter of a rich city merchant Sir John Bourchier; she was a year older than Oliver and made him an excellent wife. By her he had eight children; two boys had died when young and he was left with six—two sons, Richard and Henry, and four daughters.

It seems that during his early married life he was often ill, and some consider that it was during those years he underwent a spiritual crisis during which he was liable to fits of depression and nightmares. The puritan background of his school and Cambridge life, and his many talks with his cousin Hampden, were now to produce their fruit and he began a stern communion with his soul—a few years after his marriage. There does not appear to be any record of this spiritual struggle. But a new Oliver was re-created, and in the end he found the peace he sought —I suppose by a process of reasoning, and possibly by some personal experience.

We must mention one more characteristic—he was a man of quick temper, and sudden anger often drove him into harshness.

But here his religion stood him in good stead, and he repented quickly of his faults.

And so he lived his country life, managing his estate and riding to hounds and taking a pride in his hawks. News travelled slowly in those days, but it was often startling; it may well be that Oliver was puzzled over the foreign policy of King James. Then the old king died and the child he had met at Hinchingbrooke ascended the throne as Charles I. The new king had married a Roman Catholic, a sister of the King of France, a girl aged fifteen—who brought many papists to the royal palace in London. Oliver was disquieted. Elizabeth had supported freedom of religion, and a free England. For James he had had little regard. And now the new king, Charles, promised no better; rumour reached Huntingdon that he was ungodly and that he flouted Parliament. Oliver brooded deeply over the news from London and it seems that he slowly began to feel that it was his duty as a Christian and a lover of England to take some part in these disquieting events. He stood for Parliament and was elected member for Huntingdon in January 1628.

Parliament met on the 17th March and Oliver played only a small part, making one speech in February 1629 about religious affairs. It was his first utterance in an assembly which he was later to dominate and ultimately to destroy. It is interesting to reflect on the probable affect on his mind of his first experience of Parliamentary procedure. The session ended in a brawl on the 2nd March, 1629, Black Rod being refused admittance while a statement of grievances against the king was read. The king adjourned Parliament, and for the next eleven years it ceased to exist.

These years during which Charles governed without a Parliament saw a growing discontent in the land. Oliver spent them on his estate, managing his farm and taking an increasing hand in local affairs. The unsettled times decided him to give up owning land and in May 1631 he sold his property in Huntingdon and leased a small farm at St. Ives, a few miles down the Ouse. There are few records of those eleven years but we learn that

Oliver was often dismayed at the course of events in England. In 1636 his uncle, Sir Thomas Steward, died and Oliver succeeded to his estate at Ely, moving to a house in the town close to St. Mary's church.

But now exciting news came from Scotland. King Charles, who as king claimed to direct religious belief and worship, had, in conjunction with Archbishop Laud, introduced a new book of prayer. This had been flung back at him by the Scots, who refused to have anything to do with Rome nor with any procedures not sanctioned by Parliament and the general assembly of its own Kirk. Furthermore, that Kirk had cast out all bishops. Charles decided to coerce the Scots and to raise an army for the purpose. But he had no money and inevitably had to recourse to Parliament—writs being sent out early in 1640 for a new House of Commons.

Oliver knew that great events were impending and, like a war horse, he sniffed the coming battle. One wonders if he realised that a turning point in his career was approaching. He was now forty-one, a very different man from the young squire of 1620—and even from the man who eleven years earlier had first gone as a member of Parliament to Westminster.

He had not found himself; it is doubtful if he ever did in this world. But he had acquired a philosophy, a rule almost, of life. He had a passionate religious faith. In politics he had what I had myself until 1959—a "cross-bench" mind. In the eleven years of country life he had got to know the hearts of the English yeoman farmers, and something of the heart of England itself. They had been years of self-examination and of pondering, and possibly of dismay—until events in Scotland gave him hope.

When Parliament assembled in April 1640, it demanded reforms against the offences of the king in connection with the liberty and privilege of Parliament, the liberty and property of citizens, and the doings of Archbishop Laud and his ecclesiastical courts. King Charles would have none of it and he dissolved Parliament on the 5th May, after a three-weeks session. It became known as the Short Parliament.

POLITICAL LEADERSHIP—ALFRED AND CROMWELL

Charles then turned against Scotland, but his army was defeated on the 28th August at Newburn on the Tyne. He now had to summon a new Parliament in order to raise money.

The new Parliament, known as the Long, met on 3rd November 1640. It was dominated by Pym, amongst whose followers was Oliver Cromwell—the new member for Cambridge. Revolution was in the air; many who were to figure in the Civil War were present, both Royalists and on the side of Parliament; it resembled a parade of the soldiery before the day of battle.

There is no need here to recount all which now followed. Parliament continually stood for its rights and privileges; Charles would first agree and then go back on his word; then came folly upon folly. The climax came in January 1642 when he went to the House with 400 armed soldiers to arrest five members whom he accused of treason. He entered the chamber only to find the five men had withdrawn. Charles had now crossed the Rubicon, and it could not be recrossed. He had so lowered his dignity that neither his honour nor his judgment was trusted by the man in the street. On the 10th January 1642 he left London, and did not return until his trial and execution in 1649.

For six months negotiations dragged on but both sides were preparing for war. Essex was nominated Commander-in-Chief of the Parliament forces, and Charles set up his standard at Nottingham.

The Civil War which was now to begin was not a social war, as some have imagined. It was a struggle between two sides divided on political and religious issues. But the line of cleavage did correspond roughly to certain social divisions.

I shall not deal in any detail with the events of the Civil War which began in mid-1642 and continued until the final overthrow of Charles I and his execution on the 30th January, 1649. His son Charles II, who was in Holland, had been carrying on intrigues in Scotland with the Presbyterians, and on the execution of his father he was at once proclaimed king—arriving in Aberdeen in June 1650. Then began what is sometimes called the Second Civil War, which ended with the crushing defeat of the Scottish army at the Battle of Worcester, on the 3rd September, 1651—but its leader, Charles II, escaped to France. This second outbreak of civil war was really little more than a royalist rising in Scotland, and the people of England took little interest in it.

The Battle of Worcester ended Cromwell's life as a soldier, and that aspect of his career must be dealt with before we move on to consider his career as Lord Protector.

He was not a soldier by profession; there had been no professional army in England since the Hundred Years War. Armies had indeed gone abroad under James and Charles, but they were composed of mercenaries and press-gang men. For home defence there was merely a militia, and Elizabeth had created the trained bands; but the training was only for one day a month during the summer.

The one point in common between the rival forces of Charles and Parliament was that neither side had an army in being, and there were no generals of experience—no military reputations to which either side could turn. Under these conditions, victory was likely to go to the side which produced the best fighting machine and the greatest commander. Nobody could then foresee that the contest would lie between Prince Rupert, aged 23, who had fought with distinction in more than one campaign—and Oliver Cromwell, aged 43, one-time farmer, captain of a troop of sixty cavalrymen, whose only knowledge of war was gained by reading the campaigns of Gustavus Adolphus, King of Sweden.

It was perhaps fortunate for Oliver that he lived in a period of transition in the art of war, the traditional technique being in the melting pot. But he had certain qualities which were to stand him in good stead.

First, he was a practical man with great powers of organisation; next, he knew the way to the hearts of his men. These two assets, when combined, made him a good recruiting officer and a first-class trainer. He gave England a sound military organisation, and a disciplined army; he turned the yeoman farmers of the East Anglian countryside into his Ironsides; there lies his first claim to military greatness.

Then he turned himself into a fine cavalry leader. His love of horses, to which I referred earlier, and his own instincts, made him realise the value of the mobility given by cavalry—and the cumulative effect on the enemy of shock action by a cavalry charge at the right place and time. He must go down to history as a cavalry leader of the first order.

In the tactical sphere he was flexible, adjusting his action to the developing tactical situation. Although he had a quick temper and could at times act rashly, in battle he seems to have had a strange calmness, and the gift of being able to see his problem in the light of reality. He could be very bold, and very cautious. The great art in generalship is the power to simplify a problem and to expose the fundamentals on which all action must be based —to be followed by decision and action. The sum total of simplicity, decision, and action is the hall-mark of military genius —and this is what Cromwell had.

I reckon that if it had not been for Oliver Cromwell, the Parliament forces would have lost the civil war. If he had at that time failed England, the end of the Civil War would have seen the armed return of the Stuarts, helped by forces from Scotland, possibly from Ireland, and from foreign powers. The conflict depended on the resolution of Oliver Cromwell, which did not fail at any time.

I suppose the chief blot on his military fame was his campaign in Ireland, carried out with a ruthless severity which is difficult to excuse—and the hideous slaughter of the garrison of Drogheda, including the murder of the friars, will never be forgotten. He had erred not only against humanity, but also against military wisdom, it becoming clear later that the Drogheda massacres were a spur and an incentive to the enemy—and not a deterrent.

However, so far as we have gone we must hand him the palm, placing him in the front rank of the great commanders.

After the Battle of Worcester in September 1651 he was fifty-two years old, and the first man in England; the army was solidly behind him, the whole land acclaimed him, and he had become the central pillar of the hopes of the English people. In fact, the ball was at his feet. Let us now see how he fared during the next seven years of his life, up to his death in September 1658—with the supreme military power in his hands, and from April 1653 the supreme political power also.

Oliver realised his responsibilities but he looked to Parliament to put the government of the land on a sound basis. He looked in vain.

The crisis came on the 20th April, 1653. A bill for a new form of Parliamentary representation was being debated and was about to be given a third reading; under the bill, the present members were to keep their seats and to have power to exclude any member elected for a vacancy of whom they did not approve. Oliver was not in the House but was hurriedly sent for, and messengers told him what was afoot. He left his room in Whitehall to go to Westminster, ordering a party of soldiers from his own regiment to follow. He entered the House and listened to the debate, leaving the soldiers outside; as he listened he became more and more angry. Finally the Speaker rose to put the third reading of the bill, and Oliver rose with him. He poured out his inmost soul, telling the members exactly what he thought of them. " I will put an end to your prating. You are no Parliament." Then he shouted: " Call them in."

The soldiers filed into the chamber; the Speaker was pulled from his chair; the Mace was removed; the members were driven out. The door was locked, and Oliver Cromwell went home.

The Long Parliament had come to an end. There was now no Parliament, and no government in the land—except the man who the year before had been made by Parliament Commander-in-Chief of the armies of England, Scotland and Ireland. Oliver Cromwell was now the *de facto* ruler of Britain.

It is interesting to reflect on his career up to date. It had been brilliant in the military line. But history suggests that he made two major blunders—first, to sign the death warrant of Charles I; and secondly, the impulsive act of dissolving Parliament by military force. Both acts were committed, one imagines, against his better judgment. Parliament had secured from Charles I the right not to be dissolved except by its own consent but it had ceased to be, except in name, the body which had won that privilege. None the less, it might have been guided patiently towards self-dissolution. But Oliver's temper could stand it no longer and he turned it out by force.

Cromwell was now virtually king, and some reckon he could have had the monarchy at any time—if he had so wished. But there is no evidence that he wanted it. He now set out to govern England in his own way—as the Lord General.

His first Parliament was not a success. It met on the 4th July 1653, and dissolved itself on the following 12th December, being unable to work with Cromwell. It was called the Little Parliament, and by some the Barebone Parliament.

On the 16th December, 1653, Oliver took the oath as Lord Protector. He governed for the next eight months through ordinances. The first Parliament of the Protectorate met on the 3rd September, 1654. The break with this Parliament came over the question of the control of the army. On this point Oliver would not compromise; Parliament saw little hope of a settled government unless it had the ultimate say, and Oliver saw only anarchy if it had. He dissolved Parliament on the 22nd January, 1655.

He now had more power than any English king since William the Conqueror, but his power lay only in the fact that he controlled the army. His plan now was to devise some form of Parliament which would recommend but not dictate.

His new form of government was to divide England into eleven areas, over each of which he set a major-general—a police measure, but disastrous as statesmanship. " Merrie England " became a melancholy place under the rule of the major-generals.

In 1656 money was needed for the war with Spain and Oliver

summoned a new Parliament which met on the 17th September. The major-generals were abolished and in May 1657 a new form was given to the Protectorate; this restored Parliamentary government, with a new House of Lords to which the Protector had the right to nominate the members. But it didn't work and Oliver, seeing that a breach between the two Houses was imminent, dissolved Parliament on the 4th February, 1658.

All these troubles had made Oliver very weary and he took to his bed in March with a dangerous abscess. All the summer of 1658 he was a sick man. In August came the death of his favourite daughter, Elizabeth Claypole; he was distracted with grief and became himself very ill. He died on the 3rd September, 1658.

As a military chief I put him in the top grade. As a political chief and national leader he was not so successful. Between 1653 and 1658 he tried out five different systems of government, and all failed. He tried so hard to build; he was continually forced to destroy. He believed in government of the people, and for the people—but not by the people, who had never elected him by their votes. He tried in vain to impose the rule of a minority over a majority. He was a great improviser, desperately trying expedient after expedient, and finding every tool breaking in his hand.

And how did it all end for him?

On the 10th December, 1660, it was ordered by the Lords and Commons that:

" the carcasses of Oliver Cromwell, Henry Ireton, John Bradshaw, Thomas Pride, whether buried in Westminster Abbey or elsewhere, be with all expedition taken up and drawne on a hurdle to Tiburne."

The bodies were then to hang in chains at Tyburn, in their coffins, for some time and afterwards to be buried under the gallows. Cromwell's head was cut off and set up on a pole on the roof of Westminster Hall, for all to see; it remained there until 1684.

Another thought occurs to me about Oliver Cromwell—was he too much the servant of his Bible? His every action had to be reconciled with some biblical passage.

I am reminded of an old lady who once stayed with my wife and myself. One morning she read in a newspaper that her son had been named as co-respondent in a divorce case. She took to her bed with her Bible and spent three days trying to find some passage, some scriptural quotation, which could condone her son's action—and failed to find what she wanted. She then sent for her solicitor and made a new will, disinheriting her son!

One cannot act in that way in this imperfect world. The Bible is intended to be a guide and not a set of rules to be observed rigidly.

I get the feeling that a little more patience, more persuasion, a more tolerant approach to his problems, the use of the rapier rather than the bludgeon—all these might have helped towards a more successful ending to his political career. One of the reasons why he became a successful soldier was because he had no allies, with their petty national feelings all tending towards compromise on essentials. I myself have had personal experience of that trouble! When he became a politician, he had to compromise; and compromise was not in his nature.

A few days before he died he named his eldest son, Richard, his successor as Lord Protector. But in less than a year the Protectorate fell ignominiously. And in less than two years the monarchy was restored with almost universal rejoicing. But let us make no mistake about it—the monarchy was not the same in 1660 as it had been in 1640, and the credit for the difference must be given to Oliver Cromwell.

Without a doubt he was a most complex character. But history may well prove that he was more tolerant in the religious sense than most men of his time. He tried hard to come to an accommodation with Charles I; but Charles cheated, and anyhow the largely Independent Army of Cromwell wouldn't have it.

I believe Cromwell was an unwilling dictator, who lived in

a time when it was almost impossible for any head of state to do more than keep afloat from week to week. He certainly is a most interesting case—a man who, in the political field, did not live long enough to overcome the prevailing anarchy in church and state.

But this can be said—but for him the England we know to-day might have been a very different land.

CHAPTER FIVE

ABRAHAM LINCOLN

I WILL now move forward one hundred and fifty years. So many books have been written about Lincoln, about two thousand it is said, that it seems almost an impertinence on my part to write any more about him. But many readers of this book may know little of the man, not even being clear about the date when he was President of the United States, nor how he rose to that position and saved the Union when it could well have broken up —which would have been a tragedy for all mankind. Furthermore, for our own purpose we should try to discover the special qualities he possessed which enabled him to exercise leadership for the good of the American people. We must, therefore, take a look, a brief glimpse, at his early life and then examine how he handled the situations which encompassed him when he held high office.

The American Civil War, or, as many Americans prefer to call it, the War between the States, began a hundred years ago, in 1861—and Lincoln was born just over fifty years before that, in February 1809. He came from English Quaker stock but could never trace his ancestry beyond his grandfather.

His father, Thomas Lincoln, was a poor farmer in Kentucky; his mother was the illegitimate daughter of a domestic servant who had wandered into Kentucky with her baby. The family was very poor and Abraham's life was one of unceasing hardship, made the more so because his father was constantly moving the home in his search for better land to cultivate. Apparently Abraham differed so much in appearance from his father that stories were put around that he was not his father's son; but these stories have been proved to be utterly false. The two were not only different in appearance but also in moral and mental growth; as Abraham increased in stature, so his father Thomas seems to have slid backwards. It is clear that Lincoln had no real affection for his father and did not attempt to conceal it—he was too honest and sincere. His mother died when he was eight; he had loved her, and missed her sadly. In late 1819, when he was nearly eleven, his father married again, a widow with three children; this worked out well and the boy Lincoln came to love his stepmother as the memories of his own mother became dimmed. The love of Lincoln for his mother and step-mother, and his inability to get on with his father has always interested me because in my own case it was exactly the opposite. I adored my father, but was never able to get on good terms with my mother—the reasons, on reflection, being entirely my own fault, as has been explained in my *Memoirs*.

His schooling as a boy was intermittent. He was sent to any available nearby school, and when none was available would pick up what education he could from men he knew. All in all, one reads that he attended school less than one year. But his desire to learn urged him to teach himself; he could read and write better than anybody in the countryside and did all the writing for his family and their friends. He was a great reader, preferring to study deeply a few worthwhile books rather than skip quickly through a lot of trash. In later life he was always conscious of his lack of education and was never ashamed to admit it. There is no clear evidence that he studied the Bible; but it was undoubtedly in his home, possibly the only book, and his early reading of it can be noticed in his later speeches and writings. It seems that he was a noted story-teller and he would entertain any company with stories of his own composition—which amused friends and strangers alike.

And so he grew up and when he was twelve he was earning his own living by doing any odd jobs for the neighbours. He grew at a great rate, being about six foot four inches at nineteen, with long arms and legs, and had such strength that he was in great demand for jobs of a heavy type. And he also learnt to wrestle and became famous for his skill in that art. But all this time deep lines were early forming on his face, due, most probably, to the hardships of early life and maybe to underfeeding as a child.

The time came when he left home and set out into the world to make his own way in life. He began as a salesman in a village shop, and later became a postmaster. Then he had a short period of fighting against the Indians in the Black Hawk War, joining up as a volunteer in 1832 and being elected captain of a company by his comrades; he served for eighty days in all, for which he received in pay about 120 dollars. This was a valuable experience which taught him something about soldiering, how to handle men, and the value of morale and discipline—experience which was to stand him in good stead in later years.

He then decided to become a lawyer, which was quite a good profession in a country where there was an increasing population and everybody wanted land. About this time he became intensely interested in politics, which was almost the only subject of conversation in those days apart from farming—in fact, it was almost a national pastime. He proved a born politician; he could tell amusing stories, he was a student of his fellow men and learnt how to handle audiences, and he was a master at pulling strings. In 1834, at the age of 25, he was elected to the House of Representatives in the State Legislature of Illinois. He served four terms in the Legislature and they were an invaluable experience for him. He learned the technique of politics, and the ways and nature of politicians—appeal to the voters amounting almost to bribery, persuasion, manœuvre, and finally compromise.

And he proved to be pretty able at the game. Some have wondered why Lincoln, with his humble background and strong feelings for the mass of the common people, lined up with the Republicans, who were assumed to be the party of wealth and big business, rather than with the Democrats. So far as I can gather through reading he disliked Jackson, the leader of the Democrats, and had been greatly helped by Republican friends when he first entered politics; these things may possibly have helped to shape his thinking.

We must now turn to his love affairs, and eventual marriage. It appears that he was never at ease with women, being afraid of them; this may well have been because his uncouth figure made him shy in female society, or it may have been that sex appeal had no interest for him. Whatever the cause, his love affairs were not happy. I have read that men who grow up in ignorance of women are inclined to idealise them and, in consequence, have unhappy marriages; my own experiences would not agree with this philosophy. However that may be, his first affair was not so unhappy as tragic. He fell in love with the daughter of a tavern keeper where he once boarded, Ann Rutledge, and they became engaged to be married; then she suddenly died. Opinions vary as to whether this incident left any enduring mark on Lincoln; the general impression is that it took him some years to recover.

His next affair was unhappy, but not tragic—"humorous" might be the word. Three years later he began to associate with a lady, Mary Owens, no longer young, for whom her married sister wanted a husband. When approached by the sister, Lincoln agreed to marry Mary—laughingly, regarding it as a joke. As the days passed he realised he did not love the lady; but he reckoned it was his duty to make a formal proposal, and did so—and, to his amazement, was refused. He repeated the offer; again a refusal. He then withdrew from the matrimonial stakes, his feelings deeply wounded! I can sympathise with him, for almost the same thing once happened to me in my younger days—but few know about it and it is not a subject I enlarge upon.

Third time lucky—so it is said! In 1839 he met a vivacious, strong-willed and ambitious young woman called Mary Todd, the daughter of a Kentucky bank president, cultured and far superior socially to Lincoln or any of his friends—and with a quick temper too. With an unerring eye for the road to power, she reckoned Lincoln was the most likely man to get her to the White House—and she was right. He had never met anybody like her before and they became formally engaged in 1840. But as the days passed he realised he had hooked an awkward customer, and he tried to break off the engagement; but she used the woman's weapon of tears and he gave in. Then came the wedding day; the bride arrived first at the church, and waited in vain for Lincoln—he funked it, and failed to appear!

I have from time to time read sensational stories in the Press of such happenings, and occasionally about brides who decide at the last moment that they cannot face it and fail to get to the church. And I have always thought there must be some mental deficiency in a person who acts thus. But obviously one is wrong; Lincoln did it, and there was nothing wrong with his mental equipment. The story goes on to say that he was very ashamed at his action and consulted a mental doctor who confined him in his home for a week! It shows how the mighty can fall!

Lincoln gradually recovered and so did Mary Todd. They were brought together again by friends and this time the course of true love ran smoothly. In November 1842 they were married, and Mary bore four sons, one of whom, a boy, Edward, died when he was four, and another, Willie the third eldest, died in 1862 at the age of eleven, in the White House.

But we read that his married life was not happy. He was a simple man, with a humble background; she liked fine clothes, jewellery, and parties. I doubt if Lincoln could have been an easy man to live with; his careless ways, and periods of extreme dejection, must have annoyed Mary. Then she had a really bad temper and would lash out at him—and when he could bear it no longer he would leave the house for his office. So to him his home became a restless sort of place, with constant nagging, and little tenderness and companionship. The result was that he devoted more and more time to public affairs, and to his profession of the law, and to politics—in fact, to all those pursuits in which he could serve his fellow men. But he had learnt one lesson—that he could overcome the defects of temperament in his make-up, and go through with whatever life or fate set before him.

Lincoln was elected to Congress in 1846, and the story of his life from then onwards can be read in many books. He became a noted lawyer, travelled widely in connection with his profession, made many speeches, and gradually became very well known. At the convention in Chicago in May 1860 he was elected Republican candidate for the Presidency, and on the 6th November, 1860, was elected President of the United States. He took office on the 4th March, 1861, in Washington. He was now 52, and fate then placed on the shoulders of this lonely man a burden the like of which can seldom have been handed to any man before; it was to test him to the core—and was to lead to his assassination in April 1865, a few weeks after he had taken the oath for a second period of office as President in March.

But when the hour came for him to lead the American people, he was ready. The question at issue was the position of slavery in the United States. When the Union was created, negro slavery was firmly established in the Southern states; the use of transported African labour for the cultivation of tobacco and cotton had made the white colonists of the South rich without the necessity of working themselves. Thomas Jefferson always believed that legalised slavery was the greatest fault of his nation, and that the negro was inferior to the white man—morally and intellectually. In 1807, when carrying out his second term of office as President, he got an Act passed by Congress forbidding any further importation of slaves into America. Slavery could not have been abolished altogether at that time since this would have meant widespread ruin in the South; but it was always considered by Jefferson that its extension must not be allowed. However, as time went on more country was put under cotton and slave breeding became an industry. The six original slave states became fifteen.

The North did not want slavery; being mainly industrial, unintelligent slave labour was of little use; also they reckoned it made a mockery of the Declaration of Independence—"that all men are created equal." I have never been able to take this famous sentence at its face value; of course we are all equal in the sight of God, but we are born with very different talents and as children grow into men and women they become less equal. However, perhaps we had better not get involved in that argument!

The question of the moral basis of slavery caused much bitterness between North and South; and the crisis came when certain of the Southern states decided to secede from the Union, and to form a new Confederation based on the inequality of man, that "the negro is not equal to the white man," and that secession was necessary because the North refused to recognise this moral truth. Jefferson Davis was elected the first President of the new "Confederate States of America" in February 1861.

This was the problem facing Lincoln. He reckoned that slavery was an issue which time and common sense would solve. But once the Union was gone it would never return; North America would become like Europe, a continent torn with disunity, jealousy, economic rivalry and wars. He reckoned that the preservation of the Union was vital for the future of democracy.

He had been elected President in November 1860, but was powerless until his inauguration in March 1861. Meanwhile the outgoing Democratic government decided that the Federal government had no power to prevent any state from seceding—in fact, that the Union could not be maintained.

Poor Lincoln! He knew he would have to bear the full responsibility for what was to come, and now, while there was still time to halt the avalanche, he could do nothing.

When he assumed office he delayed the decision as long as he could. But the issue was brought to a head in April 1861 when a United States garrison at Fort Sumter in South Carolina was attacked by troops of the "Confederate States of America," the Stars and Stripes of the Union was fired on and then hauled down as the garrison surrendered.

This was too much! The North sprang to arms, as did the South, and the American Civil War began.

Abraham Lincoln was now to prove his greatness. It is not

within the scope of our picture of the man to describe all the events which now descended upon him fast and furiously, and how the crises developed in a seemingly never-ending tragedy—nor to detail how he survived the storms, and brought the ship of the Union into calm waters so that it could develop into the mighty nation it now is—the most powerful in the world. All that has been told in a thousand books, or more.

Our task is rather to examine the man himself, and to see if we can discover that "something" in his character, his make-up, which enabled this queer rough diamond of a Western lawyer to rise to such great heights. And make no mistake about it, to-day his memory is revered by all Americans the world over—rich and poor alike.

I think the basic factor in his greatness was that he loved the common man, the man in the street, the people, and dedicated himself to their service. He wanted nothing for himself, neither riches nor honours; he was utterly selfless and he didn't even try to build himself up in the eyes of the people in order to be able to lead the North successfully. Lincoln had no need to do this, nor did such a thing ever occur to him; his transparent honesty and sincerity were adequate. His sole wish was to serve the American people, and preserve the Union. Here was true and noble leadership.

Then he could listen, understand, and finally decide. Once his mind was made up, he was unshakable—accepting full responsibility for his actions.

His speeches reveal a deep knowledge of fundamentals, about which he had thought deeply and his listeners had generally not. His greatness as a politician lay in the fact that he spoke so simply that he made the people understand the issues on which all action must be based. The impression I gain is that he considered the function of a political leader in a democracy is not to impose his will, but to guide the people towards deciding wisely for themselves; he was constantly pointing out how man serves himself best in the long run by being generous towards others—and strictly fair too. In this respect his mastery of language was a strong factor in his success; for a self-taught man this mastery was remarkable.

And throughout it all his conduct was essentially Christian; he seemed to conform naturally to the teachings of the Sermon on the Mount—not in any sanctimonious way, but because he reckoned that Christian virtues are democratic virtues too, since they offer men a means of living together in dignity and respect.

I have always been intensely interested in the way he handled his generals in the civil war. As President he had to direct the war effort and to weigh political as well as military factors. His sole military experience was that obtained in the Black Hawk War against the Indians in 1832, which we noted earlier. Compare this with Churchill in Hitler's war; he had the same task and the same powers, but he had vast previous experience of war and of Service Chiefs; even so, it took him quite a time to find the generals he wanted and get them in the right places!

Knowing his lack of knowledge, Lincoln acquired military text books and embarked on a study of the art of war at his desk in the White House. It then gradually became clear to him that most of the generals on whom he could call knew so little about the game that his judgment was as good as theirs, if not better. Until trial and time could produce the right man, he undertook overall military control himself in March 1862. And all his plans were invariably sound; when failure came it was due to faulty execution by his generals. It is not too much to say that in averting disaster until he found the general he could trust, Lincoln became a master in the art of the strategical conduct of war. He eventually found the right general in Ulysses Grant, but not until February 1864—when with a thankful heart he appointed him to command the armies of the United States.

But do not let us forget that in addition to his personal direction of the war Lincoln had to handle political and economic problems, and generally hold the North together. My own study of the whole affair leads me to conclude that without his strong and sure leadership the appalling effort and loss of life of the terrible years of the American Civil War would have been spent in vain. Not only did he save the Union; he abolished slavery in America.

At the dedication ceremony in November 1863 of the national cemetery for those who had fallen at Gettysburg in the previous July, he made the soul-stirring speech which defined his feelings on the whole question of the civil war which was then nearing its end, and gave his views on the ideals of democracy. I have visited that cemetery and seen the small grass mound from which he spoke.

Let me mention one last point about Lincoln. To me, an interesting feature in his character was the tenderness of his heart, and his love of children. We see this brought out when his son Willie, age 11, lay at death's door in the White House early in 1862. There was a reception and ball that night; Lincoln welcomed the guests and then went to Willie's bedside. He was a most lovable boy and may have been a favourite son, but of this I can find no record. The days passed and he got no better, and finally died. Lincoln found it difficult, almost impossible, to shake off his grief; indeed, it was many months before he did so.

The Lincoln Memorial in Washington can move me in ways that no other can. There sits Abraham Lincoln, with his strong and rugged features, looking towards the Capitol—a noble statue of a noble man, and one of the greatest national leaders of all time.

CHAPTER FIVE

JAWARHALAL NEHRU

Now let us consider a national leader of the 1960s, the elected political head of the second largest nation in the world—Nehru.

I have known Nehru for some years, since 1946 in fact, and I have always liked and admired him. Before writing this chapter I went to stay with him in the Prime Minister's House in New Delhi for four days; I was the only guest and we lived a simple family life with his very talented daughter, Mrs. Indira Gandhi, and her children—having all meals in nursery style, with the grandchildren. We had many long talks, sometimes walking in the garden, at other times in my sitting-room, and in the evenings during and after dinner at which meal the grandchildren were usually not present. To be received into the home of the political head of a nation of 400 million people in this way, and treated as one of the family circle, is a privilege which must surely come the way of few. Our conversations, indeed the whole experience, revealed Nehru to me in a new light; here was wisdom, and a sane and practical approach to world problems which I had found in few others. By the time I left New Delhi I had put him in the category of great men. But before asking the reader to reach a decision in the matter, let us have a closer look at the man himself.

He was born in November 1889, in Allahabad, and was the only son of prosperous parents. For the first eleven years of his life he was an only child, his eldest sister, now Mrs. Pandit, being born in 1900. Being an only son, and for a time an only child, his parents lavished all their love and affection on him; in consequence his early life was very sheltered, and he never attended school until he went to Harrow at the age of fifteen.

His father was a rich lawyer in Allahabad, who reckoned that money was given to you to be spent rather than saved; so the home gradually became luxurious and the family more and more Westernised. Many visitors came to the house and the young Nehru listened eagerly to the conversation of his elders—which was generally related to the iniquities of the British Raj and the insulting behaviour of the English towards Indians. He thus developed early an antipathy towards the alien rulers of his country, although he never seems to have had hostile feelings against individual Englishmen. He admired his father but also feared him, possibly because of a tremendous thrashing which he would sometimes receive.

He went to Harrow in 1905, but he himself reckons he never fitted exactly into the life of the school. It was there that he first became interested in politics and he followed keenly the election campaign which resulted in the formation of the Campbell-Bannerman government early in 1906. He remained at Harrow only two years and then went to Trinity, Cambridge, in October 1907—being then nearly eighteen, and thirsting for greater freedom to develop his ideas and intellectual capacity than was possible at Harrow. Indian politics at that time were, as he described it, "in a state of upheaval" and it is clear that whatever may have been the impression he created on others, inwardly his thoughts were turning more and more towards his own country and its problems—which were causing him considerable anxiety and agitation.

He seems to have had no strong religious feelings in his early life, nor when at Cambridge; indeed, he disliked what he called the "repressions of religion" and searched for some other standards; he appears to be much the same to-day but, although a Hindu, his life is based on the Christian virtues.

In 1910 he took a degree in the Natural Sciences Tripos and left Cambridge. His next step was to study law in London and he was called to the Bar in 1912; he then went back to India, having been away for over seven years. He was now twenty-three, and as he himself has written in his autobiography: " I was a bit of a prig, with little to commend me."

He next took to law and joined the High Court. At first the work interested him, but he gradually became dissatisfied with the law as a profession; politics called him and he joined the Congress party.

Then came the First World War in 1914, his marriage in the spring of 1916, and his first meeting with Gandhi at the time of the Lucknow Congress during Christmas 1916.

When he was about thirteen he had met Mrs. Annie Besant and had been enthralled by her oratory. On his return to India in 1912 he met her again and worked for her " Home Rule for India" league; the eventual internment of the lady led to much excitement and played a large part in giving renewed impetus to the Home Rule movement throughout India—which Nehru now actively supported.

The end of the war in 1918 found India in a state of suppressed excitement; political agitation was widespread and unrest was being worked up among the peasants—who constitute the mass of the people.

We must now take a look at Gandhi, the leader of the movement for Independence in India, and this is especially necessary since Nehru is his disciple. I have read many books about Gandhi but doubt if any of them do justice to the man himself —whom I never met. He seems to have been a very extraordinary individual, with an amazing power to attract and influence individuals as well as masses of people—and yet without any of the tricks of public men. Nehru tells me that both he and others who worked with him often disagreed with Gandhi, but that never succeeded in breaking the bonds which bound them all to him. He was clearly a strange personality, and one who gripped the millions of India in a way which nobody else had ever done before him. As Nehru said, he had that rare quality which made him tower above the masses and left its impress on their thinking in a way which has lasted over the years. He was a man of goodwill who moved about among the masses, taking to the loin-cloth and the mud hut so as to be at one with them—and retaining these emblems of renunciation even while pleading his cause with the highest in the land. His whole philosophy was based on being "at one" with the people and educating them to the policy of *Swaraj*, which means self-rule or independence; this goal was to be achieved by *Satyagraha*—civil disobedience and non-cooperation, but by methods of non-violence. This man, miserable looking with his loin-cloth and bare body and poor physique, had something within him which drew forth the admiration of the masses of India; they literally worshipped him. The dominant note all over India at that time was one of expectation, though the hope was tinged with fear and anxiety—hope in the leadership of Gandhi towards Independence, and fear as to what might be the outcome of the inevitable clash with the Government. And so Gandhi took the lead in an all-India agitation in 1919, and began his *Satyagraha* movement—which pledged his followers to civil disobedience and to court gaol openly and deliberately.

Nehru's immediate reaction was one of tremendous relief; here was the method of action, and here was the leader, although he realised that many pitfalls and a long struggle lay ahead.

Nehru has talked to me at length about the years of the struggle which ensued. Gandhi travelled throughout India in third-class railway carriages, in bullock carts and on foot, visiting the cities and villages. The people flocked to hear him and he addressed large audiences of up to a hundred thousand; he had no loud-speaker equipment and few could have heard his voice; but that did not seem to matter since all could see their hero, and what he said soon got around. He was arrested as an agitator from time to time and spent many years in prison; he was let out from time to time, particularly when he was ill, but he was soon back again. In all he was nearly seven years in prison—less than Nehru, but then he was often ill and was let out until he recovered.

The year 1920 saw the inauguration of non-cooperation and it is not my intention to discuss all that took place from then onwards until the transfer of power, which took place on the

15th August 1947. Events by then had reached such a stage that it could not have been postponed any longer. But Home Rule brought with it Partition, Jinnah creating the Moslem state of Pakistan and Nehru becoming Prime Minister of India.

The price to be paid for all these things was high in terms of bloodshed and human suffering. By the end of 1947 the killings had mostly come to an end and they ceased completely with Gandhi's assassination in January 1948. The next year, 1949, by the Declaration of London, India became a sovereign independent republic within the British Commonwealth—and the long struggle was over. On the 26th January, 1950, the Constitution of India was formally inaugurated, that day now being celebrated throughout India every year as Independence Day.

We must now return to Nehru and see if we can learn more about him.

It has always seemed to me from my study of the struggle for Independence that the determination to carry on the struggle, come what might, was the result of General Dyer's action in the *Jallianwala Bagh* at Amritsar in 1919, when he ordered fire to be opened on a public meeting—such meetings being forbidden—resulting in some 380 Indians being killed and about 1,200 wounded. In my talks with Nehru he agreed, adding that he reckoned Amritsar was a turning point in Anglo-Indian relations. To him personally it was a great shock, and under the emotional impact of the event he plunged into politics with a fire in his belly. About this time also he became somewhat ashamed of his comfortable life, and realised how cut off the top level of Indian life was from the millions in the villages. He was ignorant of village life, but knew there was great poverty and misery among the peasants; he felt he must now make contact with the peasantry as a prelude to tackling the problem of their poverty. And so in 1920 he set out on his travels, studying the village life of India and telling the peasants about Gandhi, and the Congress party, and the battle which was being fought to abolish the alien rule of their country and bring Independence to the Indian people. He told me that at first he was shy; he had not previously bothered about the struggling village peasantry, and had taken them for granted as had most others. And he had not before addressed public gatherings. But their friendliness soon overcame his shyness and lack of oratory; he talked to them simply, as man to man, saying merely what was in his mind and heart.

He continued his visits to the villages during 1921, knowing that the peasants had little staying power and lacked the energy to carry on civil disobedience for long without continued mental stiffening—which he and others must provide.

This initial contact with the struggling millions of India has been continued by Nehru ever since those early days in 1920, and still continues to-day—as the following story will show.

I arrived in New Delhi very early on a December morning in 1959, and met the family at breakfast. On my way to the nursery wing of the house I had noticed a large crowd on the front lawn, being seated on the ground in rows by their leaders. I asked what was going to happen and Nehru replied that it was a daily event; peasants, students, schoolboys, and others who came to Delhi, all wanted to see him, and it was known that he could be seen by anybody who wished at 8.30 every morning he was at home. As he put it himself: " I am apparently one of the sights of Delhi." I asked if I could accompany him when he went out to see the gathering, and I am glad I did so since it gave one a glimpse of Nehru that one could get in no other way.

He began by walking through the rows of people, men, women and children, talking with some here and there, and being garlanded as he went. His technique with the garlands was to remove them from his neck and throw them to the children— who were of course thrilled. But what interested me was the way each individual gazed at Nehru as he moved about, each pair of eyes following him, and with a look of utter devotion on each face. I was told it is the same wherever he goes in India, as can well be imagined by what happened in Bombay a few days before I arrived in New Delhi. Nehru had gone to Bombay to open a new science building, and in the afternoon he was in a part of the city near the cricket ground where a Test Match against the

Australians was being played. Cricket is very popular in India and the match was being watched by a huge crowd. It soon became known by the crowd that Nehru was nearby, and almost to a man they left the ground to see him—the match proceeding without any spectators!

It is fascinating to hear him talking to a large crowd, as I did on the lawn of his house in New Delhi. I used to speak Hindustani fluently when serving with my regiment in India in 1908, and had passed the Higher Standard in that language, and it has not all been forgotten. So I could follow the gist of what he said. He speaks very simply to them and about their own professions —to students about learning, to farmers about farming, and so on. Each day I was staying in his house, I went with him to the lawn after breakfast—to see, and to learn more about the man.

On one occasion the crowd contained a party of peasants from Gujerat, one of whom was presented personally to Nehru because he had won a prize for his corn. Now Nehru cannot speak Gujerati; so he made the farmer address the others over the loudspeaker and tell them the methods he used to grow good corn.

When considering Nehru one has always to remember that he is a disciple of Gandhi and uses many of his methods. Such as India is to-day is largely the result of the influence of Gandhi on the masses of his countrymen in general, and on his immediate group of followers in particular. But the more one studies Gandhi, and the more I talked to Nehru about him, the more I come to the conclusion that he seems a very strange figure in the modern world, and perhaps he would not have fitted in to any other country. It was the utter sincerity of the man which compelled the admiration of the teeming millions of his fellow countrymen; Nehru would often argue with him and get angry, but the anger passed, leaving him ashamed at his lack of balance. Of course, once Gandhi began his campaign for Independence, and to do away with the alien rule of his country, all of the 400 million Indians lined up solidly behind him. And one cannot wonder.

I spent some seven years in India and during that time saw

most parts of the country. On one occasion I served as transport officer to a British column which was changing station; this involved a march of several weeks through southern India and its villages, and I saw something of the squalor of the peasants in their miserable rags, the thousands of uneducated children, and the general misery of the people—unable to do anything to better their lot. I used to compare this squalid picture with the splendours of the British Raj and of the Native Princes; and since then I have sometimes wondered if we British can have a very clear conscience about the years of our rule in India.

Nehru has worked on the same principles as did Gandhi. He has developed an intense interest in the masses of the Indian people and their problems, and here lies the key to his political power—the millions of India have given him their utter devotion and trust, they are solidly behind him. " *Chacha* Nehru" they shout when they see him—Uncle Nehru—and that is how he is known.

He himself is fully aware of this power, and of the problems it creates. In our talks he emphasised the point constantly that *a leader cannot act to a degree beyond what the people will take;* he must, of course, have courage, but if the people will not follow his decisions he will inevitably fall. He must therefore be a persuader, and this is what Gandhi was; he would persuade the masses by his transparent honesty.

For these reasons, and possibly others, Nehru's view is that a national leader must have home affairs uppermost in his mind at all times; this is not to say that he can neglect foreign affairs, very far from it, the two must be nicely balanced; but he reckons to-day that there is a general tendency for heads of governments to devote too little of their time to the problems of the people they govern.

He considers, like me, that Ministers give themselves insufficient time to think and to be with the people they represent in a parliamentary democracy. He told me that recently he asked his colleagues in the government if he could lay down his office of Prime Minister for a while, say for one year, and have time to renew his contacts with the peasantry in the villages, and as he put it: "re-charge my batteries." He promised to return, if they so wished. His colleagues decided against such action on his part, and Nehru thinks wrongly; however, he abided by their wishes. As I pointed out to him, it may well be that their decision was influenced by the difficulty of nominating his relief!

One morning when walking in the garden I asked him for his views on the need for "selflessness" in a leader, national or military —and his reply was interesting. He agreed that selflessness is essential in that the true leader must have no thought of personal gain or aggrandisement. But he added that complete selflessness insofar as the outside world is concerned is not always possible. In order to lead successfully, a man may have to build himself up in the eyes of his followers—and this will create unfriendly criticism among his pseudo friends and political opponents that he is not selfless. Nehru was insistent that the build-up may be necessary, and if so the leader must not falter—but must put up with the criticism, knowing in his own heart that it is unjustified and that all will work out rightly in the end.

Nehru is interesting when you lead him on to talk about his years in prison—which totalled nine years in all, the longest continuous period being $2\frac{1}{2}$ years. His great occupation was gardening, not only because he likes it and knows a lot about plants and flowers, but also because it provided exercise. Smoking was not allowed. The prison fare was not too good; but his friends would hand in food parcels for him at the prison gate and most of the contents reached him—after the warders had taken their share!

In those days the governors of prisons were officers of the Indian Medical Services; these may have been good doctors but they knew little about the organisation of prisons. However, on the whole he and other political prisoners were well treated. And one good result has followed—all who were political prisoners of those days are now deeply interested in prison reform and the need for good governors!

Nehru was most interesting about his fellow prisoners. He said the ones he liked best were the murderers, at which I expressed surprise and asked him to explain. He said that in India very few men murder by intent; most killings in normal times are due to the results of a beat up, or a sudden blow given in anger. Anyhow, he reckoned the murderers who were his comrades in prison were decent and sincere people! The ones he disliked most were the pickpockets; they were basically bad characters. It would appear that in India you cannot be a sincere pickpocket—nor anywhere else, I reckon!

When talking about his prison life, Nehru would remind me that he has himself changed from a political agitator to a respectable Prime Minister. But he once remarked that he sometimes thought that the most effective and vital part of his work was done in those old days of agitation and national struggle. I replied that in my view his real work lay in the years which lie ahead, and perhaps we should consider that before closing this chapter.

Nehru's contribution to India up to date has been tremendous; but for him India might well have left the British Commonwealth, so bitter was the feeling against the British and the memories of their rule of the country. But he faces a tremendous task. The movement for Independence in India was based on the people and their economic prosperity; there is no apparent ideology to which the 400 millions adhere and subscribe; there is no discipline in the movement, except the discipline and obedience demanded by Gandhi from his immediate followers. In fact, the movement was based on the idolisation of one man, Gandhi—and now Nehru.

And on the northern frontiers of India are nearly seven hundred million Chinese, increasing at the rate of fifteen million a year—China having an ideology, strict discipline, and stern leadership. Will the Chinese one day look outwards, hoping to join forces with India—thus creating a bloc of some fifteen hundred million people within the next twenty years? I hope not; India is needed in the Western camp.

But one can say this about the movement for Independence in India—it was very different from those in other countries such as Egypt, Iraq, Burma, Ceylon and the Congo. In those countries the movement had its origins in exciting the people to flare up; there was mob violence worked up by political agitators. And, of course, India is a vastly larger country than any of those I have mentioned, a sub-continent of over 400 million people—but it has held together.

None the less, much of what happens in Asia in general, and in India in particular, in the foreseeable future will depend on Nehru.

If he can solve the Kashmir problem, and can move towards friendship and co-operation with Pakistan, and his health lasts (he is seventy-two)—all may go well in Asia. If he fails, there is nobody of his wisdom and stature in sight to succeed him—and the worst may happen.

" *Chacha* Nehru," shout the millions of India. If ever a man has the hallmark of greatness it is Nehru, and I place him in the front rank of great national leaders.

I have often thought it interesting to compare Nehru and Abraham Lincoln; their lives were totally different, yet each rose to be the political head of his country. As we have seen, Nehru was the only son of a wealthy, aristocratic and distinguished lawyer. He had the best education that money could provide—private tutors, Harrow, Cambridge, and the Inner Temple in London.

Abraham Lincoln was the son of a poor farmer who had never learned to read and could only with difficulty scrawl his name; his mother also could neither read nor write. Lincoln himself spent only a total of one year at school, and that at very irregular intervals of a few weeks at a time.

Both men reached the pinnacle of fame. But on the way to the summit Nehru became a political agitator and spent some nine years in prison. Lincoln managed to escape such indignities, but was assassinated when he had completed only half his task.

It should be noted that Nehru has also completed only half his task in India, and has some formidable problems yet to face—Indian rural poverty has to be tackled, and the mass of the peasants have to be fired with a sense of national unity and purpose. It is a tremendous and challenging task, yet I believe he will carry it out successfully.

We must now leave him for the time being. But such are the hopes for the future in Asia which depend on him that we cannot finish with him altogether just yet; we will return to him again in a later chapter.

CHAPTER SEVEN

GENERAL DE GAULLE

I ONCE read an article by Maurice Edelman which described de Gaulle as:

" a father-figure, a sometimes angry but long-suffering Moses leading his people out of the desert of mediocrity to the uplands of greatness."

This comparison between the two leaders seemed to me to be so interesting that my first idea was to consider them together in the same chapter—because both had the same problem, the re-building of the soul of a nation. But on second thoughts it seemed more suitable to consider de Gaulle in the "setting" of the present times, as I have done with others of his day. We can have a backward look at Moses and his activities later on.

In 1940 France suffered the humiliation of collapse, occupation by the armed forces of Hitler's Germany, and finally despair leading to a disease of the soul—a *tristesse*.

A leader was needed to lift the nation up from its sorrowful state and place it on the way to its rightful destiny.

After many years of political strife, during which France was blown about like a ship without a rudder in a rough sea, she found her leader in de Gaulle.

Charles de Gaulle

He was the son of a soldier who later became a lay master at a Jesuit college in Paris; the boy Charles was educated at a Jesuit school before he went to the military college at St. Cyr. It can therefore well be imagined that he is a staunch Roman Catholic and deeply religious. When he passed out of St. Cyr in 1911, he asked to be appointed to the 33rd Infantry Regiment because he admired its colonel—who was Pétain. He could then hardly have known that the time would come, and did come in August 1945, when General de Gaulle would have to order Pétain, Marshal of France, to be tried by a military court for collaborating with the enemy in wartime. Pétain was so tried and was condemned to death. But de Gaulle reprieved him; his intention was that after two years of detention in a fortress, the Marshal should be released to live in his own home near Antibes. However, we have got ahead of the story.

When Pétain first came across de Gaulle in the 1920s, he realised he was a very unusual officer and employed him on his staff at various intervals. De Gaulle was a great student of war and a military thinker who was well ahead of his times—at any rate, in France. His book, *Vers l'Armée de Métier* (title of the English edition—*The Army of the Future*), published in 1934 shortly after Hitler's rise to power, was in fact a classic—though not recognised as such at the time. It advocated:

> "the creation, as a matter of urgency, of an army of manœuvre and attack, mechanised, armoured, composed of picked men, to be added to the large-scale units supplied by mobilisation."

The quotation is from Vol. I of his *War Memoirs*. This force was to be composed of long service professional soldiers; it would be a *corps d'élite* of some 100,000 men, its three thousand tanks being the spearhead of all offensive operations. He was right, and events in 1940 might well have turned out differently if his military doctrines had found favour with his political masters. But his call for a mobile striking force was linked to the philosophy of a professional standing army in France; this was anathema to the French politicians, who considered such a force might well become a military menace to the régime and thus endanger the Republic. The French Parliament set its face against all change, preferring the large conscript army to the smaller professional force.

It is possible that at this moment in his military career de Gaulle's thinking was influenced by Hitler's success in Germany, which resulted in the German Army being remodelled soon after Hitler rose to power in 1933. De Gaulle referred in his book to the need for a leader to appear in France, thereby showing great foresight—but when the crisis arose in 1940, France lacked the leader.

Pétain backed the young soldier, who dedicated his next book to him. Pétain had become godfather to de Gaulle's son—called Philippe in honour of the Marshal. De Gaulle, now a Colonel, also impressed Paul Reynaud who put his military doctrines before the Army Committee of the French Chamber—only to have them rejected.

In March 1940 Reynaud became Prime Minister in place of Daladier; I remember that time very well. I had paid a visit to the active front in the Saar, where part of my division was serving in the Maginot Line—to gain experience in contact with the enemy—and I returned full of alarm about the state of the French Army; my thinking on this subject is explained in my *Memoirs*. Reynaud also was apparently not too happy about the course the war was likely to take, and about the ability of the French Army to play a full part in checking the flood of German military might; he remembered the energetic young infantry colonel who was then making a name for himself in command of an armoured division—being now a general.

In early June 1940, when the British Expeditionary Force had been evacuated to England from the Dunkirk bridgehead, Reynaud brought de Gaulle into his Government as Under-Secretary of State for National Defence. But events were moving too quickly for de Gaulle, or anybody else, to do any good; the German Army swept forward to victory, driving the defeated and dazed French Army before it.

The French Government had moved to Bordeaux, and on the 16th June Reynaud had resigned and Marshal Pétain was forming a Government. De Gaulle knew what that meant—a defeatist Government, and surrender to the Germans. He took an immediate decision to leave France, which he did in a British aircraft at 9 a.m. on the 17th June. France fell that day; a nation had lost its soul. That night he broadcast from London to the French nation.

From that moment he made it his purpose to rally to the cause of Fighting France the members of the French forces who had made their way to England—and indeed Frenchmen everywhere. He agreed that France was, for the moment, conquered —but the French Empire was not. The leadership being given by Vichy France was not what was needed for a great nation, and he set out to provide the true leadership from a headquarters in London. He was not too easy to deal with during the years which followed, particularly when the time drew near for the cross-Channel invasion of Normandy in June 1944. But his unshakable faith in the greatness of France, and his solid confidence that she would rise again under his leadership, eventually established his position as the true leader of French revival.

On the 30th June 1940 General Weygand, who was Minister of National Defence in the Vichy Government of Pétain, ordered de Gaulle to report at once to the prison in Toulouse, there to be tried by court-martial for desertion. He was tried (in his absence) and was condemned to death by the court!

The rest of the story is well known and, indeed, has been told by de Gaulle himself in the three volumes of his *War Memoirs* "Gaullism" was born. Then was created an organisation for the administration of the forces of Fighting France in Britain, together with a secret service for travel to and from France for dealing with the Resistance Movement in that country. And finally de Gaulle himself returned to France in 1944 to form the Fourth Republic. He was at one time accused of co-operating with the Communists when he became head of the Government after the Liberation of France. My own view is that he was determined to save France from Communist domination, and has done so.

I well remember his visit to Normandy on the 15th June, 1944, soon after we had established a secure bridgehead. He was anxious to set foot again on the soil of France—and very naturally. Winston Churchill was not at all keen that he should visit the front at that time; but I said it would help me greatly if he would come and advise us how to handle civil affairs as we enlarged our bridgehead and liberated more of France. So he came, accompanied by General Koenig who had commanded the French troops on the southern flank at Alamein—and who later became a firm friend of mine. He also brought with him a member of the French Foreign Office—a M. Coulet. I found de Gaulle very helpful and I sent him by car into Bayeux and suggested he should establish M. Coulet in that town to take all French civil problems off my plate—and this was done. There were certain "rumblings" from Whitehall about it, because they didn't want to let de Gaulle establish his government in France until we had won a bigger area from the Germans; but I welcomed his taking over my back areas as early as possible. M. Coulet was a great help; he took over the local government and this enabled me to concentrate on the battle. And he was particularly helpful when rumours began to circulate in London that British troops were looting in Normandy. I put the matter in the hands of M. Coulet and his investigations proved that the rumours were without foundation. The full story is told in Chapter 14 of my *Memoirs* page 264—in which it will be read that I myself was accused of looting by a colonel on my staff!

During the war de Gaulle was often touchy and irritable, and so were a lot of other people—many with less right than he. But his escape to England in June 1940 was the one bright piece of good fortune that France, and indeed the whole free world, had in a most dismal year.

He has certain qualities which are the hallmark of greatness. Chief among these are his sincerity and integrity, which not even his opponents have ever called in question. Then he has two qualities which appeal to me enormously—decision and action. He may not always reach the right decision; nor does anybody else. He doesn't wear himself out by fussing overmuch about the unimportant details of current tactics; he spends much time in quiet thought about the grand design of future strategy. He had plenty of time for thinking when he withdrew in January 1946 from the somewhat sordid politics of the Fourth Republic to his home at Colombey-les-deux-Eglises—to spend the next twelve years in the wilderness. I often motored past his home when I lived in France, but never stopped to call on him; I was advised by Western diplomats in Paris that I should not do so, because it might annoy the Governments of the Fourth Republic—which changed about every ten months! I accepted the advice although I disagreed wholeheartedly with the motives behind it.

During his thinking period at his home he worked out in his mind the details of a new constitution for France—the Fifth Republic. This was later approved in a referendum by the people and, because it is a sound common-sense measure, de Gaulle is forging ahead, and under him France will rise again to become a great nation—in my judgment.

When I was a boy, and indeed up to the time of Hitler's war, a great nation was one which possessed a powerful Navy. After Hitler's war, navies were down-graded somewhat, and to be reckoned a great nation it was necessary to have a powerful Air Force. To-day, to be a great nation it is considered that you must have the nuclear bomb—and to be able to make it. That is why de Gaulle has insisted that France shall produce her own nuclear weapon, and test it—which was done in the Sahara. And as things stand to-day in the world, we cannot say he is wrong. It was a remarkable sense of timing (and perhaps of humour too!) which led him to arrange that France would test her *second* nuclear bomb during the time of Khrushchev's visit to Paris in March 1960!

If anybody ever had any doubts about de Gaulle's leadership in the Fifth Republic, those doubts could not fail to be dispersed after his broadcast to the French nation on the 29th January, 1960, about his Algerian policy. I was in Switzerland at the time and I listened to his speaking. It was terrific! Here was real courage; an appeal to the people of France to unite and give him their support, "whatever happens." Such a broadcast could have been made only by a great leader who was sure of himself. I put him in the top category of national leaders.

I doubt if he likes Britain particularly. I lived in France for ten years, from 1948 to 1958, and I reckon most Frenchmen think we British are pretty good hypocrites! Those who think thus are, of course, referring to our politicians and not to our nation as a whole, and maybe they are right. Some writer has said that to be able to appreciate fully the true hypocrisy of the British politicians one has to be 100 per cent British—foreigners haven't a chance! Maybe he was right too!

My own experience in this respect is interesting. In October 1948 I ceased to serve the British Government only, and became an international soldier serving fifteen governments. I then learnt to look at every problem from an international point of view, and not from a purely British one; the political and military problems of the free world looked very different when viewed in this way. I also learnt that we British are very difficult people to deal with —stubborn, and thinking we are always right and others always wrong. All in all, therefore, I can sympathise with de Gaulle! And I would add that to get a clear view of British Governmental policy and diplomacy one has to go and live abroad for a while.

In September 1958, de Gaulle conferred on me the *Medaille Militaire*, the highest honour which France can bestow on a soldier—and seldom given to a foreigner in peace. It was a tremendous honour. In that same month I relinquished my NATO appointment and returned to England—having lived the past ten years in France.

I did not meet him again until he paid his State visit to London in April 1960, as President of France. He appeared to me on arrival to be a bit nervous, as if he was not too sure of the reception he might receive. One can never be certain how a London crowd will welcome a foreign visitor; sometimes the reception from the pavements is a bit chilly, as for instance in the case of the State visits paid by the Presidents of Federal Germany and of Italy. I was on the pavement outside Westminster Abbey when the carriage procession from Victoria Station passed by;

the crowd was not enthusiastic and such cheers as were given were more for the Queen than for de Gaulle, it being her first public appearance since the birth of Prince Andrew.

"Nous Londoners," as the Lord Mayor referred to us in his speech at the Guildhall luncheon, cannot be ordered to give a warm welcome to anybody; what welcome is given will depend on the visitor himself—or herself. I well remember the tremendous reception given by Londoners to Queen Salote of Tonga at the time of the Coronation in 1953. In the case of de Gaulle, British reserve thawed when he left his escort and mingled with the crowd after laying a wreath at the statue of Marshal Foch—shaking every hand stretched towards him. Londoners saw at once that he was no cold, proud, unbending soldier, but a very warm-hearted human being. He went from strength to strength after that. His address to the members of both Houses of Parliament on the 7th April was a wonderful achievement; he praised British institutions and our parliamentary system, and practically said that if they had such a system in France he might not have had to suspend normal democratic processes. He won our respect at once, with the dignity of his bearing and the grandeur of his words. Possibly his remarks about the British parliamentary system were meant for home consumption in Paris!

I had two talks with him when he was in London—one at the State Banquet at Buckingham Palace, and the other at the French Embassy when the Queen was his guest at dinner. After dinner at Buckingham Palace he sent for me—a high honour indeed and a proof of his friendship. I told him about the book I was writing on leadership and asked if I could visit him in Paris later in the year and get his views on the difficult problem of leadership in a democracy. He replied: "Ah! That's a difficult problem, but perhaps less so in your country than in mine. Of course come and see me in Paris whenever you like, and we will discuss it."

At the French Embassy, encouraged by his friendliness I approached him on my own, and we talked more about the same subject. I saw him again at the Royal Opera House on the last night of his State visit, and observed him closely from my seat in the stalls. I thought he looked tired, and well he might; he had had a very strenuous three days. The warmth of the greeting he received from the distinguished audience moved him greatly and I thought I saw tears in his eyes.

I had an amusing experience on leaving the Opera House that night. I was with Field-Marshal and Lady Harding and we tried unsuccessfully to find a taxi. Finally a friendly Police officer bundled us into a " Black Maria " which was waiting in the vicinity of Bow Street Police station, and this took us to the Savoy where I was staying and where a taxi was procured for the Hardings. I don't suppose two field-marshals have ever before been whisked away in a " Black Maria "!

Let us have a closer look at the man himself. We also want to understand his thinking, his ideas on the problem facing us in this split world; that will best be done by a reference to the talks we have had together.

First, what of the man himself?

He is tall and loosely built. Some will say that his manner is cold and that he lacks the personality to be an outstanding national leader. On the surface he may appear thus, giving the impression that he lacks a sense of humour and has few real and personal friends. I would not agree with this appraisal of his make-up. The point is he is shy and doesn't open up too easily. But he has a warm and generous heart, and this very soon becomes evident once you get to know him.

I have had many talks with him and I not only like him, but also admire him enormously. Each of us goes along in life in his or her own way. Not everybody likes de Gaulle's way. But we must remember that he considers France cannot be herself unless she is in the front rank; we think exactly the same about Britain. He wants nothing for himself; he wants everything for France. The central theme of his philosophy is that he will restore France to her former glories. One thing is very certain—if he can't do it, nobody else can.

To many de Gaulle may seem a strange figure in this world of politics and war—cold, aloof, and a difficult character to understand. The same could be said of many others; but in his case it is not true. If he likes you, he unbends at once; possibly he is not good with those he dislikes, and he is not alone in this respect.

He possesses in full measure the qualities I mention in Chapter twelve as being essential for successful leadership in Western countries—conviction, transparent honesty and sincerity, tenacity, political courage. And above all, he possesses the quality of decision —as I have said earlier in this chapter. He is a soldier, and he would never sacrifice his principles for office or for power—as too many politicians do. Indeed, he deliberately resigned his high office in 1946 and went into the wilderness, and waited—during which period he indulged in no intrigues to regain power. He had confidence that in due course France would need him again—and he was right, being recalled by the nation in 1958.

Now let us look into his thinking—examine what is in his mind.

I have already referred to the broadcast he made to the French nation in January 1960 about his Algerian policy. Later, in conversation one day, I asked him to tell me in simple terms the underlying difficulties about a lasting solution to that problem. He said a major difficulty was the one and a half million white settlers in Algeria, mostly French, who must stay there; they have no other home and they are the hard core of the Algerian economy; without them the country could not carry on—at any rate until the local population reaches a higher degree of education and civilisation, and this will take time.

Then there are nearly half a million Algerians working in France; these send money back to Algeria, which money supports nearly three million Algerians—who otherwise might starve. All-in-all, without France and French help it would be impossible for Algeria to carry on, and to have an adequate Civil Service and a viable economy. The problem is twofold: to quell the rebellion, and to discover a way by which the two communities—French and Algerian—can live together contentedly and happily.

In de Gaulle's view this twofold problem can be solved only in the following way:

First: Cease fighting.
Second: The population to vote for what they want.
Third: All parties to abide by the majority vote.

These three points constitute his policy, which seems to me eminently sensible and sound. The conflict in Algeria is very expensive for France; the bulk of the French Army is in that country, and it must be brought back to France and reduced in size if the money is to be found for equipping the armed forces with nuclear weapons under French control—which is de Gaulle's intention.

I once discussed with him his plan of frequently broadcasting to the French people and explaining his policy—what he was trying to achieve, and how, and when. He said it was only what I myself used to do during Hitler's war, when I used to speak to the soldiers and tell them the task, and explain their part in the next battle. He made another remarkable broadcast on the 31st May, 1960, in which he explained to the French people the policy France should adopt in the East-West conflict; it was after that that I went over to Paris to see him and asked him to explain his policy to me. He began by stating that the greatest evil of the times in which we live was the division of the world into two armed camps, or political blocs, and under such conditions that it depended only on a decision taken in Moscow or in Washington whether a great part of humanity should be wiped out in the space of a few hours. It was his view that when confronted by this monstrous peril, no territorial nor ideological dispute had any importance; the peril must be banished, and to effect the banishment three measures are necessary:

First. Reduce the suspicion between East and West, which itself leads to tension between the two blocs. In fact, create a better atmosphere by getting to know each other, by more cultural exchanges and tourism, and by cutting out all provocative acts and speeches. Unless this could be done, the world would one day find itself at war again—"as has happened twice within my lifetime, because an Archduke was dead or because somebody wanted Dantzig."

Next. Introduce a measure of controlled disarmament. He would prefer to begin with weapons which could send nuclear bombs over great distances, i.e. strategic offensive action. But he didn't want to be too dogmatic on the subject; the great point was to get some agreement, and make a beginning. He reckoned we would get no progress by just talking at Geneva; in fact the first step must be to reduce the suspicion between East and West, and until that was done it was useless to assemble a conference about disarmament.

Third. Organised co-operation between East and West, devoted to the service and welfare of mankind—both to bring economic aid, education, and improved standards of civilisation to under-developed nations, and also to work together on scientific research on which the future of mankind depends.

While waiting for these measures to be implemented de Gaulle is determined that France shall be able to defend herself, and to do so better than was attempted in 1940. He is clear that if the Western Alliance is to be an effective reality, France must have her own "personality"; this implies that if other nations have their own nuclear armament, France must have hers too—so that the security of her territories may depend on herself. In short, he believes that whilst being associated with her allies, the destiny of France shall remain in her own hands. It is difficult to disagree with any of this thinking—indeed, I told de Gaulle that I agreed wholeheartedly with him on all three points.

I once discussed with de Gaulle the United Nations Organisation; he has no great opinion of it, and this is really an understatement! I said the voting power was becoming unbalanced. Only about seven per cent of the world's population was black; but in a few years, if all newly independent states are admitted, this black seven per cent of the world will have about twenty-eight per cent of the votes in the Assembly. Against this, the Chinese total twenty-five per cent of the population of the world and have no votes—not even being a member of UNO! De

Gaulle said that the United Nations had ceased to be an effective organisation, if indeed it ever had been.

I always find it interesting to discuss the late war with him—Hitler's war. I once asked him what difference, if any, it would have made in May 1940 if Gort had directed the British Army in a south-westerly direction so as to join up with the French Army in the south—as indeed the War Cabinet in London had wanted him to do, sending the C.I.G.S. (Ironside) over to France with instructions to that effect. De Gaulle said it would have made no difference, and he reckoned Gort was right to refuse to carry out the instructions, and instead to plan for evacuation back to England through Dunkirk. It was too late for any other action; the rot had set in and it was necessary to rescue whatever could be saved, so that it could live to fight another day. He said the right answer to the tragic situation was to withdraw the French Army to North Africa and the British Army to England; and he considered Churchill was right to refuse to allow the remaining squadrons of British fighter aircraft to be based in France once the crisis began to unfold. With her army in North Africa, France would have been better able to help Britain in the war against the Axis powers; in the event, the British people carried on the fight alone, for which he considered Western civilisation will always be grateful.

I then switched the conversation to the "Declaration of Union" which had been proposed on the 16th June, 1940, by the British Government to the French Council of Ministers, of which Paul Reynaud was Prime Minister. Since the reader may have forgotten about this unique proposal, the text of the final draft is given below—taken from Volume II of *The Second World War* (published by Cassell), by Churchill.

DECLARATION OF UNION

"At this most fateful moment in the history of the modern world the Governments of the United Kingdom and the French Republic make this declaration of indissoluble union and unyielding resolution in their common defence of justice and freedom against subjection to a system which reduces mankind to a life of robots and slaves.

" The two Governments declare that France and Great Britain shall no longer be two nations, but one Franco-British Union.

" The constitution of the Union will provide for joint organs of defence, foreign, financial, and economic policies.

" Every citizen of France will enjoy immediately citizenship of Great Britain; every British subject will become a citizen of France.

" Both countries will share responsibility for the repair of the devastation of war, wherever it occurs in their territories, and the resources of both shall be equally, and as one, applied to that purpose.

" During the war there shall be a single War Cabinet, and all the forces of Britain and France, whether on land, sea, or in the air, will be placed under its direction. It will govern from wherever it best can. The two Parliaments will be formally associated. The nations of the British Empire are already forming new armies. France will keep her available forces in the field, on the sea, and in the air. The Union appeals to the United States to fortify the economic resources of the Allies, and to bring her powerful material aid to the common cause.

" The Union will concentrate its whole energy against the power of the enemy, no matter where the battle may be.

" And thus we shall conquer."

General de Gaulle told me that the idea of such a Union originated in the brain of M. Monnet, and he asked the general, who had come over to London to discuss shipping problems, to get Churchill to persuade the British Government to agree to it, and to make a definite proposal to the French Council of Ministers under M. Reynaud, then at Bordeaux—which was done, only to have the proposal rejected. As Churchill has written: " rarely has so generous a proposal encountered such a hostile reception."

I asked de Gaulle if he, personally, thought at the time that there was the slightest chance of the Declaration being accepted by the Bordeaux Government; he said he never thought so for one moment; in any case, he said, the grandeur of the conception made its rapid realisation quite impossible. He agreed to go along with it because he reckoned it might provide what he called a "psychological shock" to the French Ministers and nation, a manifestation of solidarity, all tending towards a postponement of surrender. But in the event it had no such effects.

I then asked him what would have been the result if it *had* been accepted. He said the conception was not a practical proposition; it would have led to interminable arguments about the relative positions of the British Sovereign and the French President, about Parliament and the French Assembly, together with all sorts of legal and other problems; it could never have worked—and he didn't think Churchill ever thought it would. I later checked this with Winston Churchill and it seemed he was rather inclined to agree with de Gaulle!

I found the general's views on European unity to be interesting. He considers that a United States of Europe—a Federated Europe —is not possible in any future that can be foreseen. His view is that to-day (1961) the nations of Western Europe are no longer afraid that a military threat will develop from Russia; indeed, such military aggression can be ruled out. Therefore, political federation being impossible, the nations should exploit economic unity, e.g. the Common Market, and as that unity grows and develops it might after a number of years be possible to move slowly towards a Confederated Europe—a confederation of Sovereign States. I said that having travelled widely through all the nations of the Western Alliance, I personally did not see even a Confederated Europe. After further discussion it emerged that he thought as time went on, say twenty years ahead or even longer, a threat might possibly develop from Asia—and when that happened Europe would have to unite or go under. On that subject, I remarked that having visited China and talked with the most powerful figures in that country, and seen how poor and backward are the people, I reckoned that China had enough on her plate to keep her fully occupied for the next twenty years and possibly longer; what might happen after that time was anybody's guess.

I asked de Gaulle in June 1960 who would give the lead in Europe, and "jolly" the nations along towards working on the fundamentals of his policy—with which I so wholeheartedly agreed. I suggested that France, under his direction, must provide the leadership we so badly needed, and guide the nations of Western Europe towards that unity which they have always lacked. I said we British are much to blame; we were the only country which had neither been defeated nor occupied; we could have had the leadership of Europe after Hitler's war, but we looked inwards at our own affairs and deliberately turned down the leadership. The judgment of history will be severe on this point, and rightly so. I added that it interested me to hear his views about economic unity leading eventually towards political agreement. My view has always been that the problem confronting the nations of the West is primarily political; economic fusion and collective military strength cannot be obtained until the political association between the nations concerned has first been clearly defined—and it has never been so defined. I also gave it as my opinion that both the political and command structures of NATO are in need of drastic revision, and unless this is done soon his ideas for solving the difficult situation confronting us to-day (as explained in his broadcast to the French people on the 31st May, 1960, to which I referred earlier) cannot be implemented.

In any talks I have with de Gaulle, I am always left with a feeling of confidence in the man himself—in his wisdom and quiet dignity. He considers that we must just go calmly on, working for economic agreements, trading with each other, visiting each other, and generally trying to influence the people of Europe to see the problem whole and true. The threat of any military aggression from Russia having passed away, we must now try and put our own political and economic affairs on a satisfactory basis. How right he is!

I reckon the future of the Western Alliance, and the successful handling of the conflict between East and West, depends greatly on de Gaulle. He has brought about a change of spirit in France which has to be seen to be believed; he has given the nation back its soul and its pride—something which seemed to me to have died with old Clemenceau, and with the great and suicidal French offensives of 1914 and of 1917. It is indeed a wonderful thing he has done; France is such a great nation when she is "whole" and at one with herself, and the world needs her wisdom and her spirit.

Will he stand up to the strain of this tremendous task? Will his health last? I have seen a good deal of him since he came back from retirement and founded the Fifth Republic; he seems to me to be in good health, and full of vigour and confidence. He knows exactly what he wants, and has the drive and determination to achieve it. His eyesight, about which some have doubts, appears to me to give no cause for alarm. I reckon he is good for another ten years at least; and, indeed, that is necessary, since there is no successor in sight. He is seventy-one.

He has those qualities of leadership which I admire so greatly —calmness in the crisis, decision, the ability to withdraw and have time to think. And overall, he has the ability, will and courage to express clearly what he wants to do—in fact, his master plan—without being overwhelmed with unimportant details. And he is genuine—a very great quality. All these qualities, particularly decision and courage, seem to me to be lacking in so many political leaders of the present day.

The general has a great asset in his wife; Madame de Gaulle is a most gracious host in the *Palais de l'Elysée*. She has a nice sense of humour and laughed heartily at a lunch party one day when I described to her a visit I once paid to a mannequin display at the business house of Christian Dior in Paris!

I reckon de Gaulle is definitely one of the great men of our time; indeed, he is a genius. He is the greatest political leader in the Western world, and is indispensable to France and to Europe.

CHAPTER EIGHT

CHURCHILL AND ALANBROOKE

I HAVE DECIDED to devote a chapter to these two men because they form a good example of the relationship between the statesman and the soldier in war. All great men are difficult to serve and Churchill, being a *very* great man, is no exception to the rule. Alanbrooke, being also a great man, certainly found it so, and his wartime diaries, which have formed the basis of two volumes by Sir Arthur Bryant, have quite a lot to say on the subject!

I served under both. Alanbrooke was, of course, my military chief throughout the war, and after it—from the early days of mobilisation in 1939, until I succeeded him as Chief of the Imperial General Staff in June 1946.

Churchill, as Prime Minister and Minister of Defence, liked to deal direct with the British commanders-in-chief in the various theatres of war, often by-passing Alanbrooke who was not only C.I.G.S. but also chairman of the Chiefs of Staff—thus making him very angry, and I don't blame him.

The sparks used to fly quite a lot in Whitehall and elsewhere on such occasions, and sometimes I myself became involved—and had the worst end of both worlds, military and political! But as a commander-in-chief in the field, I could retire to my headquarters when the storm clouds gathered and get on with the war—in a somewhat strong position actually, since I couldn't be sent for to No. 10. I could, of course, have been sacked, but so long as we won our battles that was unlikely. I once said to Churchill: " You like generals who win battles." His reply was interesting, simply: " You're telling me ! "

Alanbrooke was not so well positioned as me to deal with the great man. He could never escape, day or night, and I watched him with interest throughout the war—wilting a bit sometimes, at other times with a murderous look in his eyes, but overall taking it in his stride!

I am a great personal friend of both men. So much criticism has been aroused by the publication of portions of Alanbrooke's wartime diaries, that I feel impelled to include this chapter in the book—if only to show how two great men of strong character and will-power, one a statesman and the other a soldier, can work together in wartime—and successfully as regards the result.

It is going to be a difficult chapter to write because their relations and actions were so dovetailed. It may be best to give a brief sketch of each man, and then put the two together in a final analysis. Of course I do not know the details of what went on in Whitehall behind the scenes—except by hearsay. But I knew when the cold blasts were blowing strongly down the passages of the Whitehall ministries—such as when the Chiefs of Staff were trying to get agreement with the Americans about the best plan for defeating the Germans in Europe, and the great man reckoned that the best plan was first to capture the northern tip of Sumatra from the Japanese!

I propose to discuss the two men as known personally to me, Alanbrooke for thirty-six years and Churchill for twenty-two, and then their relationship with each other and with me during Hitler's war and since—all as experienced personally by myself. It should be quite an interesting study and may throw some new light on both.

Let us begin with Churchill.

Winston Churchill

It will be unnecessary to cast back and describe the early life of this very great man. Of all the books about him he wrote the best one himself, entitled *My Early Life*; this is a classic, and in my view, the best of all the many books he has written.

I first met Churchill in June 1940, after returning from Dunkirk in command of the 3rd Division. In those days I knew few politicians and was suspicious of most of that profession; I reckoned they were largely responsible for the troubles which had descended upon us. But he impressed me at once as a man of decision and action, knowing what should be done and having the courage and determination to do it.

Courage is one of the greatest of human qualities. There are two kinds of courage, physical and moral. It is not given to everybody to have great physical courage and if it is lacking one just has to do the best one can without it. But we can all have moral courage, which to me means standing firm by what you believe to be right and giving a firm lead to others in that direction.

Churchill has both kinds of courage, physical and moral. Sometimes his courage was aggressive and sometimes modest. But overall it was a clearly defined quality which shone forth in wartime, and in peacetime in the House of Commons—and also during periods of illness, when he fought so bravely to continue his duties.

Then he has imagination to a high degree. Some would say that his imagination was a bit too much at times, which may well be true—and it was no easy job to restrain him. In the military sphere the trouble was that he reckoned he knew, and did know, a good deal about the conduct of war; he had once been a soldier, and of course he had had great experience of the governmental side during the Kaiser's war; and he had written many books on the subject. He was a great student of history. On reflection, my view is that in the larger strategic issues he was often right; in the smaller issues, such as in the tactical sphere and in the details of organisation in which he loved to wander, he was often wrong.

But it is as a national leader in critical times that he rose to the greatest heights. When our very existence as a nation was threatened in 1940, he knew well that the British spirit was there but needed to be called forth. So he spoke to us through the B.B.C., and brought the crisis home to the nation in words which rang and thundered like the Psalms. All will recall the eagerness with which we looked forward to his broadcasts and speeches in the early days of Hitler's war. I doubt if any man in history has ever made such grim utterances and yet given so many people such a feeling of strength and exuberance—even cheerfulness and light-heartedness—and a sense of having got one's teeth into something. He was British to the core, with a sturdy refusal to be carried away by the temporary storms and stresses of the moment. He was a rock-like figure in an emergency, on whom all could lean.

When the storm burst upon us in 1940 and developed in ever-increasing fury, he adapted himself to the crisis, and to the unexpected—the latter being the sorrowful fact that our hoped-for ally, the United States of America, did not join the fight for freedom until she herself was directly attacked. By standing firm when all seemed lost, Winston Churchill saved Western civilisation—including the United States.

When it came to fighting wanton aggression as practised by Hitler, Mussolini and the Japanese, he had a "fire in his belly" which swept everything before it; it sometimes took all one's strength to stand firm against the persuasive arguments of the man when he was "hell-bent" on some unsound course of action for which the military resources were inadequate.

However, when all is said and done, was it not this very "fire" which carried us all through the weary years of Hitler's war? Never has any land found any leader who so matched the hour as did Winston Churchill in 1940. He towered head and shoulders above the leaders of all other nations. He inspired us all. There was a certain magnificence about him which transformed the lead of other men into gold.

I do not know how many Prime Ministers have guided the fortunes of our nation over the past two centuries, but I suppose the men of genius among them would be very few. In the twentieth century I would name only two—Lloyd George and Winston Churchill. I never met Lloyd George. But in his heyday, Winston was a towering personality, and an outstanding national leader.

I have used the words "in his heyday" and this causes me to reflect for a moment on the man as known personally to me. When I first met him after the Dunkirk campaign, he was at the very height of his powers, and, insofar as my knowledge and experience goes, he remained so until towards the end of 1943. Then he became very ill when in North Africa, and I noticed a change from then onwards. I used to see a good deal of him in the pre-Normandy days, and of course from then onwards until he went out of office in 1945, and I reckoned he had slipped back a bit; he didn't seem to be the man of unbounded and fearless decisiveness I had met for the first time in June 1940. I gained the impression that the artist and perfectionist was too often interfering with the man of action. If he couldn't get his way he would sometimes carry the process of "persuasion" to most unjustifiable lengths! The war was beginning to take its toll of this great man; the man of decision and action of 1940-1941 was tending in 1944 and 1945 to be inconsistent; all the noble qualities which had shone forth in the early days of Hitler's war were finding it difficult to keep their heads above water. And can anybody wonder? As the war drew to its closing stages he had the mental anguish of watching the Western powers losing it politically *vis-à-vis* the Russians, with all the difficult problems which that must bring to post-war Europe—which he, and only he, saw clearly.

We are apt to forget that great men, men of genius like Winston Churchill, are, after all, only human beings like the rest of us. There is a limit to what the human frame can stand, and yet still maintain full vigour—bodily and mentally. Winston Churchill stood it for over five years, leading the British people through the greatest war in history, and to my knowledge he never had a day off duty, or a holiday of any sort. Indeed, such was the intensity of his hatred of Hitler and all he stood for, he would have scorned to take even one day's rest. I did once suggest it, but never again; I received a proper "blasting," a back-hander which kept me quiet for some time!

And then the war ended, and he was discarded by the British

people. I well remember the first visit I paid him after the general election of 1945; he was like a man who had been pole-axed; he couldn't understand it. But I reckoned it was for the best. He who had carried Britain through the weary years of Hitler's war was completely worn out, and needed a rest—although he would never have admitted it. Anyhow, he had the rest he needed and returned six years later to lead the nation again—but this time in peace.

And now let us have a closer look at the man himself, a more personal look. It wasn't until the war ended that I began to know him really well and our true friendship began; we have now been close friends for seventeen years, since mid-1945, and I reckon I know him better than most others—I mean "as a man," not only as a wartime Prime Minister.

He is a very good friend, at least I have always found him so. He has his enemies and detractors of course, and I know some of them; but all they can say will never dim my affection for him. He is a wonderful story-teller. It is a real delight to get him talking about the past and to listen to stories of his Sandhurst days, or about the battle of Omdurman, or how he was captured by the Boers and of his subsequent escape. I have often sat with him until the small hours of the morning listening to his accounts of bygone days, forgetting that my normal bedtime is early— and glad to forget. He can be very interesting about the personalities, political and military, of his own lifetime. But all in all, he is a very fair critic, and a man had to be pretty bad before he would comment adversely on him. Latterly it has not been so easy to get him to talk, and if you ask him to tell you about some contemporary of his earlier days he will perhaps say a few words and then shrug his shoulders and stop—but you can generally guess his opinion from the nature of the shrug! After all, has he not written about the men of his time in *Great Contemporaries*, first published in 1937?

Churchill has his faults, like all humans. He is impatient, he can be very intolerant; he can be suspicious, and—dare I say it? —a touch of jealousy has appeared at times. But when you weigh up the virtues and the faults, what a tremendous balance of virtue is found. He is intensely loyal. He revelled in responsibility. He could listen, but with considerable impatience if he did not agree with what you were saying! And he could decide but, as I have already indicated, as Hitler's war drew to a conclusion he seemed to find it increasingly difficult to give quick decisions.

He has a great sense of humour. Of late years this has become of the quiet type. For instance, when I stay at Chartwell he will offer me wine at dinner—as the gesture of a host, but also as a joke. He knows well what the reply will be, and when it comes he will look at me with a shy smile and say: " You don't mind if I do! "

I visit him frequently and I reckon the more his friends rally round him and keep him interested the better—because he is now old and tired, and must not be allowed to feel we have no further use for him. We discuss the past a great deal; he delights in talking about his visits to my headquarters during the war. And occasionally I try and get him on to the future, but that is not so easy; he seems to think that the future is for others to handle— and so it is.

An interesting point occurs to me about Winston Churchill. In his school life at Harrow, and at Sandhurst, he cut no ice at all; he didn't like either place. This shows perhaps that it is a mistake to develop your powers too early, since they may fizzle out. He developed his powers in no uncertain manner in due course! But it is interesting to reflect that if it had not been for Hitler's war he would very possibly have gone down to history as a political failure! His reputation would, of course, have been firmly established as an author and a painter.

How was it then, that when the call came in 1940, Winston Churchill was able to play his part as a national leader? Of course he had tremendous experience of the governmental machine; he had held many ministerial appointments and he understood the fighting Services better than any other Minister of his time. He had been a successful war correspondent and knew what went on at the headquarters of a C.-in-C. in the field—or perhaps I should say, what formerly went on! He had travelled widely and had a good knowledge of the British Dominions and Colonies. He knew the people of Britain better than most, and he knew how to speak to them.

All these things are well known, but there must have been something else. I have often talked with him on this subject in order to extract from him the information I wanted—what was that "something" which completed his equipment, and ensured he was ready when the call came? Here is the answer to the conundrum.

Winston believes with Machiavelli that whereas fortune or fate will decide one half of our life, *the other half will depend on ourselves.* If we prepare ourselves for what might come, master our professions, and study how the great men of the past tackled and overcame their problems—then all will be well. So he read widely, and in particular studied the lives of great men. When studying their problems he didn't bother overmuch about details; what he wanted to know was *the conditions* of the problem facing the man, and what were the reasons which influenced the statesman or military commander to reach the decision he made. This study taught him, when faced himself with some difficult problem, to consider the actual facts of the situation as they appeared to him *at that time*; he refused to allow himself to be influenced by a decision given on a similar problem at some other time, because the conditions of that other problem were different from those surrounding the problem he now faced. He considers that what was done in bygone ages bears no relation to what should be done now; the actual conditions *at the time* are what will influence a decision.

Then he is a master at finding out what others think. He would make some quite outrageous statement to the Chiefs of Staff, just to arouse their heated opposition and get their real views. I suppose this might be termed "teasing," but it gave him the information he wanted.

It would be wrong to talk about Winston Churchill as known personally to me without mentioning also Lady Churchill—who to me, and to her many friends, is always "Clemmie." She is a beautiful and talented lady and I am one of her most devoted admirers. She is very well read, has great wisdom, and it is a real delight to talk with her. And she has courage, which quality has been needed at times—particularly when Winston was ill, or under great strain, and outwardly she had to make it appear that all was well. This must have been difficult during times when she herself was not too well; but however unwell she felt she carried on, and never let her guests know she was in pain. I recall particularly the dinner-party at No. 10 on the night of the 4th April, 1955, when the Queen and Prince Philip dined with Sir Winston and Lady Churchill. Clemmie was in great pain from neuritis, but only a few of us knew; she stuck it out and was a most gracious hostess the whole evening; it was one of the bravest acts I have seen. She had to be brave for another reason; it was her last party at No. 10, since Winston was to resign as Prime Minister the next day.

I will never forget that evening. I was living in France because of my NATO appointment at SHAPE, and I came over to London for the dinner; it was, of course, a tremendous privilege to be asked, since the dinner-party could not be large. I don't know how many of those present knew that Winston was to resign at 4.30 p.m. the next day, the 5th April, but I did. I had arrived early to have a talk with him while he was dressing for dinner, and he told me.

At the end of dinner Winston made a speech, quite short, but wonderful in his references to the Queen; he was clearly greatly moved by the occasion, both of them knowing what was to happen the next day. He finished, and stood there glass in hand; there was absolute silence in the room for some seconds, perhaps ten, and we all wondered what was coming next. Suddenly he raised his glass aloft, and with a shout of triumph his voice rang out—" The Queen." We all sprang to our feet, and drank the loyal toast. It was most dramatic, and only Winston could have made the scene. Then the Queen spoke, very simply and quite short, her object being to ask us all to drink the health of " my

Prime Minister." We all wondered whether a Queen of England had ever proposed such a toast before, and I still don't know the answer.

On the following Sunday, the 10th April, Easter Day, I drove to Chartwell and lunched with them both—and had a quiet talk. It was a sad moment in some respects. Nevertheless, I reckoned Winston was glad to be clear of the hurly-burly of political life and to be able to live in peace and quietude, and have time to travel—and I am certain Clemmie was. Many are the talks I have had with her, and many are the occasions when I have sought her advice, which is always willingly given and very sound. If she doesn't agree with you she says so very definitely, at least to me, and I prefer it that way—indeed I do the same myself!

One of the greatest privileges which has come my way has been to be admitted by Winston and Clemmie to the family circle, and to be allowed to invite myself to Chartwell whenever I like. One of my great friends is Mary Soames, their youngest daughter, and I am godfather to Jeremy her second son, whose photograph stands before me as I write these words—a delightful boy for whom I predict a great future, perhaps second only to his grandfather Winston.

I do not believe Winston could have achieved all he has without Clemmie at his side, and I reckon he would agree. After all, are not the last words of *My Early Life*:

" I married and lived happily ever afterwards."

There can be no doubt that in political leadership the right wife is essential, a vital essential—and here Winston made no mistake.

I have hanging in my home two paintings by Winston. This is somewhat of a triumph since he, who is so very generous, is not inclined to give away his paintings—and I don't blame him! He loves them, and he delights to sit in his studio and talk about the memories each picture recalls; he has a great many, and the pleasant hours I have spent with him in the studio will always remain in my memory.

There was no difficulty about getting the first one; I was moving into my home at Isington Mill late in 1948 and, since all my belongings were destroyed by German bombing during Hitler's war, I asked him for a picture for my study. He gave me a painting of a scene near Marrakesh, in Morocco, not far from where we had a picnic when I spent New Year's Day 1943 with him on my way back to England from the Eighth Army in Italy.

The second was more difficult. When I had got things sorted out in my study I needed another picture and, when I reckoned the moment was right, I asked for one. I was wrong, the moment was not right; there was no downright refusal, he merely ignored my question and changed the subject! I then adopted the tactics of the indirect approach, a very useful tactic in battle—but which I had not tried before at Chartwell. I enlisted the help of Mary Soames and we extracted from the studio a delightful painting of the pond at Blenheim; this I took to his room and praised it which pleased him greatly. I added that Mary reckoned it was exactly right for my study; only one thing was needed, he hadn't signed it. He saw the battle was lost, sent for some painting materials, and signed. When I took it to be framed in London, the dealer pointed out that it had been signed twice; the first signature was in red on a dark background, and neither Winston nor I had noticed it. I have never before seen a painting which has been signed twice by the artist. Perhaps it is unique; I hope so!

Both paintings are of water scenes, at which I consider he excels. His painting I like best is " The River Loup," which hangs in the Tate Gallery. The incidents of the pictures he gave me shows the kindness of heart of this great man.

Well, we must now leave him. He doesn't paint so much now as he did formerly; he is old, and quickly gets tired. But we can all be glad that he is still most happily with us, enjoying in dignity and quietude the evening of his splendid life.

Let us pass on and take a look at his wartime counterpart—Alanbrooke.

Alanbrooke

As I have said earlier, I have known Alanbrooke for thirty-six years. He is not an easy person to get to know well, and he gives the impression to some that he is cold and "distant," and perhaps a bit callous. This is not a true picture of the man in any way; once he has given you his friendship, which must be admitted is not quickly done, you find he is warm-hearted and generous to a degree.

It is not generally known that his early life was spent in France; he speaks French fluently, almost as well as a Frenchman. Shortly before I first met him, which was in 1926, he was involved in a motor accident with his first wife which had a tragic ending. The car was smashed to bits, he and his wife were carried unconscious to hospital, and when he recovered consciousness he saw his wife in the next bed—dead. He was left alone with their two children. This would be enough to shake the nerve of most men, but not him; he rallied bravely. And in due course he married again, and found perfect happiness once more—as his wartime diaries reveal.

He is emotional to a degree, maybe due to his French background. And he gives the impression that he is trying to hide his feelings and hold himself in check; it is possibly this which makes people think he is very reserved—which he is to those who do not know him.

In the days when we were both instructors at the Staff College, Camberley, in 1926, I got to know him pretty well. I remember well one summer vacation when we were both going over to Ireland; he offered me a lift in his car to Stranraer, and we crossed by the night steamer to Larne. It was a lovely evening and after dinner we leant on the rail on deck and talked far into the night; that quiet talk showed me the true man, his convictions and his sincerity, and it is a moment in my life I have never forgotten.

He is a very able soldier. Indeed, I reckon he was the best soldier produced by any nation during Hitler's war—and I have said so many times. He has a very high-class brain, quick and clear. He thinks very quickly, and speaks quickly too—like a machine-gun! And when he writes to you in his own handwriting, which was his normal custom with me, he writes at speed—but the resulting letter often showed that his pen was well behind in the race with his brain, and his spelling was not always very accurate!

In Chapter Two I expressed the opinion that Alanbrooke possessed all the qualities essential in a leader. I also said that I doubted if he would have been such a highly successful commander in the field as he was a national Chief of Staff, giving as the reason that he wouldn't have got himself over to the soldiers in the right way. I do not know whether this will be generally agreed, but having served with and under him, I reckon I am right; I wonder if anybody will take me up on this point?

He is quick tempered, and when he does fly off the handle and bite you there is no room for doubt about what has happened. I had many back-handers from him during the war; I think I deserved most of them, and I certainly never resented being ticked off by him—as he himself admitted in his diaries.

I would like to say a word about these diaries. Alanbrooke kept one during the war and I did too. I believe there is a regulation to the effect that an officer is not to keep a diary in the field, presumably in case he and his diary might get captured; there was never any danger of my headquarters being captured. My diaries, kept during Hitler's war, and when I was Chief of the Imperial General Staff after the war, and during the ten years I was an international soldier in the Western Defence Organisation, are of intense interest to me. I use them to refresh my memory, as for instance when I wrote my *Memoirs*. I would never dream of publishing them, nor even of letting anybody see them; such action might well cause another war, since they contain some very plain speaking!

I think Alanbrooke knew I kept a diary. I certainly knew he did. But his diary was written every night to his wife in order to unburden the anguish of his soul, and gain some relief from the tremendous burden he bore and the irritations he suffered.

They are intensely interesting historically, as showing what stresses and strains are suffered in war by those who carry great responsibilities. He spoke about these things every night to his wife, using his diary as his medium; and when each little booklet was completed, he sent it to her by a sure hand for safe keeping. It is very right and proper that his feelings, as expressed in the diaries, should be made known to a wider public; unless this is done the historians will not get the true picture when they come to write the story—as they certainly will, and, indeed, have begun.

I always reckoned Alanbrooke, or "Brookie" as I called him, showed great wisdom in the way he handled me. I like to be told by my boss what he wants me to do, and then to be left alone to do it—being given all possible support, but without any interference or fuss. If I make mistakes I am quite prepared to be ticked off, and if I prove unequal to the job I fully realise I will be sacked. In hunting parlance, I like to be ridden on the snaffle, not objecting to a good blasting if I stumble; what I do not like is to be ridden at all times on the curb, and kept under tight control.

By the time the Dunkirk campaign was over, and after a further two years of training in England, Brookie had got to know me well as a commander. Throughout he rode me on the snaffle; but on occasions a proper blasting was received. And a Brookie blasting—by gum!

I recall particularly one incident. It occurred in France during the winter of 1939-40, the period of the phoney war as some call it, before the Germans overran Western Europe. My division was in an area to the south of Lille and when we had been there for some months the incidence of venereal disease in the division gave cause for alarm—and in spite of all our efforts the figures increased. It finally became so bad that I decided to take drastic action; I wrote a circular letter on the subject, giving my views on how to stop the disease. This letter produced the required action and the disease practically ceased throughout the division; the incident is described in outline on page 60 of my *Memoirs*. But it had awkward repercussions when the chaplains at General

Headquarters complained about my methods to the Commander-in-Chief, Gort. He said I must hand over my division and return to England! Alanbrooke was my Corps Commander and, for reasons best known to himself, he didn't want to lose me; so he persuaded Gort to let him handle the case. I did not know about the storm which was blowing up, and when I received a message that the Corps Commander was coming to see me, and I was to remain in until he arrived, I thought in my innocence that some urgent tactical problem was to be discussed. I was mistaken! He arrived, and I could tell by the look on his face and his abrupt manner that I was "for it"—and I was right. He let drive for about ten minutes, and I listened. When he had run out of words he became calmer, and even smiled. I then plucked up courage and said I reckoned my circular letter was rather a good one, and extremely clear. That finished it; he began again and I received a further blasting! I have since come to the conclusion that it is better to remain silent on such occasions and take all that comes to you!

The great point about Brookie's anger was that it didn't last long; he would flare up very quickly, and calm down equally quickly—having done which, he would forget all about it and resume the old friendly relationship.

I have said that my circular letter was very clear, and it certainly was. But the subject of clear expression reminds me of a story I once heard about the old Duke of Wellington. Whether the story is true, or not, I don't know—but here it is.

A man called London wrote to the Duke and asked if he could visit Stratfield Saye and inspect his beeches, particularly those which had been planted at the time of Waterloo—and the letter was signed "A. F. London." Possibly the writer had not been very clear about what he really wanted, and who he was. Anyhow, the Duke thought the letter was from the Bishop of London, so he wrote to the Bishop in the following terms:

" The Duke of Wellington presents his compliments to the Bishop of London and will be glad to allow the Bishop to inspect his breeches. But the Duke is not clear why the Bishop particularly wants to inspect the breeches he wore at Waterloo, which are not now in very good condition."

History doesn't relate what happened when the Bishop received the letter!
Not all of Brookie's "tickings off" were justified, at any rate not in my opinion; one in particular comes to mind. Peter Fraser, Prime Minister of New Zealand, came to visit me at my headquarters outside Portsmouth on the 24th May, 1944—shortly before D-Day. The New Zealand division under General Freyberg had served under my command in the Eighth Army, in the desert and in Italy, and I was able to tell their Prime Minister what a fine division it was. Peter Fraser then asked me what would be the best way to employ General Freyberg after the war. Without any hesitation I replied: " Governor-General of New Zealand." He told Brookie what I had said and when next we met he reprimanded me sharply, saying I frightened him at times —D-Day was approaching, and instead of devoting all my attention to that operation I was discussing the affairs of New Zealand with its Prime Minister! Why couldn't I mind my own business? Anyhow, Freyberg was made Governor-General of New Zealand—and proved extremely good at the job!

Another incident connected with Alanbrooke comes to my mind—a sad one. It took place in the Dunkirk bridgehead, and the scene was the headquarters of my 3rd Division in the sand-dunes on the outskirts of La Panne, in Belgium. The general situation was so bad that it had been decided to get some of the more experienced commanders back to England, to handle affairs in the home country in the event of a German invasion. Alanbrooke had been ordered to hand over his Corps and leave that day, the 30th May. He arrived at my headquarters to say goodbye and I saw at once that he was struggling to hold himself in check; so I took him a little way into the sand hills and then he broke down and wept—not because of the situation of the B.E.F., which indeed was enough to make anybody burst into tears, but because he had to leave us all to a fate which looked pretty bad. He, a soldier, had been ordered to abandon his men at a critical moment—that is what disturbed him. He told me I was to take over command of the Corps. I comforted him as best I could, saying that we would all get back to England somehow and join up with him again—but I must confess that at that moment it wasn't clear to me how it would be done, but it became clearer later that day when I had time to study the problem at Corps H.Q.

There are moments in the life of each one of us when the pressure of events is too great, and we break down; and it is right that we should give way in the face of great emotion, rather than bottle it up inside us. But when the reserve of the English heart is broken through, most of us like to be alone—as I was with my wife when she died in my arms in October 1937. And so when Alanbrooke broke down and wept on my shoulder, I knew it meant his friendship was all mine—and I was glad to have it that way. That scene in the sand-dunes on the Belgian coast is one which will remain with me all my life. I was allowed to see the real Brookie for the second time; the first time was when we crossed together to Ireland by steamer from Stranraer to Larne in 1926, which I described earlier.

I have said that if it had not been for Hitler's war Winston Churchill would possibly not have risen to the top post in political life. This cannot be said of Alanbrooke; I reckon his outstanding military qualities would have taken him to the top in peace time, as Chief of the Imperial General Staff—the professional head of the British Army.

It will be clear from what I have writtten that I have an enormous admiration, respect and affection for Alanbrooke—a very great soldier and human being. The same applies equally to Winston Churchill. Fate decided that these two should work closely together during Hitler's war. Let us see how it worked out.

Churchill plus Alanbrooke

When two great men, each of tremendous strength of character and strong will-power, each reckoning he is right and determined not to be "seen off" by the other, both men of decision and action, and each inclined to be somewhat emotional—when two such men are yoked together in harness there are bound to be fireworks, even though both have at heart the same cause. The sparks were bound to fly when the two men were Churchill and Alanbrooke.

You might just as well put Dr. Verwoerd and Nehru together on a common task and expect a calm partnership!

In the case of Churchill and Alanbrooke, the wonder is not that the sparks used to fly. The wonder is that the two didn't part company. Churchill, being supreme in the political and military spheres, could have sacked Alanbrooke whenever he liked; Alanbrooke could have thrown his hand in at any time and asked to be employed elsewhere. Neither of these things happened, which proves the greatness of each man. If either had been unable to stand it any longer, which would have been very understandable, it would have been a tragedy. I believe that these two men between them played a greater part in ensuring that the Allies won the Second World War than any other two men; I have always thought thus, and nothing which has emerged since the war ended has caused me to change my opinion. They provide a superb example of the relationship between soldier and statesman in war—and of how the two must work together, come what may.

There is no doubt that Winston thought the world of Alanbrooke; he told me so many times during the war. He is capable of great affection for those he likes and who serve him well, and during the war he developed a genuine affection for Brookie. I reckon his affection cooled off somewhat after Brookie's diaries revealed the strain from which he suffered—which, after all, is but human!

I have seen both men in a real temper, but never with each other because I was not present when the sparks used to fly. Both have at times been pretty angry with me. On such occasions

Winston's anger would be restrained, since as a Commander-in-Chief in the field I was not his servant—his immediate subordinate—and he was always very correct on such matters, particularly when he was at my headquarters. His anger would express itself in a painful silence, broken occasionally by somewhat inaudible mumblings! I knew my place and always remained silent. In the end I won, because it was made clear that if he insisted on a certain line of action we would lose the battle!

Sometimes he would get very angry with me in Whitehall. Brookie would protect me and Winston would then turn on Brookie—referring to me as " Your Monty," as if he himself had completely cast me off!

When Brookie got angry with me, the scene was different; I have already described one such scene when I commanded the 3rd Division and he was my Corps Commander. He being my senior in army rank and my superior in all army matters, had a perfect right to tick me off—and often did, in no uncertain voice. His anger never lasted long—possibly because he reckoned I was some use to him, or because we were very old friends, or because I took it well and never got upset or answered back. My admiration and affection for him was such that I would take any rebukes he gave, even when they were undeserved. I knew the difficult task he had, and it wasn't for me to make it any harder.

He was always a help to me when I myself looked like heading for trouble with the Prime Minister—and the following incident is a good example.

Early in March, 1945, my tactical headquarters were located in the village of Geldrop, near Eindhoven, and Winston visited me there—accompanied as always by Brookie, who was Chief of the Imperial General Staff. Now Winston knew very well that I was making plans for 21 Army Group to cross the Rhine later in the month, and I had been warned by Brookie that he was determined to be present at the crossing—because I had always told him that once we were over that barrier and into the north German plain with our tanks, the war could not last much longer. I had told Brookie he must keep away; it might well prove to be a difficult operation to handle and I didn't like visitors on such occasions. I rather think Brookie had told Winston he wouldn't be very welcome, which didn't improve the *bonhomie*! That night I was invited to dinner by Winston in his train, and took my Chief of Staff with me, Freddie de Guingand. The visit for the Rhine crossing was not mentioned during dinner, and naturally I laid low, returning to my headquarters after dinner to attend to the war. I left de Guingand behind to talk to the Prime Minister, who at once raised the question of the visit, and Freddie, not being so skilful at playing the hand against Winston as I was, promptly declared that the Commander-in-Chief (myself) would never agree to such a visit! This infuriated the great man and he returned to London the next day in a flaming temper. I then received a letter from Brookie warning me that Winston was determined to come, and I had better watch my step! My strong card was that I had never *myself* told him he mustn't come; I had only told Brookie and de Guingand. I quickly decided there was only one thing to do—to write as if nothing had happened and invite the great man to come and stay with me and witness the operation of crossing the Rhine; and this I did, sending the letter by a special messenger direct to No. 10. He was, of course, absolutely delighted. He duly arrived and we all enjoyed his visit. I tremble to think what might have happened if I had played the hand badly; Brookie's advice was exactly right—as always.

One of Alanbrooke's great qualities is sympathy; he was ever ready to help and I felt I could go to him at any time with my troubles and get the benefit of his wisdom and advice—even when he was himself struggling with his own troubles. Another outstanding quality in his make-up is sincerity and loyalty; he is selfless, utterly sincere, and entirely loyal. There has to be two-way traffic in this matter of loyalty, by which I mean that you cannot expect loyalty from those below you unless you yourself are loyal to your superiors. And when this principle is applied at the lowest level, the discipline demanded of the soldier must become loyalty in his officer. There was no question about the two-way traffic in this matter with Alanbrooke. We in the Army knew that we could trust him absolutely; he is incapable of any intrigue, or of anything mean or underhand. I would trust him with my life.

Alanbrooke couldn't have carried out his task as senior military adviser to Churchill unless others had been available to run the internal affairs of the Army. He was the senior military member of the Army Council and, as such, professional adviser to the Secretary of State for War. The Secretary of State was Sir James Grigg, the best we have ever had in the Army during my military career; and Alanbrooke's Vice-Chief was Archie Nye, a brilliant staff officer. These two relieved Alanbrooke of all possible detailed work in the War Office; there was complete trust and loyalty between the three and no intrigue of any sort.

We might pause for a moment on the subject of intrigue. During the First World War, the Kaiser's war, I was too junior to know what went on in military circles, or between the soldiers and politicians; but one has read that both sides indulged in intrigue. In the Second World War, Hitler's war, there was undoubtedly intrigue during the Hore-Belisha régime, and possibly after it, but of that I have no knowledge. But after Alanbrooke became C.I.G.S. there was none in the Army; neither he nor Grigg would have tolerated it for one moment— nor would Churchill.

And so these two men, very different in temperament, worked together during the war, sinking their feelings in order to ensure that the war effort of the Allies didn't suffer.

It is far better to have such men at the head of affairs, men who know what they want and can give decisions; we could so easily have had men of indecision, who expect others to produce the answers for them—there were plenty of them about, and still are to-day.

Neither of the two, Churchill and Alanbrooke, could have done without the other, and in their hearts they both knew this to be true. And so they both carried on, sparks and all, to the lasting benefit of the British people—and indeed of Western civilisation.

CHAPTER EIGHT

A GREAT CIVIL SERVANT—
SIR JAMES GRIGG

HAVING CONSIDERED certain military and national leaders, and the interplay between the military and political fields, we should now take a look at a Civil Servant—a member of a Service forming the link between the political and executive agencies of government. I have always had the highest admiration for the Civil Service—for its impartiality, and for the manner in which it gives loyal and devoted service to the government of the day, irrespective of which political party is in power. As I understand it, that Service is charged with the administration and direction of government, under political chiefs; therefore a first-class Civil Service is indispensable to any nation, and that we certainly have in the United Kingdom. The man I have selected as an example of the Civil Service is the greatest I know —Sir James Grigg, known to all his friends as P. J. Grigg, or more often as just P.J.

The writing of this chapter is not made any easier by the fact that I have a tremendous admiration and affection for this great man and for his lady wife; they are two of my greatest friends. On the other hand, it is difficult to judge a man if you don't know him, and here I am on sure ground because I know P.J. very well indeed—as will become obvious to the reader.

To be great, to be a person of stature, a man must have character, judgment, high intelligence, a special aptitude for seeing his problems whole and true—for seeing things as they are, without exaggeration or emotion—and above all the ability of decision, the right decision, of course. P.J. has these qualities. Nevertheless, it is very difficult to depict on paper the true character of a man, the whole of what a man is, being sure of what one writes and linking metaphor to fact—the illustration fitting exactly. It is much easier to do this in conversation because then there can be cross-examination and explanation; in the written word there is no reply—at least not until somebody replies in the Press!—so it is the more difficult. However, I can but try, adding that P.J. himself has not been consulted—otherwise I am certain he would object vehemently! In one respect the task is made easier in that he has himself written the story of his life—*Prejudice and Judgment*, published in 1948. I do not know how widely it has been read; I recommend it to those who have not yet done so.

It may not be generally known that Grigg's father was a carpenter earning twenty-three shillings a week, and his mother a nannie. From these humble beginnings he paid for his education by scholarships, gaining a senior scholarship at St. John's, Cambridge, becoming a mathematical wrangler, and finally passing top into the Civil Service—beginning his career at the Treasury.

But overall things were not easy for him at Cambridge; he had great difficulty in living within his scholarship income, his life and meals were Spartan in the extreme, he could not afford to take any part in the organised athletic life of the college or join any of the social clubs—nor could he return hospitality. This latter inability must have caused him much grief and, as he himself wrote, it " increased the natural reserve due to shyness." This puts it shortly but very well; P.J. is naturally reserved and shy if he is with those he does not know, but once he is with his friends or those he knows well he opens up and becomes the life and soul of the party. He admits that he didn't get the best out of Cambridge because of the narrow life he was forced to live; maybe so many inabilities developed in him an inferiority complex. I have always thought that if a man has to struggle in early life and fend for himself, it toughens and develops his character; in his case there is no doubt about the strength of character which ultimately emerged. It takes a good man, one with a tough character and a strong sense of purpose, to undergo all these trials and tribulations and come through unscathed—and that he did. The natural reserve and shyness remain to this day; but they can be broken down since he responds quickly to the friendly approach; and then, underneath, will be found a warm and generous heart and intense loyalty to those to whom he extends his friendship. On the other hand, he is very sensitive and will withdraw into his shell at the first sign of snobbish superiority.

We all have our faults, and in my own *Memoirs* I have attributed to myself most of the bad qualities we humans can possess! If I was forced to specify a weakness in P.J. I would say it is "intolerance"; he either likes you or dislikes you; you are either white or black; there are no greys or half-tones. He is on dangerous ground (or perhaps you are!) when he meets brains less quick and clear than his own; and since he has the clearest and most brilliant brain of anybody I have ever met, the occasions when intolerance can hold sway are frequent! There are two faults in others which he will never forgive—one is insincerity or deceit of any kind, and included in this is, of course, intrigue; the other is an inclination to immorality of any sort. Anybody who errs in these respects is finished as far as P.J. is concerned; there can be no excuse, no suggestion of the frailty of human nature; the two sins often go together and then the person concerned is past redemption. If he thinks that way about anybody he will express his feelings in language which is quite impossible to misunderstand—and which is often quite unprintable! Some will add another fault—that he is too critical, his tongue often running away and getting him into trouble. Maybe that is true; many will say I am like that myself; and certainly many other are the same. But the point here is that P.J. is generally right in his criticisms of things or of people; where he differs from most others is that he had the courage of his convictions and is prepared to say what he thinks. Perhaps it was for this reason that he did not make a successful politician;

he is too sincere, and will never sacrifice his principles for ministerial office or to get people to vote for him. A further point is that he is so well read, and devotes so much time to quiet thought and reflection, that any opinion he may express is well considered; he doesn't give off-the-cuff criticisms and if you demand one he will ask for time to think the matter over—which modesty is a trait in his character known possibly only to a few, of whom I am one.

He is a great debunker of persons. It is, of course, much easier to debunk than to give credit for virtues—and perhaps one should remember this when discussing P.J. and his characteristics.

I first saw him in the spring of 1942. He had become Secretary of State for War in April and General Paget, C.-in-C. Home Forces, gave a lunch party for him at his headquarters in London after a conference of army commanders—of whom I was one. I was introduced to Grigg but we had no conversation. I do, however, remember Paget saying that he was likely to prove a really first-class Minister in charge of the War Office. This left little impression on me at the time, probably because my first view of our new Secretary of State did not impress me —and I don't suppose he noticed me although he must have heard of me, but possibly as an opinionated general whom he must watch!

Soon after that first meeting I went off to command the Eighth Army in Africa, and the next time we met was when he visited the Middle East towards the end of June, 1943—shortly before the invasion of Sicily. By that time I was pretty well known; the sudden publicity, and the curious wording of some of my telegrams to the War Office (considered by some to be a bit dictatorial!) had caused him some alarm—so I was informed. My Chief of Staff, Freddie de Guingand, was always very good at sensing trouble ahead and he warned me that Grigg might be critical, and possibly even deliver a back-hander! So he invited the Secretary of State to drive with him from Cairo down to Suez, where I was inspecting the divisions of 13 Corps, and meet me—holding out the bait that he could attend my talk to the officers of the divisions about the plan and problems of the Sicily operation, which was our next task. Exactly what was discussed during the drive to Suez, I do not know; at any rate, Grigg was in good form when we met, listened to my talk, and, at my request, said a few words himself to the officers, creating a good impression. He left Africa pleased with what he had seen of the Eighth Army—and presumably satisfied with its commander! At any rate, when later in the year there was some argument in Whitehall about which general should be selected to command 21 Army Group for the invasion of Normandy and the campaign in North-West Europe, he voted wholeheartedly for me.

However, there was to be one small bust-up before we became firm friends. I had arrived in England from Africa on the 2nd January, 1944, and it didn't take me more than a few days to see that the control exercised by the War Office over the armies in England which I was to prepare for the invasion of Normandy was too tight; nothing could be done in the way of minor changes in organisation or tactical doctrine without War Office approval—which either took time to obtain, or was refused. I tackled this problem in my usual robust manner; I summoned all the general officers of the armies to a conference on the 13th January and gave my views on battle fighting. During the subsequent discussion it became apparent that if divisions were to fight in the way I had outlined, certain minor changes in organisation would be necessary; I approved the changes and ordered them to be implemented at once. Some officers from the War Office were present at the conference and they were quick to report my action to their superiors—and glad to do so! There was quite a storm and the C.I.G.S. (Brooke) told me that the Secretary of State strongly disapproved of my apparent disregard for War Office authority; he then suggested to Grigg that he should ask me to lunch—which he did, and we had a good talk. That gave me an opportunity to explain how much there was to be done and how little time there was in which to do it; I asked him to trust my judgment on the operational necessity for what I had done. I remember driving back to the War Office after lunch at his club, and saying that I much preferred to be sent for and "ticked off" if I went too fast or offended in any way, rather than to have unpleasant criticism under the surface; he had given me the hell of a job to do and it couldn't be done without full War Office support, and I asked for that support. And I most certainly got it; after that talk he backed me to the hilt, and it was the beginning of a friendship which has lasted to this day.

P. J. Grigg is like that; he can be very critical. But he is chockfull of sound common sense and is very quick to see whether a project is sound or not; once he is satisfied, you have his full support. Of course he can fly off the handle and tell you in no uncertain voice, and in his own illuminating language, exactly what he thinks of you—and he is generally not far wrong!

When P.J. became Secretary of State for War he had to leave the Civil Service, and become a politician. I don't think he enjoyed politics; he found it a hard and disagreeable trade. But one must hand it to him—from humble beginnings he had become one of His Majesty's Principal Secretaries of State. And he proved to be the best Secretary of State for War we have ever had in the army within my personal experience. During the campaign in North-West Europe he visited me many times, beginning in Normandy and continuing at intervals right up to the end of the war in May, 1945. We were always glad to see him, and he entered with a boyish enthusiasm into the life of the mess at my Tac. H.Q.—enjoying the fun and charming us all with his lively conversation.

When the war was over, the Labour Party won the General Election of 1945. Grigg lost his seat in a three-cornered fight in East Cardiff and was in the wilderness—no longer a Civil Servant, no longer a politician, and with no other profession and no assured means of livelihood. This is the moment in his life when his own story, as told in *Prejudice and Judgment*, ends, and few people know what happened then. But I know, and it is right that all should know.

P.J. and his devoted wife bought a small cottage near Tilford in Surrey and lived there alone—he wondering how he was going to earn a living for them both. She became the cook and did all the housework; P.J. did the fires, chopped the wood, and stoked the boiler.

In his book he mentioned his joy at passing top into the Civil Service in 1913: "I could look forward to a prosperous and useful career with the assurance of a pension at the end of it." But when he accepted ministerial office as Secretary of State for War in 1942 he forfeited his Civil Service pension, and he who had been comparatively well off financially, now found himself in 1945 with no income. It was not an easy time for him and I have a feeling that some of his friends neglected him; it happens thus sometimes, particularly when a successful man departs into the wilderness and some think he can be of no further use to them. For myself, I stuck to him; he had been a good friend to me and I wasn't going to desert him in his hour of need.

I was C.-in-C. and Military Governor of the British Zone in Germany at that time, from May, 1945, to June, 1946, and I used to come over for periods of leave to the home of my friends at Hindhead (the Reynolds family who had looked after my son David for me during the war). On these visits I never failed to visit the Griggs in their cottage at Tilford; I liked to discuss my problems with P.J. and get his advice—which was the best I knew.

I recall particularly one visit. I had asked myself to supper, expecting a simple meal; but Lady Grigg had managed to procure some partridges and these she had cooked herself, superbly; I had not known before what a splendid cook she was. I have never forgotten that meal.

This is the right moment for me to bring Lady Grigg into the story—or Gertrude, as she always is to me. P.J. first met her when he was working at Woolwich on range tables and fuse scales, having been sent home from the Salonika front at the end of 1917 for the purpose—he being a skilled mathematician.

Gertrude (then Miss Hough) was working as a computer in the same department of External Ballistics. At first P.J. took a dislike to her because of "her air of brisk competence"; I can well imagine it, intolerance having already begun to show its head at that age of twenty-seven! However, he gradually had the opportunity to learn how wrong he was, and they were married in July, 1919—she being a few years older than him.

I have a tremendous admiration for Gertrude Grigg; she is wise, kind, and with a sound judgment. In my study of the lives of great men I have realised how important is the right wife; the two must be a team, and one sees how hopeless it becomes when this is not the case. Gertrude has been, and is to-day, exactly the right wife for P.J. With increasing years he has become a bit crotchety and argumentative; she handles him beautifully and remains completely unperturbed, even when he gets angry with her—which he does whenever she expresses an opinion with which he disagrees, which is very often! They are a wonderful couple, completely devoted to each other—each one miserable when the other is away—and they understand each other perfectly.

One interesting point must be mentioned—neither of them is good in illness. I have at various times seen each of them in the doctor's hands, once or twice rather bad; these occasions produce a loss of morale in the home, gloom descends on them both, and they become depressed—particularly the one who is not ill. Gertrude is not a good nurse when P.J. is ill, and openly admits it; P.J. gets fussed if she is ill. On reflection, I am inclined to think the true reason is their intense devotion to each other; the feeling that one may not live, and the other be left alone, is too terrible to contemplate—so much are they part of each other's life.

P.J. didn't remain unemployed for very long after he lost his seat in Parliament and his ministerial office in 1945; he has far too brilliant a brain, and many firms and organisations competed for his services. To-day he is a successful financial adviser to several well-known business houses and banks. And he is happy in his new life, with perhaps one exception. In conversation with me he has frequently deplored the fact that he is only an *adviser*; he can never make a *decision*. My reply is that it is exactly the same with me; indeed, more so. As a soldier my whole life has been based on decision and action; now, in the evening of life, one can give decisions only about one's own private affairs!

He and Gertrude live happily in a flat in Albany. On Saturday mornings P.J. may be seen sallying forth with a string bag to do the household shopping for the week-end, and I am sure he has many friends in the shops of the West End—always getting the best cuts and the choicest vegetables.

They frequently stay with me at my home in Hampshire, and when my son and his family are abroad they like to come and spend Christmas with me. They are ideal guests; they don't want to be amused, but like to be left alone and to be quiet in their own sitting-room—which suits us all well, as none of us is exactly young. But they do enjoy a good talk and we have much stimulating conversation—at least I find it so. And when one can get P.J. to talk on a subject which he really knows about, it is a sheer delight to listen; as I have already said earlier, he is very widely read, and his views on most subjects are worth hearing.

They remain, and always will remain, two of my greatest friends. I find in both that complete and absolute integrity and sincerity which is so rare; I just cannot imagine either of them doing anything mean or underhand. And both are modest withal.

Should you say to me:

"If P.J. Grigg is the great and wise man you say he is, with such a brilliant brain and so much sound common sense, can you explain why he did not rise to great heights?" my reply would be that he did rise to great heights. Remember his early days and boyhood! He had none of the advantages of wealth; he did not go to an expensive public school; he had to fend for himself, paying for his own education by his sheer ability and hard work. And from those beginnings he rose to become the *constitutional* head of the British Army—and the best one I have ever known.

I like to think I didn't do too badly myself, rising to become the *professional* head of the British Army, but I had not the same disadvantages in early life as had P.J. My regret is that the two of us were not together at the War Office in the post-war years, since his brain-power and wisdom would have enabled me to achieve more than I did—if, indeed, I achieved anything at all when Chief of the Imperial General Staff from 1946 to 1948.

If you sometimes meet a smallish man with a very alert and intellectual face, walking to the City, or having lunch in the Athenæum, or shopping with a string bag on Saturday mornings in the West End, and you ask me who he is, my reply will be: " That is Sir James Grigg, a former Civil Servant, full of wisdom and common sense, modest and unassuming, who, from humble beginnings rose to great heights by his own sheer ability and hard work."

And I will add with pride: " He and his wife are two of my greatest friends."

CHAPTER TEN

A CAPTAIN OF INDUSTRY—
NUFFIELD

MY OBJECT in this chapter is to analyse the life of a successful business man—a captain of industry. I have selected Lord Nuffield for this purpose for two reasons—first, because I know him well, and secondly, because he started from the bottom and built up his own business. He did not take over an existing organisation or firm; he was educated at the village primary school in Cowley, and at the age of sixteen started work on his own with a total working capital of four pounds.

This subject is going to involve me in the question of leadership in industry—a terrific problem which cannot be dealt with adequately in a few pages, when even volumes already written on the subject have been unable to determine the answer. It seems to me that before dealing with the life-work of a great industrialist like Nuffield I must not shirk the main issue—but rather use his life to illustrate the broad principles of leadership in industry which have formed in my mind of recent years, and which must be dealt with first.

It is a difficult subject for me because it is one in which I have had no practical experience. But leadership in industry has to do with the same human factor, the handling of men, and that is a subject which I know something about—or like to think I do. So I must have a shot at it, however difficult the task. What follows is my own view, formed after conversations with certain industrialists whose opinions I value.

It appears to me that industry in any country is affected by certain " external " factors over which it has little control, if any. Chief among them would be the international political situation and its effect on world trade, and also the home and overseas policy of the Government. In this particular respect and in some others, a government has a role to play in relation to industry which must be understood and acknowledged. Obviously a strong and stable Government with a declared financial and commercial policy is necessary. Given this, directors of industrial concerns can plan ahead with reasonable confidence —without it they cannot.

But I am more concerned with " internal " factors in industry and that brings me directly to the problem of human relationships, the factor which overrides all others—which must, therefore, be considered in some detail. The raw material of any business is " men," whether it be soldiering or industry. To succeed, a proper understanding of human nature is essential— whether you want to win battles or have an efficient factory.

Let me digress for a moment and say how I handled men in the army *at all times* and particularly in war-time in the Eighth Army and in 21 Army Group. I made the soldiers partners with me in the task which lay ahead. I took them into my confidence, explained the problem and how we would solve it, told them what *they* had to do and how success or failure on their part would affect the master plan, and finally told them how the job would be done—and when. In war, the soldiers then won the battles; I didn't. And when we weren't fighting, I saw to it that they had every possible amenity in the way of good meals, newspapers, mail from home, concert parties, leave, and so on. In peace-time the men's wives were visited by the officers' wives, and their families were looked after in times of need. All this produces a comradeship between officer and man, between a general and his troops, and the comradeship of the army is a great and wonderful thing—as I know well. But, of course, it is not so easy as that in industry. Then the army chain of command is pretty well absolute and *inflexible*; it is not for the soldiers " to reason why," or to strike if they don't like the sergeant-major. I read recently of an unofficial strike at a works because a foreman used a swear word when speaking to an operator. In the army if a sergeant-major told a soldier he was a bloody fool, there would not be a strike—not that I am suggesting a sergeant-major would ever use such language!

On the other hand, workers are independent to a degree. The essence of an army is discipline, whereas the essence of democracy is freedom; soldiers have to obey orders, workers have to be persuaded. Here lies the great difference between the handling of the soldier and the worker.

All of us, soldiers and industrialists, have got to realise that the man of to-day, soldier or worker, is more knowledgeable and better educated than formerly—and more curious. Education and the progress of civilisation have extended his capacity to think, and to criticise, and because of this he needs better leadership than formerly. And so do soldiers; what counts with them is the sure knowledge that a man will get justice, that his problems and troubles will be understood, that he "belongs," that he will always get a fair deal. There is no difference here between the soldier and the worker.

If the worker thinks that the leadership from the top is not all it should be, the discipline of the workers on the shop floor is often far from good—indeed, it is sometimes thoroughly bad. Something is very wrong when a body of men can withdraw their labour at a few hours' notice, against the advice of their Union leaders, and by so doing throw many thousands of their comrades out of work; and if one or two men of integrity refuse to take part in the strike, they are sent to "Coventry" and their lives made miserable.

A tremendous problem in industry in modern times appears to me to be that of redundancy. In some industries, Trade Unions have been able to co-operate with management in the introduction of new automatic processes, and a compromise has been reached; in other industries this has not been possible. The chief difficulty is that of dealing with the redundancy which often follows the invention and introduction of labour-saving machinery, because there is reluctance to work new processes which involve the displacement of even a single worker.

So it is all very difficult, and we don't have such problems in the army—thank God!

From talks I have had from time to time with groups of shop stewards, I am left with the impression that there is a good deal of suspicion on the part of the workers about what goes on at the top—and jealousy too. The ones I have met reckoned there was too much secrecy, and that they are not taken sufficiently into the confidence of the management. They think they just work for their employer, and there the matter ends. But they don't realise that the employer works for the man too, and one wonders if this is always explained and put across to the common sense of the workers. I once asked the Chairman of a works if he ever addressed gatherings of his workmen, told them what is going on, and made them his partners in the battle of production and the fight against rising costs. He said he did not; if he did it in the firm's time they would lose money, and if it was in the men's off-duty time they wouldn't turn up. I replied that such talks must, of course, be given during working hours; one half-hour talk once a month might result in the loss of a few pounds, but the resulting dividend in goodwill and mutual trust would be terrific.

As in the army, so in industry, I reckon that " communications," downwards and upwards, is probably the best way to maintain good relations with the workers—and I imagine it becomes more difficult as a company gets larger. But this is a living problem in industry, and a sincere desire on the part of the management of a company to maintain good relations with the employees must be apparent—however large the company. In this connection it must be important, indeed essential, that the top management of a company should seize every opportunity of meeting the rank and file by going round the factories, being seen " on the job," and passing the time of day with as many individual employees as it is possible to contact. Nothing is more distasteful to the British working man than the unhappy thought that he is working for a nebulous boss—one he never sees. He does not like the picture of a Board of Directors sitting in remote luxury and taking decisions which affect his own well-being and that of his wife, his children, and his mates. He wants to see in the flesh the human beings who are striving and worrying to create business in which he will participate and benefit, and he will then work *with* his employers—and not at variance with them.

A disturbing feature in British industry in my lifetime has been the swing of the workers' loyalty towards the Trade Unions and away from the employer. Surely we must attract the mind of the workers to the realisation that their best friend is the man who is in a position to pay good wages for good work? But there is certainly a problem here. The job of the Trade Unions is ever to get better conditions for the workers, and the individual workers are quite happy to leave it to them. So long as there are Trade Unions they will be fighting for something; if they did not, or were never successful, the men would stop paying their Union levies!

The history of Trade Unions shows that they have done a good job in raising the standards of the workers; they are an essential part of industrial life and provide a healthy opposition. But they must maintain discipline within their Unions, and act with courage in cases of indiscipline—particularly with regard to unofficial strikes, and the disregard of signed agreements.

We pride ourselves on being a democratic country, with free elections and a constitutional system of government—and in all democratic countries elections are by secret ballot. But when some major issue is to be decided by the workers in an industry, the vote for or against is taken by a show of hands and not by a secret ballot. I reckon there would be fewer unofficial strikes if the decision was by secret ballot; this would be genuine industrial democracy.

And here is another point. I remember somebody, I think Sir Miles Thomas, once told me that in industry there was a basic two-fold problem which has always been difficult to solve.

It was this. On the one hand, the employer wants to get as much work as possible from his workmen for the smallest possible pay packet, so that he can sell his goods at a profit in a hotly competitive market; on the other hand, the worker wants to do as little work as possible for the maximum pay! This may be a somewhat crude way of propounding the problem and, of course, there are undoubtedly many noble exceptions; but human nature being what it is, the above can well be understood. Presumably this prickly nettle must be grasped by the Trade Unions; they must somehow equate the two aspects of the problem, and they don't seem to have had much success at present.

I sometimes wonder if the relationships between master and man have not deteriorated during the years since the end of Hitler's war. Most firms devote large sums to *external* public relations; possibly if some of this money were diverted to the task of developing better *internal* relations, we might have greater harmony in industry and less strikes.

There are, one supposes, bad or inadequate leaders in industry as there are in other walks of life; but the problem of selection in industry is not easy. For instance, in the army we train and produce leaders by selection in a well-defined chain of command until, after a period of years, one can be certain that the right man has been picked for the right job. Not so in industry. There, leaders must of course be men of great integrity and devotion to duty as in the army; but they are also highly individualistic, with strong personalities and varying accomplishments. They have arrived at the top by hard work, of course, but by different routes and various means—some on account of technical skill, others because of financial knowledge, others by pure salesmanship, and so on. There is no common denominator. They are all men who have the drive to get things done, and they command respect by the example they set—which is an essential quality in a leader. But how precisely can one define such an individual?

My feeling with regard to industrial peace and contentment

is that it falls definitely into the realm of human relations—in which realm to-day politics intrude into the picture, which is a pity. However persevering the leader, the worker in a free democracy has definite rights to voice his opinion regarding wages and conditions of work. But unfortunately he is at times swayed by political thought. However much conservative and socialist ideals may approximate in regard to labour, there will always be a break-away so long as an extreme " left " exists. This is a most difficult problem in a free democracy which is based on freedom of speech.

I hope that this short introduction has opened the door to the subject so that we can now discuss the methods adopted by a particular individual.

Let us, therefore, have a look at Nuffield and see if we can discover the secret of his success.

Lord Nuffield

William Richard Morris, now the Viscount Nuffield, was born in October, 1877, which makes him ten years older than me. He was born in Worcester, but the family moved to Oxford when he was three and he has lived in that county ever since. It is sometimes said that he rose from nothing or, at least, from very humble circumstances. This is not true; his ancestors were landowners in Oxfordshire in the thirteenth century.

We should have a look at his parents as this will give us a guide to the character training of the son—who was the eldest of seven.

His father, Frederick Morris, had moved about more than most of the Morris clan, going at an early age to Canada, then working in a drapery business in Worcester, and finally returning to the family occupation of farming near Oxford. He seems to have been a man of strong character who brought his family up wisely. In 1893 he developed asthma so badly that he had to give up active work.

The boy William was then nearly sixteen and he realised he must leave school and get a job at once; indeed, he had to become the main bread-winner for the whole family. So he got work in a shop in Oxford where he learnt the bicycle trade, but he stayed there only a few months because he had always wanted to have a business of his own. With complete confidence he opened a workshop in 1893 with only four pounds to his credit; but he had made such a good name for himself and his work in his first job that a number of people transferred their custom to his new workshop—which was a brick building at the back of his father's house in Cowley. Later his father, as he got better, helped him by handling the accounts of the bicycle shop. He died in 1916.

His mother must have been a remarkable woman; she devoted the best years of her life to her family. Very often successful men are said to have had a dominating mother, but not so W. R. Morris; his mother certainly encouraged him, but she never attempted to interfere in his affairs. He loved her dearly and it was she who moulded his character towards that simplicity of life which he has always had. She died in 1934.

Nuffield, as we will now call him, realised that repairing bicycles and selling accessories would not take him very far, and so he began to build his own machines. Orders for bicycles soon began to flow in, and this meant hard work and long hours; he was prepared to work far into the night—sometimes all night. His business grew with his reputation, and he then launched out to become a bicycle agent and dealer. But this was not enough for him and his thoughts turned to motor bicycles; in 1902 he machined and built a one-cylinder engine which he fitted into one of his own frames; he was now well launched into industry.

It has been said of Nuffield that when he was a schoolboy he had wanted to study medical science and become a surgeon; but he couldn't carry out this ambition because his father's illness made it necessary for him to get work at once to support the family—when he was not yet sixteen, as we have already seen. He had always been very good with his hands, so much so that he used his hands to help his head—with the result that he became a skilled mechanic very quickly. This led me to think that he might well have become a famous surgeon. But when I suggested this to Nuffield in conversation one day, he said there was nothing in the rumours that he once wished to become a surgeon; it had never entered his mind seriously, and anyhow he couldn't have pursued a career which required a long period of training because he had to earn money when fifteen in order to support his family. He told me that he always wanted to be an engineer, and never had any other ambitions.

However that may be, he has, during his lifetime, made very generous donations to the medical school at Oxford University, to hospitals generally, to St. Dunstan's and to many other medical organisations too numerous to mention. I suppose he has been the largest single contributor to the alleviation of pain and suffering that our nation has had.

He has also given generously to the fighting Services. The Nuffield Trust for the Forces of the Crown totalled over eight million pounds, and since 1939 the three Services have received in income a sum of nearly £2,500,000. All in all, he has given away in his lifetime a total of forty million pounds.

It is not my intention to trace for the reader the growth and development of the Morris Motors organisation from the small beginnings we have seen in the bicycle workshop in Oxford to the mighty British Motor Corporation of to-day—which led to Lord Nuffield becoming one of the richest men in England. That can be read in various books. We must now pass on and have a more intimate look at the man himself. But before doing so we must mention his marriage which took place in 1904, he and his wife making their first home in a small house in Oxford not far from the business premises of:

W. R. Morris
Practical Cycle Maker and Repairer
48 High Street, Oxford

I never met Lady Nuffield; but I have seen a photograph of her and it shows a most attractive face. The two were close companions during the whole of their married life. She died in the spring of 1959 and he, who has always been somewhat shy and reserved, and perhaps a little lonely, became more lonely than ever he was before. The reason may possibly be because he devoted his whole soul and all his energies to his workaday world, and never became attached to any hobbies—except those which have to do with the profession of a mechanic.

I first met Nuffield in 1944, before the Normandy campaign. I had been ordered to return to England from the Eighth Army to take command of 21 Army Group and to prepare the Allied Land Forces, British and American, for the cross-channel operation—under the Supreme Command of General Eisenhower. Besides visiting the soldiers, I also visited many factories which were producing military equipment for our use, and some of these were in the Nuffield organisation. I will never forget our first meeting. He had offered to take my war caravans into one of his works in Birmingham and overhaul them in readiness for the invasion of Normandy. They certainly needed it; they had become a bit battered during the march from Alamein to London —via Tunis, Sicily, and half-way up Italy! We visited the factory in Birmingham together and saw the work on the caravans being carried out; we then drove to another of his works in Coventry and during the drive we discussed the handling of men. He had heard about the methods I used in the army, and I remember telling him of my underlying philosophy that battles are won primarily in the hearts of men, and that once you can gain the trust and confidence of those who serve or work under you, then the greatest achievements become possible. His reply was most illuminating—it was that exactly the same principles applied in industry, that his policy had always been to have a body of workers who were interested in their work, and I think his closing words were: " If you look after your men they will look after you, and the result will be contented workers who are proud to work for you."

After studying his life, and also seeking information from some who have worked with him, I tried to decide what was the basic factor in his make-up which led to his success. Of course, he was a good business man. And he was a good judge of men, a good picker of subordinates—men who would carry out his policy. But there was obviously something more than that to him; what was that " something more "?

I think it was " courage." He had no advantages in the family sense; although of good yeoman stock, the family was poor and there was no money to spare. He had always kept himself fit by abstemious habits and bicycle racing; and he had a most attractive personality—quick, dynamic, and warm. But it was his courage which really set him apart; that was the basic quality which guaranteed most of the others. Chief among " the others " were decision, action, and a single-minded devotion to his business. He had a sort of personal magnetism which ensured that when he turned his abilities, energy and courage to the task ahead, he would be backed by a devoted staff who knew that their best interests were secure in his hands.

In conversation with Nuffield one day I asked him if there was any moment in his life which he has never forgotten, and which taught him some lesson for the future. He said there was such a moment, and he told me the following tale.

By 1903 he had been in business on his own for ten years, and was well on the way to becoming firmly established in the motor-cycle trade; his thoughts then began to turn towards motor cars. At this time he was approached by an Oxford undergraduate, a Christ Church man, who had inherited a hundred thousand pounds and a steam car, and who wanted to put his money into the motor industry. He persuaded Nuffield to go into partnership with him, together with a third man who was a salesman; Nuffield was to be the works manager; and on this basis the partnership of three was established. But the undergraduate had no idea of business finance and spent money on a scale which was not justified by the trade available; the salesman, who was also a general manager, could not resist the enthusiasm of his young colleague who had put up all the money; and Nuffield, working long hours on the engineering side of the works, gradually saw disaster looming ahead—and it duly came. The business failed in 1904, after one year of the partnership. The debts were all paid by the sale of the assets; but nothing was left over. After ten years of struggle, Nuffield was " broke "; all he possessed was his kit of tools. His courage now stood him in good stead; he began again from the bottom, but he took a firm decision not to share control of his business with others— he would retain overall control in his own hands.

During the same conversation he told me of another difficult moment in his life, and this was one which I remembered myself and which made an impact on me at the time. It was in 1920; I was a student at the Staff College, Camberley, and needed a car. There was a slump in the motor industry due, I suppose, to the general rise in prices in the immediate post-war era of the 1914-18 war and, in particular, to the high prices being charged for cars. In the Morris works the accumulation of unsold cars was making it difficult to find space to continue the assembly of new cars coming off the line. Nuffield quickly decided to reduce his prices substantially, in spite of the protests of his sales manager, and of the bitter reaction of some other firms in the motor industry—who still regarded him as an upstart who did not know what he was doing.

Within three weeks he had sold all his completed cars. I bought one myself! He had, of course, lost money in the process; but within three months it had all been recovered and the firm was forging ahead again.

I don't think it would be possible to describe Nuffield as one of the greatest leaders of his time; he is not sufficiently extrovert for that role. He is shy and doesn't like meeting people. He has always been happiest with a spanner or a pair of pliers in his hands; he was a born mechanic and retained a perfect co-ordination of hand and eye until he reached an advanced age. But for all his shyness, he was always sure of himself and never wavered in his confidence in his own abilities and judgment. Some might say that he was lucky in that the times were right for him, and that others did not make the same use of the times. Nuffield certainly seized every opportunity which came his way; but he also created opportunities for himself. He was never upset by misfortunes; indeed, they rather spurred him on to take risks which would have daunted a less courageous man. Always it was his courage which carried him forward; and, added to courage, he had the drive to get things done.

Even with all these splendid qualities, it is doubtful whether he would have succeeded to the extent he did if he had not been a terrific worker; he was prepared to work early in the morning until late at night—and all night, if the need arose.

In conversations I have had with Nuffield, we have discussed many subjects—mostly about his own life, and about personal relationships between master and man in industry. I once asked him why more time was lost to-day by strikes in the motor industry than in any other industry of comparable size. He said the chief trouble was that firms in the motor industry do not control their own supplies; the component parts of motor cars are made in factories all over England; in no other industry are the component parts of any product spread over so many independent firms. A strike of a few skilled men in a factory making a key component can stop the production of the whole British Motor Corporation, and throw many thousands out of work.

As regards industrial unrest generally, and strikes whether official or unofficial, he considers that men do not work to-day like they used to when he was a worker on the shop floor. He deplores the lack of discipline among workers, and the absence of a sense of duty, of responsibility, and of loyalty to their leaders. He is a firm advocate of the secret ballot when votes are taken at mass meetings, and of not reaching a decision to strike by a show of hands—and all will agree with him here.

I once asked Nuffield if he would like to have his life over again, and, if this were possible, would he act differently. His reply was that his early life was a constant struggle, and very hard at times; he couldn't go through with it all again. At the age of fifteen he had to support his father, mother, and sisters. After ten years of struggle he was just beginning to make headway in his business, when suddenly he was let down by his partners, became "broke," and had to begin all over again. No, he couldn't face it all a second time! One must remember that when he said this to me he was eighty-three, an age when one has earned a rest. But he doesn't rest! He goes every morning to his office at Cowley and works there until late in the afternoon; he is Honorary President of the Nuffield Organisation and the many charitable trusts he has created take up much of his time. He also continues to keep in close touch with the motor organisation he created.

After a great deal of pressure from me, he did at last admit that if he had his life over again he wouldn't work so hard next time! For myself, I doubt that; he loves work. Indeed, he did say that nothing is so difficult in life as knowing what to do when work is over, and, unless this problem can be resolved, leisure can be boring.

I said earlier that Nuffield is to-day a very lonely man; and I said it because he told me so himself. But I did also say that he is shy and reserved, and while I think he appears thus to many people, there is a side to his character which gives a very different impression. I recall a visit I paid him in Cowley in March, 1960. I had not seen him since his wife had died ten months earlier. He welcomed me in his office with enthusiasm and we talked at length. Indeed, once I had opened a subject it was difficult to get a word in at all! He was friendly, and delighted to see me, and I drew him out and worked on his sense of humour. His office is in what used to be his old school, the village school of Cowley. Every Monday morning his father gave him twopence, which he had to hand to the schoolmaster—that being the fee for a week's schooling!

We lunched together in his private dining-room in the office block, just the two of us—alone. I had to leave soon after lunch, and I pictured him going back to his home later in the afternoon, to a lonely evening. During our conversation I had remarked that in old age one has a great interest in the progress of a son in his chosen profession, and in one's grandchildren. He agreed, and then remarked sadly that he had no children and when he died his title, home, and everything else would disappear.

The picture I like to have of Nuffield is of a warm-hearted, friendly and generous man who delights in meeting his friends —but quietly, and in his own time, and one at a time, to talk about the past. He may appear shy and reserved; but once you show that you really do want to see him, and to talk to him, and to get his views on things, he opens up at once. I like him very much, and I admire him enormously.

He was a good " captain of a team," a man of decision and action; he had within him those qualities which enable a man to influence and control other men for their own good. Clearly then, in industry it is " captaincy " which counts—as indeed it is in the professions of all those men whose careers we examine in this book.

Good relationships in industry are really nothing more than human relations, and that has been made clear in what I have written. A major trouble is that in civil life it is rare to find directors or top executives who are experts in human relations, or any who have made an intense study of leadership. In the army the subject of leadership is studied by the potential officer from the day he joins the Royal Military Academy at Sandhurst —and is continued throughout his career.

We must remember that at the turn of the century when Nuffield was operating, the mind of the employee tended to be " dependent "—that is to say, he was content to carry out instructions. To-day, the employee has a more " independent " outlook. As we have seen, Nuffield realised this to the full; he regarded human beings as the most important part of his business, and no major move was made without first considering its effect on those people who were concerned. To-day in the motor industry it does not seem to be quite the same, and certain of the principles on which Nuffield worked in the past have clearly been discarded.

CHAPTER ELEVEN

LEADERSHIP OF YOUTH

IN THE SUMMER of 1948 I delivered an address to the Mothers' Union in London, the subject being "The Youth of Britain." Certain organs of the Press when commenting on the address said that a man of sixty, which was then my age, had no mandate to speak on the subject of Youth! At the time I reckoned that my experiences in handling the young manhood of Britain, helping to turn them into the tough warriors who fought and beat the once-renowned German Army from Normandy to the Baltic, and later in testing others in the fire of National Service, gave me a certain entitlement to speak my mind about the boys of our nation. And this I did, saying that I was not too happy about them.

Nearly fourteen years have passed since that address was delivered. Let us now take another look at our British boys and see how we stand in 1961. We must "understand" the human material at our disposal before we can decide the type of leadership and training it needs.

During the years of so-called peace since 1945, it has been my good fortune to have been brought into contact with the young men of every nation in the Western bloc, seeing them carrying out their National Service or military training. In addition, when I visited a country in the Western Defence organisation it was my custom to go to a boys' school and learn about that age group. Thus I gained a good working knowledge of the youth of the Free World—from Norway across Europe to Italy, due east to Turkey, across the Atlantic in Canada and the U.S.A., and of course in Britain and Northern Ireland. To-day I am a Governor of two English public schools.

I find nothing wrong with the boys of our nation as regards the material they offer; they are splendid material, and will stand comparison with the young people of any other nation. I find a good deal wrong in our handling and training of this fine material, and if the boys of to-day are considered to be not so good as they should be, I reckon it's our fault. What follows has reference only to boys since I have no experience of the education or upbringing of girls; but it is possible that, in principle, the lessons are comparable. And in the particular problem we are discussing, girls are just as important as boys—and maybe more so. Generation after generation of boys are perpetually passing through our homes and schools, and passing on to manhood; each generation is distinctive and personal to those who belong to it, but each overlaps those which precede and follow it—a river of young life in unbroken continuity. One generation is always in the forefront of my mind—the generation of those who served, and who offered and gave their lives, in two world wars. The war memorials in our cities and towns, and on the village greens of Britain, stand in gratitude for what they were and what they did.

The " distinctiveness " of each generation, to which I have referred, is due to the progress of civilisation over the years. For instance, I was a boy in the Victorian and Edwardian eras; those were the days of large families; my parents had nine children and we were a self-contained little community within ourselves. There were no cinemas; we had little pocket money; living was cheap; we made our own amusements and didn't have to go outside for them. And a very important point—girls were not allowed to go out alone with boys, to dances or elsewhere.

The generation after mine, that is after the 1914-18 war, had very different conditions. There were cinemas; girls went out alone with boys; families were smaller due to economic pressure; boys began to go outside their families for their amusements. And consider the *next* generation, that would be the boys of to-day—what freedom they have!

I am sure it is all for the best; but the changes which have taken place over the years must be understood. They are the same boys as regards flesh and blood. But just as the soldiers of to-day need a different kind of leadership than those of say the South African War of 1900, so the boys of each successive generation need a different kind of handling—and particularly the boys of to-day, in the 1960s.

In every generation some boys come from good homes, some from bad; some are the sons of rich parents, some come from the working classes. But, overall, a common humanity unites them. The proper study of mankind is man, so let us consider the upbringing of the boys of our land in the present times.

The boy of to-day is the man of to-morrow; the object in his training should be to build up his character so that in due course he can influence others for good. Let us make no mistake about one thing—the foundations of character must be laid in the home; the basis of all training must take place *there*; it is *that* training which will influence a boy all his life, for good or for ill. On the sure foundations for good laid in the home, the schoolmaster will build when the boy comes his way; if those foundations have not been laid, neither the schoolmaster nor anybody else can do much about it. We hear a good deal these days about " juvenile delinquency "; this, of course, is often a very convenient expression for " parental neglect."

My own experience leads me to believe that the foundation of character-building—what is right and what is wrong, speaking the truth, chivalry, to mention the most important—must be instilled into a boy by the time he is six years old. This is necessary because of the world we live in. As the boy grows up the time will come when he has outgrown his family, or thinks he has—which is the same thing in the end. He is now about fourteen, and the foundations of character which *should* have been instilled into him eight years ago ought now to have blossomed and borne fruit. If they have not, the boy is in danger. Why? Because he sees a world in which the scientists are producing things about which mankind has dreamed for centuries—

and it could be such a happy world. But he also sees that it is a world split in twain by two conflicting ideological doctrines or moral codes—one half Christian, the other half atheistic. He sees fear abroad, international tension, much talk of war, and much unhappiness in many parts of the world—such as millions of refugees wandering about, not only homeless but also stateless. There were no such happenings when I was a boy, nor was I subjected to the temptations which confront a boy to-day —due to the progress of civilisation.

But in my adult life, during two world wars there has been the most incredible cruelty inflicted on humanity by nations calling themselves civilised. The contrast is clear—a world of immense and wonderful possibilities, a happy and beautiful world, and man's ugly misuse of the same world.

When this is put to people in conversation, many say: " It makes you think." But does it?

Are we not all living in a mist of self-deception, in a world in which materialism holds sway and spiritual values have been discarded? For example, consider the many advertisements which confront us wherever we go, and which undoubtedly influence many people. They suggest that the answer to every problem can be bought with money. Do you want happiness in your home? Then buy this vacuum cleaner, or that kind of breakfast food, or this soap, or drink that beer! Of course, not everybody is deceived by all this, but the adolescent boy is in danger when living in such a mist of self-deception.

"What shall it profit a man, if he gain the whole world, and lose his soul."

Our British boys have, we hope, been brought up in Christian homes; they have probably heard sermons about Christ, and been told that the world would be a better place if there were more of His kind. But that is no answer to a boy's troubles. Christ does not ask the boy to idolise Him; what He asks one and all to do is to support His cause. Not " idolise Me," but " follow Me." He then gives us all a set of principles and an unforgettable example. If we Christian people can understand

and accept all this, then our duty is plain. It is this—if the world is to come through the present turmoil and unrest safely and sanely, we must live the real life, we must follow His example instead of groping in the dark. He claims to be the light we need; no other man has ever made that claim.

Now we can see how difficult it is for the boy of to-day, and what a gigantic task confronts the parent and the schoolmaster—to explain all this to boys, and to influence them to take the right road. And the task is made far more difficult by modern conditions of life—a life in which the boy faces temptations and problems greater than any of us had to face when we were young. The thrillers, gangster films, broken homes due to laxity in the marriage obligations, the advertisement of sex in certain newspapers—all these impose a severe strain on the adolescent boy, and the development of character under such conditions is not easy.

Then the progress of civilisation and science has introduced other problems. As the boy passes through the adolescent stage and grows to manhood, he will find that his visual world has been extended. He can go to the cinema and see how people live and behave in other parts of the world. In the home he has the radio and the television; he can " listen in " to world affairs and home affairs; he can hear specialists talk on almost any subject. He can read in the newspapers about socialist agitators, the cry for more pay and less work, and present-day industrial problems. Because of all these things, the adolescent boy can measure his everyday environment in a way impossible fifty years ago; and as he grows up he will be unlikely to accept conditions of work not in keeping with the ideas he has absorbed.

Hence it is essential that he should absorb the right ideas. He must learn to co-operate in a community. He must learn that one of the fundamentals of democratic life is voluntary self-discipline in the interests of the group to which he belongs; he must acquire the quality of subordination of self for the benefit of his comrades and the community in general. Above all, he must gain a balanced view of things, a balanced outlook on life.

He must learn to keep his inward sense of proportion when outward things are distorted and difficult.

I have mentioned the word "discipline." This word has a somewhat unpleasant sound to some people, possibly because it is not properly understood. The true basis of discipline is self-discipline; it embraces the idea of self-control and self-restraint, and implies a life ordered and bounded by certain voluntarily imposed limitations. These limitations may be considered as duties, or obligations, which we feel it necessary to fulfil.

This conception of duty underlines the whole of Christian teaching on personal conduct, and must be impressed on every child from his nursery days onwards—and certainly before he is six. Discipline may, in fact, be defined as "the performance of duty." It has, I believe, a moral foundation which none of us need be afraid to admit.

Discipline has also what I call, for want of a better word, a social basis. All civilised communities demand a degree of self-control from their citizens. In the interests of the community as a whole, each of us willingly submits to the supremacy of the law and to the authority of its agents—the police. If anything is in short supply, we stand in a queue for it and do not fight for it in the shops—in England, at any rate. We all realise that the community as a whole makes demands on us as individuals; and in order that we may all live freely and happily together, we voluntarily impose upon ourselves a certain restraint.

Therefore discipline has both a moral and a social foundation. And it is vital that this fact be impressed on the youth of our nation.

The root of discipline is that "something" which a boy, a young man, must set above himself, and for whose greater value he will give up his own wishes in order that the Cause may prevail—in order that his community can continue.

I have thought it right to include this analysis in order to clear my own mind on the subject. We now come to the difficult part of our task—to indicate how all these things are to be done and who is to do them. It would appear to be a gigantic task.

But I don't think it need be if we define the object clearly and then outline the basic principles to be followed in achieving it. We must avoid becoming involved in detailed methods, since these will vary with the boy and the area in which he lives.

What is the object? It is to instil integrity, moral courage and enthusiasm into the ranks of youth and thus erect a bulwark which will defy the undermining influences which are seeking to destroy the characters of our boys. They must be taught to be " strong points " in the nation, standing for honesty amid the temptations to be dishonest, for team work and loyalty, for genuine effort, for a high sense of duty, and, in fact, for everything which works for the good of the country.

Where must the teaching begin? In the home. *That* is where the formation of character must begin. The boy must be taught that certain things are right and certain things are wrong; he must learn the foundations of honesty and sincerity, to speak the truth, and in the face of temptation to stand firm by what he believes to be right. The foundations of this teaching must begin early and be firmly in his childish mind by the time he reaches the age of six, so that when he begins to go to school he will not be " easy meat " for any evil influences he may encounter. Both parents must take part in this teaching, the mother initially, and the father taking over as the boy increases in years—and most certainly before he approaches the age of about ten.

We now come to the age when a boy leaves his primary or preparatory school, and moves on to a secondary, grammar or public school. This is a period when he will meet temptation. Will he throw overboard all he has been taught in the home, or will he hold fast to the principles of Christian behaviour? Which is to happen will depend a good deal on the type of company he keeps at this vital stage in his life, and also on what use he makes of his leisure time. There is a danger in too much leisure unless a boy is taught how to use it; aimless leisure leads to boredom and can be a menace; at this age a boy should be encouraged to have a hobby.

He is now about thirteen and this is the time when he should find an outlet as a member of a really good youth organisation, or boys' club; a good Cadet unit, or the Scouts, provide a first-class type of organisation, because there he will learn discipline and physical training and acquire a sense of duty. I believe in these movements because they provide a boy with a sound democratic group in which to grow up—while he is still young and struggling to form his own opinion. Through membership of such a group a boy will learn self-discipline, self-reliance, and " to give " rather than to get. Furthermore, through the friendships which he makes he will begin to learn the true meaning and value of comradeship. He does not merely enjoy the benefits of being able to take part in the games and other activities organised by his club; he learns by practice and example that he must play his full part as a responsible member of a team. A good club, with a good club leader, can set standards of behaviour, taste and endeavour which will influence the life and growth of a boy. As he grows to manhood he will become conscious of his responsibility to the club as a whole; he will learn that duty comes before pleasure, and that privileges are enjoyed only if obligations are willingly shouldered. In fact, under a good club leader a boy's character can be moulded in such a way as to fit him to become a man of high integrity and courage, moral and physical, who is prepared to do a hard day's work and to find happiness through his achievements. For all these reasons, I am convinced that a boy needs the membership of a youth movement as he approaches and passes through the age of adolescence—say from thirteen to eighteen.

I would like to mention two interesting contacts of my own with boys' clubs.

In 1946 an officer who had been on my staff during the war, and who had returned to civilian employment, wanted to start a club for very poor boys in his town and asked me if I would help financially—which I did. I suggested that there should be one basic rule which must be agreed by all the members:

" In this club we speak the truth."

This rule was to be written up on a large notice in the club.

If a boy told a lie to his comrades, he was to be tried by the boys themselves; if he was proved guilty, he was removed from the club. All this was agreed. An old deserted house was acquired as a club centre; the boys themselves carried out the necessary repairs, painting, etc., and I attended the opening ceremony. It was a great success. The point here was that there was no book of rules; the boys made their own rules and did all the necessary work themselves. All they were *asked* to do was to speak the truth—very simple, and it paid a good dividend.

In 1948 I went to live in France and one summer I invited six of the boys to spend ten days at my chateau near Fontainebleau; we all enjoyed that visit. One of the boys had very definite Communist tendencies when he arrived; but we cured him before he left!

The second incident which comes to mind is a visit I paid in 1959 to a youth centre in the East End of London. I was shown over the centre, and then the club manager asked me to go with him to a room where the members of a well-known London "gang" were boxing; this gang, he said, were a tough lot, well armed when on the war-path, and able to take on the police or any other gang in London—and when up against it would shoot to kill. The members of the gang all belonged to the club, about sixteen in number and aged from, say, seventeen to about twenty. I was intensely interested and went along with the club manager. They had finished their exercise when I arrived; I expressed disappointment and asked if two of them would give me a demonstration of their skill. The gang leader at once ordered two boys to take off their jackets and get into the ring; I then witnessed a tough scrap, more fighting than boxing with some hefty blows exchanged. Then they gathered round and we talked—or rather I got them talking, and I listened. It was for me an intensely interesting experience to meet these boys—east London boys, from poor homes but all at work and earning good money, in fine physical condition, quick on the uptake and with that Cockney sense of humour which is so attractive, and with a tremendous sense of comradeship and loyalty to the "gang." They all seemed to me to be very decent lads, not a bit afraid and very willing to talk to me; there wasn't what I could describe as a "bad face" among them. What a lot of good one could do with boys like that if only they could be taken in hand early enough! After all, it was those very types of Cockney boys who were my comrades-in-arms on the battlefields of Africa and Europe; and how gallantly they had fought, many giving their lives that we who survive might have the freedom we now enjoy. But we must pass on in our study of youth.

After a boy is about sixteen, I doubt if there is much anybody can do to mould his character, except by influence and example. You can no longer force him to do *this*, or not to do *that*; he will do what he likes. And what he does, and the life he leads, will depend on how far his parents have been successful in building up his character in the home—helped, of course, by the schoolmaster and the club leader. I must make the point here that the parents and the schoolmaster, and the club leader, too, are partners in the battle for the boy—for his character, and to help him to stand firm in the buffeting he's going to get in this life. It would be fatal if the schoolmaster has to fight a losing battle with the parents, or vice versa. For this reason I believe there should be consultation between the two. If the school is attempting to put forward one set of values and the home is practising another, then a conflict may be set up in the mind of the boy. It is the duty of the school to present with courage and conviction the values for which it stands, and to be prepared to discuss these values with parents. Probably no part of the work of a schoolmaster will be more important than personal interviews with the fathers and mothers of the boys he teaches; they may range from some straightforward matter such as the choice of a career, to a discussion of the reasons behind some serious problem of truancy or juvenile crime. The parents of many boys now receiving a secondary education and perhaps going on to a university may never have had these advantages. It may often be necessary to smooth some of the strains set up in a family by the development in a gifted child of certain unfamiliar tastes and ambitions. The schoolmaster must be prepared to help in these matters.

We must now endeavour to formulate some conclusions, some principles which emerge from what I have been trying to say. There are many youth organisations in Britain, but their activities do not appear to me to be co-ordinated in any way; this is a weak point and it leads to disjointed effort and to a waste of resources. I do not believe that a Government Department like the Ministry of Education is the proper authority to handle a Youth Service. The Civil Service is an admirable organisation; but it is bound by red tape and regulations. A Minister of the Crown is so busy with answering Parliamentary questions, and is so involved with party politics, that he has little time to spare for quiet thought and reflection about what is best for the boys of Britain. The result of the present system is merely a stream of circulars which have resulted in haphazard development, all leading to the Youth Service of Britain being in a state of acute depression. Some headquarters, divorced from Government control, needs to be organised to handle the matter. It should be headed by some well-known personality, to whom all will owe allegiance because of his record and single-mindedness. Boys are inveterate hero-worshippers, always willing to follow a known and trusted leader; they cannot be expected to follow with enthusiasm a party politician, or the Civil Service, where the warmth of leadership is entirely lacking because the subject of leadership has probably never been studied. I place this matter of organisation first and foremost.

Next, the units of the Youth Service must be given some ideals to which they subscribe. Some already have very high ideals; I refer to the Boy Scouts, to Cadet units, to the Boys' Brigade, and many others. But most boys' clubs have no high ideals; something more is needed than merely to take a boy off the streets so that he can play darts and table-tennis indoors. We have in the last half century done a great deal to abolish unfair privilege and unmerited poverty, and to give a chance to everybody whatever his origin. But in doing so we have not been very successful in making it clear to our boys that privileges and benefits bring responsibilities; a boy must shoulder his fair share of responsibility and not merely stand out for his " rights." In fact, he must learn to understand that life has a purpose. We have got to make it clear to the boys of Britain that they have something to be proud of in the past, and something to do in the future. We must develop in them a realisation that true happiness comes from achievement, and that we achieve something in this life only by hard work. They must be taught that " service " to others is one of the most satisfying experiences of life, provided it is voluntary; this spirit of " service " should flower naturally in adolescence, and must not be allowed to wither and die in later life. I cannot imagine the hard-worked Civil Service putting all this over from a Whitehall Ministry with any success; it is not the sort of stuff to go out to local education authorities in " Circular No. 1000 "!

Let us have a look at this matter of " ideals." There is a general tendency to-day for great ideals to become lost, and for the inspiration which can influence a community to become watered down in a maze of detail. Where are the great ideals for which words like " England " stand? It is not enough to say simply that such words are unfashionable. In parliamentary elections little or no appeal is made to idealism; even words like " freedom " and " justice " are only thrown in as a kind of makeweight to the boasts and promises of a higher standard of living, better social services and less taxation. But is this the right sort of stuff for our young people? Are we to teach our boys that they need not care what happens to England so long as " the State " arranges for their material welfare? If we do not care, then the chances are that we are liable to be rudely awakened. The citizen who uses his country simply to make money, or to acquire social status and power, may quickly find that his country becomes second-rate, and that the empire of finance or prestige which he has selfishly created becomes valueless and liable to swift destruction. In order to serve England,

and to be proud of being English, we do not have to possess as many atom bombs as America, or as many scientists as Russia. It is not the countries who lack the atom bombs or the big battalions who should be called " second-rate powers," but the countries who lack the big ideals. Unlike big battalions, big ideals have a habit of surviving. Our boys must be taught to make "England" mean something more than just a Welfare State; they must think and work for our community in an idealistic way and not in an egocentric one. By all means let us have our material benefits; we have virtually completed that step. We cannot now stand still; we must move forward, or perish. One of the first requirements is to remedy the widespread ignorance of the elementary facts of the Christian faith; many of our young soldiers have little knowledge of these facts. A recruit was recently asked what he knew about Good Friday —did it mean anything to him? He thought for a moment, and then replied that he had once read about Good Friday, and as far as he could remember he was a batman to Robinson Crusoe!

I cannot say that my own boyhood days were very happy, the main troubles being outlined in my *Memoirs*. For this reason it has been my object in later years to give help and encouragement to those boys who seemed to need it, and who came my way. There is not any great problem with boys who go to the public schools or grammar schools, since these mostly come from good homes. There is a very great problem for those boys who leave school at the age of fifteen and go to work, mostly coming from poor homes; it is these boys who need help. The following examples may be of interest.

In July, 1947, I went to New Zealand at the invitation of the Prime Minister of that country. My tour took me right down to Invercargill, at the southern end of Southland, and I was accommodated in the Grand Hotel; there was a large crowd outside the hotel and the police had some difficulty in getting me inside. But a small newspaper boy pushed his way through the crowd and handed me a copy of the *Southland Daily News*; I offered him payment, which he refused and disappeared into the crowd. Later that evening I remembered the boy and asked the Commissioner of Police to find him for me so that I could thank him for his friendly act; he was found in Sunday School the next morning, was removed and brought to me in the hotel; he was eleven-year-old Clive Adamson, who lived with his parents at 90 Fox Street. That meeting was the beginning of a friendship which has lasted to this day; at my request he wrote to me regularly and kept me in touch with his life and hopes and ambitions as he grew up—and told me of his troubles as they arose. In my replies I gave him the best advice I could; once or twice this was very necessary, such as when he seemed unable to settle down for long in any occupation. He never asked for money, nor did I send him any—except once on his twenty-first birthday. To look after him I enlisted the help of the Mayoress of those days, Mrs. Mabel Wachner, who proved a very good and faithful assistant. And now the little paper boy is married and has his own home, and I like to feel I was some help to him in the difficult years of his youth and adolescence. If ever I am able to visit New Zealand again, I will most certainly include Invercargill and Clive Adamson in my itinerary.

Then there is the story of the English schoolboy, aged 16, who had to write an essay on somebody he knew by reputation —and he selected me. He read all he could about me in the Press, much of it very uncomplimentary, and having described my army career, finished by saying I was a very unpleasant person—conceited, vain, ruthless, and so on. His father sent me the essay to read, which I did with interest! I then wrote to his father, saying that the boy should at least be fair; he had never met me, indeed had never seen me, and yet had made definite statements about my character. I suggested that he could have begun his critical remarks in this way:

"I have never met him but *it is reported* that he is . . ."

I asked the boy to visit me in my home, and he duly came. He was a delightful lad, very intelligent, and with a most attractive personality; we had an amusing talk and he is now one of the greatest of my young friends—and he visits me every time he returns from school for the holidays. I have persuaded him to go to Sandhurst and become a soldier—and he will make a good one.

I have another young friend, a working lad aged 19; he speaks the broadest "Lancashire" I have ever heard! He left school at fifteen and became an apprentice fitter in a big engineering firm. In 1959 I was asked to give the prizes at his Apprentice School and he won all the top awards for skill at his trade. He impressed me enormously; he seemed full of character. I asked the firm if they would send him to stay a week-end with me in my home, so that I could get to know him; he came, and told me about his life and hopes for the future. His ambition was to become a professional footballer and he had already signed as a part-time professional for a Fourth Division club. I found that, although he was technically very good at his work, he was very uneducated; and I proved to him that he must put this right if he wanted to succeed. I also proved to him that there was no real future for him in professional football; at the age of about thirty-five he would be discarded, with no profession. A better aim in life would be to work hard at his chosen profession of engineering, marry a nice girl, have a good home, and give his children a better education than he had been given. He agreed with all this advice. I then asked his firm to help in his education, and they agreed to send him to a Technical College for a four-week period every three months until he was twenty-one. The point I want to make is that Eric said nobody had ever talked to him in that way before, or advised him how to plan his life sensibly. However, all is now well, and when he has improved his education his firm will get a good dividend for the trouble they have taken over Eric.

All these friendships have convinced me that some of the best boys in our land come from the poorest homes; if contact can be made with such boys in early life and their characters developed on the right lines, they can rise to great heights. There is no doubt that if a boy, a young man, has to struggle against adversity when young, it can toughen his character to a remarkable degree. But he must be advised, and helped; he doesn't want money, he wants sensible advice.

I have mentioned earlier that a boy needs to belong to some youth movement or organisation so that he can come under the influence of a good club leader. But it may not be generally known that some two-thirds of the boys of Britain belong to *no* youth organisation—about 200,000 boys between the ages of seventeen and twenty are uncared for in this way, out of a total of 300,000. These are the boys we want to make contact with. The Youth Service deals only with existing clubs and organisations, and for such events as the Duke of Edinburgh's Award a boy must come from one of these.

In my opinion the best character training given to boys in Britain is that provided by the Outward Bound Trust, through their sea and mountain schools. Their aim is to select a boy from a poor home, remove him from his local environment, and then to spend four weeks developing his character in completely different surroundings in the mountains or by the sea—and then return him to his home surroundings, where he will be a " strong-point " for good in his street or community. Boys thus trained must be between the ages of seventeen and twenty; they are given tough and hard work, excitement, a challenge, and responsibility—to which any boy will always respond. Unfortunately Outward Bound can take only some 4,000 boys a year; but only ten per cent of these come from known existing organisations, ninety per cent coming from the 200,000 boys who belong to no organisation. If ever an organisation was worthy of support it is Outward Bound; its Patron is Prince Philip.

I first made contact with Outward Bound in 1947, when I was Chief of the Imperial General Staff. I was greatly interested and said I would like to pay for a boy from a poor home in the East End of London to go to one of their schools. They selected a boy called George Stiles, a member of the Fairbairn House Boys' Club and a young lorry-driver. George came to see me in the War Office before going to the school, and I said he must visit me again on his return—which he did. He was a changed boy and, what is more, he admitted it; the course had done him a world of good, chiefly in that it had helped him to get his moral values right and, by mixing with other boys from many different walks of life, to learn that life has a purpose and that he had a part to play. He is now happily married and lives in Walthamstow, and I am told he often speaks of his talks with me and of his four weeks on the Outward Bound course. And he writes to me from time to time.

I was recently allowed to see a letter written by a boy on his return from a course at an Outward Bound school. This is what he wrote:

"There was one person in my 'watch' whom I greatly admired—indeed whom we all admired, because he was so selfless. He never gave up working—however futile it was to go on. He never asked others to pull their weight. He hardly ever spoke. He possessed only the clothes he stood up in. He always smiled even at the worst moments, and although he never said anything to make someone work or join in, by his very example and love to others, there seemed to be a sense of unity whenever I was with him. This chap inspired me, and although his inspiration didn't show itself very clearly or successfully in me, it 'made' the course for me and gave me a glimpse of wholeness which I have never experienced before."

It is a wonderful tribute; I would like to meet that boy.

This short chapter gives, in outline, the type of leadership which I would advocate for the British boys of to-day—and for the girls too. My ideas may not be generally agreed, but at least they are simple. They are based on ideals, and on the eternal verities—which do not change, whatever age we live in. But I consider that the organisation and running of the Youth Service must be taken out of the hands of the Civil Service, which is in no way fitted to handle the problems which arise; also, we must cater for the large number of boys who are not in the Youth Service.

LEADERSHIP OF YOUTH

I am sorry that National Service is to come to an end. It has been good for the boys of our land to come into the Services for a period, where they learn discipline, a sense of duty, comradeship—and each one to find his own level in a bigger community than is possible in his own home. The National Service entry was a cross-section of the young men of Britain; they came from the public schools, the government schools, the factories, the workshops, and from industrial concerns of all kinds; from their ranks came a first-class type of young officer, and a great many N.C.O.s up to the rank of corporal. We will miss them.

SUGGESTIONS FOR THE ELDERLY

I believe that we older people have got to exercise a sense of proportion, and find a sensible and practical approach to the problem of helping young people over a very difficult period in their lives. A boy leaves school and goes straight into a factory or office; up to this moment he has had little pocket money, and not much free time because of homework in the evenings for the next day's school; then he finds himself with a pay packet, and with leisure in the evenings to spend it. It is this transition, sudden and abrupt, which is the danger period—because this is the time when a boy wants some fun, very naturally, and without any responsibility. Those who are trying to tackle this problem need humanity and imagination, remembering that they were once young themselves. The answer will not be found *only* in boys' clubs. Many of the "bad hats" come from families completely incapable of bringing up children —spoiling them up to the age of six, losing control over them afterwards, and denying them the affection which they have a right to expect. *Is it not the parents who need instruction?* Perhaps there should be a joint effort by employers and parents to search for the answer to this tremendous problem—sponsored and helped by leaders in the Youth Service.

A boy ought to be encouraged to plan his life intelligently, beginning to think about it when he is, say, fifteen; if he neglects to plan his life, his future is likely to be accidental. He will begin a new phase of life when he leaves school, which may be any age between fifteen and eighteen, and he needs an objective— a goal. Possession of a goal does not necessarily mean that it will be reached; but if there is no goal there is nothing which can be reached, and advancement then comes haphazardly.

A major factor is that a boy should enter a profession in which he will be happy, and where his special aptitudes will find the greatest scope—and this may not be one in which he will earn most money. The parents should guide him in this matter, helped by the schoolmaster.

Education must play a full part in all this business, but its purpose must be properly understood. What is " education "?

First I suggest that education enables a boy, a young man, to face up to some problem, some crisis in his life, to analyse it and sort out the factors which matter from those which are unimportant, to reach a decision—and then *to do* something. Decision, and action. This is a facet of education which appeals to many; but there is more to it than that.

Education is not primarily the acquisition of factual knowledge, although this is necessary in modern life for examination purposes. Education is the training, guiding and influencing of *people*, of human beings, each one of whom has a body, a mind and a soul which are all highly susceptible to every influence which surrounds them—and, above all, to the influence of *other people*. Ultimately, therefore, *education is a form of human relationship, a relationship in which some people train, guide, and give what they can to others—who in their turn must respond to the guidance, and themselves learn how to give.* Class-room instruction is one important element in this, but it is only one; another and more important element is the building of character, a definition of which was given in Chapter One, and to help a boy to get his sense of values right. I am a great believer in aiming high with young people, making it clear what they have to do, and explaining the reason. This is important because the future is in the hands of youth; they will have to take over the torch from us.

Our task is to inspire the youth of Britain and of the Commonwealth with a common moral purpose, which is based on a conscious and ardent belief in the Christian faith. If we can then unite our youth behind leaders who regard that faith as the Communists regard theirs, we will have nothing to fear—neither enemies nor economic troubles; both could be overcome. The most important thing in education—and in life—is a sense of purpose so strong as to enable a boy, a young man, to face and overcome all difficulties. Such a purpose can be built only on faith; that faith can be given only in youth. But it must be a good faith; bad faith lies at the root of most of our troubles to-day.

I mentioned the word " torch " in connection with youth. That word was used by John McCrae in the poem " In Flanders Fields ":

> " The torch, be yours to hold it high.
> If ye break faith with us who die
> We shall not sleep."

In memory of those who died that we might have the freedom we now enjoy, we hold Memorial Days—Armistice Day in November, Battle of Britain Sunday in September, and remembrance days of other kinds. On such days, in every town and village where we live the people gather round the war memorial, and lay wreaths in honour of those from the village who fell. Do our young people, do any of us, understand that Memorial Days have a challenge? What is the challenge? It is this.

They gave everything for me. Am I worth it? If so, what am I doing about it? And finally—our generation owes much to the past; what am I doing to ensure that the future will owe something to us?

That is the challenge; and some of us might find it difficult to answer the three questions. But our young people must be taught to see their life in that light.

Let me suggest four points for our consideration.

First, in dealing with a boy, a young lad, we should work initially on the assumption that he is good; we should not begin by considering him bad purely from hearsay; he is good until he shows himself to be bad.

Second, having analysed his good points we should concentrate on strengthening them—rather than " getting at him " always about his faults. As the good points begin to flower they will over-shadow the faults—which will eventually wither. The analogy of the gardener applies—the man who spends all his time digging up weeds will never grow good flowers.

Third, I was once asked what, in my opinion, was the worst crime a man could commit. Without any hesitation I replied:

" To lead a boy, a child, morally astray."

and added that no punishment would be too severe for that man.

Fourth, I recently asked a young friend of mine, a schoolboy aged sixteen, what he reckoned was the really important point which will have most influence with young people. Without any hesitation he replied—" example." Perhaps we can all take that to heart—and act on it. We have seen in the letter written by a boy on his return from an Outward Bound course, quoted on an earlier page, the effect which example can have.

IN THE DAYS OF THY YOUTH

If the above suggestions to older people are considered sound, what advice can I offer young people—how can they attain the glory of youthful character? I offer the following four points.

First, have a certain seriousness of mind. This does not mean that a boy, a young man, is not to be happy, not to be bright—far from it. But it will be brightest of all for him whose brow is open, whose heart is innocent, whose conscience is clear, and who is trying, humbly and heartily, to hold fast to the golden rule of David in Psalm 37:

" Keep innocency, and take heed unto the thing that is right; for that shall bring a man peace at the last."

Endless amusement, wasted opportunities, abused privileges

—these things cannot make up for the loss of virtue, the loss of manliness, the loss of self-respect.

Second, I place obedience. That high virtue, the true school of empire, means the law of duty cheerfully accepted as the law of life. From our earliest years God delegates some of His authority to our fellow-men—first to our parents, then to those set over us. Therefore, respect for authority is a sacred duty, as it is also a divine command. Never has there been an age when that command has been violated which has not become a corrupt age. In the loyalty, in the humility, in the obedience of youth—in their respect for their elders—have ever rested a nation's hopes.

Wherein lay the greatness of Sparta? It is revealed on that epitaph over the Three Hundred at Thermopylæ:

" Go, tell the Spartans, thou that passest by,
That here obedient to their laws we lie."

Is not obedience—is not simple loyalty to simple duty—the basis of all that is greatest in England's honour? What happened at the wreck of the *Birkenhead* in February, 1852? She was a troopship bound for South Africa, and she struck a rock in the early hours of the morning off Danger Point some fifty miles from Cape Town. The women and children were got away in the few boats which could be lowered; the officers ordered the men to stand firm on the deck, and not to risk swamping the boats by jumping overboard; the order was obeyed, and the soldiers went down with the ship, standing to attention on the deck—an officer and forty-seven men of my regiment, The Royal Warwickshire, being included in that gallant band. Here is an instance where scores of disciplined men preferred death to disobedience.

Third, I place diligence. The time for work, for study, is short. Swiftly, imperceptibly, boyhood flows into youth, and youth into manhood. When Napoleon visited his old school at Brienne he addressed only these words to the assembled boys, and said nothing more:

" Boys, remember that every hour wasted at school means a chance of misfortune in future life."

A boy, a youth, must not find himself on the threshold of manhood bankrupt in strength and wisdom, because of idleness; and this will happen if he squanders the vigour of his youth which is meant to be the capital of his future—instead of living on the income of the present. My advice to youth is " never be idle." A boy who gathers learning when young has taken the first steps to possess when old the riches of knowledge and wisdom.

Fourth. In my own life I have learnt that three qualities are vital for success: hard work, absolute integrity, and moral courage—which means not being afraid to say what you believe to be right, and standing firm in that belief.

A FINAL THOUGHT FOR US ALL

Do we realise that most of the suggestions about the state of youth to-day, the problems facing them, and the best methods to help young people on the road to maturity, are put forward by men and women well past their own youth? If this disparity in age is not understood, the final results may not be what is needed—however valuable the suggestions, and however sincere the intentions.

The fact is that the question of age cannot be disregarded. People who live differently, feel, think, and act differently. The motives which influence young people, and the aspirations which excite their imagination, are rarely the same motives which are in the hearts of the middle-aged; this is because the hopes and fears of youth are unique to their age. The simple danger is that we may fall into the error of suggesting to young people those things which *we* think ought to occupy *their* minds and feelings. We may be unable to help them because we do not understand them, or we make them feel that we do not understand them.

The material background of the times has changed greatly in recent years, even during the lifetime of the present generation. Our prosperity has given a new sense of significance and power to many thousands of adolescent boys who have had little training in the responsibilities involved. Indeed, few are aware of any responsibilities! Much of the delinquency which confronts us on a mounting scale may partly be the result of this unawareness. The spirit of the times, of which the Welfare State is a symbol, underlines this problem and teaches the adolescent boy that he has rights—but fails lamentably in driving home the fact that these rights imply complementary obligations. We have got to learn how to guide the social imagination of our boys without being too solemn about it. However refreshing the existence of the Welfare State may be, we will live in the menacing shadow of indifference unless we can spread the idea on a grand scale that a society is only healthy and virile when its members believe in its democratic purposes—and are willing to play their part in maintaining its vitality.

We will never achieve mental, moral, spiritual and emotional health in boys and girls merely by exhorting them to be good, honest, truthful and helpful. If the matter was as simple as that, then religious sermons would long ago have overcome human frailties! Children who have been exposed to a background of moral and emotional insecurity, will rarely feel morally or emotionally secure in their youth and adult life. What a little child most needs is to be loved, and to feel safe; he wants to be accepted and recognised; he needs to feel that his parents are strong and dependable, and that their authority is sensible and fair. The lessons of love, co-operation and truthfulness must be learned by the child in the first six or seven years of his (or her) life—as has been emphasised earlier in this chapter.

Later, and particularly during adolescence, the wise parents are those who slowly step backwards and allow their children to grow in moral stature and independence. The only way to become self-reliant is to have continuous practice; young people will soon learn to accept responsibility, and with alacrity. Parents, school teachers, industrial managers, youth leaders, ought to focus their attention on this important problem, and provide frequent opportunities for boys to assume limited areas of responsibility. Only in this way will our nation produce the leaders we so badly need in all walks of life.

It is true that in the Western world much has been done to solve the basic problems of fear and material wants—freedom from fear, freedom from want. But have we paid sufficient attention to the foundations of *behaviour*? Are young people willing to make use of their freedom in order to take responsibility, and to achieve something? Or have we all become so frightened of real positive freedom that we have renounced the challenge it poses by imprisoning ourselves, and our children, in a dull routine of conformity?

These are some of the questions we should ask ourselves.

CHAPTER TWELVE

LEADERSHIP IN THE WEST

THIS is going to be a difficult chapter to write by any standards, more particularly because if I speak the truth it may well cause annoyance in certain quarters. But one is entitled to one's opinion and, after all, it can always be said that truth is many-sided! Anyhow, I must have a shot at it, the more so since we are going to examine communist leadership in the next chapter —and we must get our own troubles sorted out first.

Western leadership to-day (1961) is a bit uncertain and perhaps we had better begin by searching for the reason. When Hitler came to power he began a policy of territorial expansion outside the legal frontiers of Germany, and finally in 1940 embarked on total war to achieve his aims more quickly. In Europe the nations were quickly overrun by the armed forces of Germany.

The world then saw the British Commonwealth fighting alone against the combined might of the Axis powers, Germany and Italy, which at that time controlled the whole continent of Europe. One should add here that if it hadn't been for the English Channel, Britain herself might well have gone under— and if we had the lights would have gone out on Western civilisation. But we stood firm, and by grim determination we weathered the storm in those dark days of 1940 and 1941.

Why did we stand firm when all seemed lost?
First, because we are British. We are an independent and an individual people. Our long freedom from oppression has made us self-reliant, and our one passionate belief is in the liberty of the individual to live his own life and go his own way—within the law, of course. Most people in Britain accepted Hitler's war as a fight for survival. The idea of Britain, free, independent

and powerful was deep in the breasts of her people. The catchword "freedom" didn't mean very much to the mass of the people; indeed the reality of freedom was often absent, many being subjected to economic pressure of one kind or another which drastically curtailed their freedom of action. But the illusion of freedom was valued almost as much as the reality; freedom of speech, freedom of the Press, freedom to live your own life—here were things worth fighting for. If the Germans intended to stop Tom Jones going to the pub, then Tom Jones would fight the Germans. But he fought more for his own liberty rather than for any abstract principles connected with it —such as "Cause."

We British fight the better because we make up our minds to it. What did Pericles say during the war with Sparta?

> "They toil from early boyhood in a laborious pursuit after courage, while we, free to live and wander as we please, march out none the less to face the self-same dangers."

How often do our enemies fail to recognise this fact! I do not believe that British soldiers are greatly influenced by "Cause"; they do not advance over dangerous and fire-swept ground in the conscious pursuit of an ideal, or for such catchwords as freedom or democracy. The soldier goes forward into battle because of the leader in front of him and his comrades around him— having confidence in his leader, and a feeling of being at one with his comrades. In fact, it was leadership and unity which disciplined us British, and helped us to stand firm in Hitler's war. *Secondly*, and obviously from what I have said above, we had the leader ready to hand—Winston Churchill. He called forth the spirit of the British people, inspired the nation and gave it a sense of purpose, and gave confidence to those nations which had been overrun—or which were waiting on the touchline to see which side was going to win before they joined the contest. The point to note is that Winston Churchill gave leadership to the Allied nations in the fight against the Axis powers, and unified them; these two factors, leadership and unity, gave us victory in the end. But basically, it all turned on leadership. It has always been my opinion that Churchill did more to ensure the Allies won the war than any other single man—because of his leadership.

UNITED STATES LEADERSHIP

When Hitler's war was over the leadership of the free world passed to the United States. I consider that we could have established British leadership in Western Europe at any time between, say, mid-1945 and 1950. The blame for not doing so can be laid at the door of the Labour Government under Attlee, and possibly Ernest Bevin was primarily responsible for our lack of vision. The Labour politicians of those days devoted their attention to the creation of a Welfare State in Britain, to the nationalisation of industry, and to raising the school age at a time when there were not the buildings nor the teachers to cope with the increased number of pupils. All these things were no doubt very desirable; but they all had to be done at the same time, and quickly, and this was not possible. With Britain looking inwards, overseas problems were pushed into the background. The American Alliance was given priority over British leadership in Europe, and maybe rightly so, but not to its exclusion; both policies could have been carried out simultaneously.

After I went to live in France in 1948, I frequently came over to London and visited Bevin, for whom I had the highest regard. I emphasised to him again and again the need for Britain to be less insular and to put her foot into Europe—adding that it was possible to do this without in any way damaging the American Alliance or our Commonwealth responsibilities. But it was of no avail. There finally came a time when Europe could wait no longer and we lost the leadership of Western Europe.

How has the West fared under United States leadership? I think it must be admitted that United States leadership has been intermittent in its pulsation, for all sorts of reasons. She began well; as a result of Hitler's war much of Europe was in ruins and the economic framework of the world had become disrupted. America gave generously in economic aid and military equipment to friend and foe alike; the result has been that the nations of Western Europe have recovered economically far quicker than they did after the 1914-18 war, and Federal Germany and Japan have achieved a degree of prosperity which is possibly greater than that of some of the nations which fought against them.

Many might think that the United States would have earned the gratitude and affection of the nations to whom she gave such generous help; but she has not. What is the reason?

If a nation is very rich and there are a number of poor nations it wants to help, much will depend on the way that help is given—particularly if the poorer nations are proud, with old civilisations and traditions. The American leaders didn't seem to understand that history would measure their leadership not so much by the quantity of dollars that were given away as by the quality of the leadership that was provided. Americans generally reckon they can buy anything with dollars; they soon found out that you cannot buy with cash the affection and loyalty of proud nations, nations who want to decide their own destiny and not have it decided for them by the United States; this is particularly the case with emergent nations. A further point is that the Americans want so much to be liked; they got upset when they realised that they were heartily disliked in Europe, in spite of their dollars.

We British are different; we never expect to be liked, which is just as well because we have at various times in our history been pretty well hated! Of course, we don't have any spare dollars to hand out, and therefore do not run the risk of being considered arrogant, or vulgar!

Then, again, it has puzzled some nations to find that the American people, who in two previous world wars were very reluctant to join the fight and only did so after the rest of the free world had struggled on for some years without them, now look like being the nation most likely to lead us all into a third world war! I always think this is due to the shock their pride suffered when the Japanese surprised them at Pearl Harbour on the 7th December, 1941; they are determined not to be surprised again, and now insist on a state of readiness for war which is not only unnecessary but also creates nervousness, perhaps jitteryness is a better word, among other nations in the Western Alliance —not to mention such great suspicion among the nations of the Eastern bloc that any progress towards peaceful co-existence or disarmament is not possible.

Anyhow, the net result is that under American leadership the general world situation has become bad—worse than it has been for many years. In Britain we all hoped that the *détente* between the United States and Russia, which seemed likely to follow the Camp David talks, would lessen world tension; Eisenhower is known the world over as a man of great goodwill and sincerity; it did seem at last that Khrushchev was going to show some goodwill—or at least be reasonable. But the asset of the Eisenhower goodwill ceased to be of any value to the West in May, 1960, when he assumed personal responsibility for the U-2 aeroplane incident; this admission was a tragedy because he still had some eight months longer as President and his goodwill might have achieved a further relaxation of tension during that period. If he had been able to carry out his original intention of visiting Moscow in June, 1960, and then going on to Tokyo, all might have been well. But the unpleasant fact is that United States leadership failed to handle the U-2 incident in a manner which would have enabled their President to continue to exercise his sincerity and goodwill for the cause of world peace. It is not too much to say that once the intelligence flights over Russia had been exposed by the Russians, the United States Government bungled at every step taken, with the result that the Western Alliance lost one of its greatest assets—the goodwill of President Eisenhower.

It is well known that all nations have a secret service, and that these exploit their own methods of getting information. But Washington broke the three basic rules of secret service work, which are:

1. Don't be found out.
2. If you are found out, don't admit it.
3. Always fasten the blame firmly on somebody else.

My information is that at the Camp David talks Khrushchev mentioned the intelligence flights, which were known in Russia, and Eisenhower said they would be discontinued—thus creating a good atmosphere for future talks. But when later Eisenhower assumed personal responsibility for the flights, and said they would be continued, Khrushchev was forced to adopt the line he took in Paris—or else suffer a great loss of prestige in Russia, which he couldn't risk.

It is a tragedy that the post-Summit atmosphere has completely destroyed the post-Camp David atmosphere. It is more than likely that there will be hurled at me the taunt of hindsight in all these matters, and of course things do look clearer when seen through the spectacles of that intruder. But I would reply by saying that there is such a virtue as foresight, and also flexibility in planning; and one cannot escape the conviction that the trend of events in Russia and the East was not realised in Washington.

WESTERN ILLUSIONS

A major trouble in the West is that the foreign policy of the United States in Europe, and in Asia, has been based on illusions. The same might be said of Britain; but in our case we have refrained from taking the right and logical action for fear of causing offence in Washington, and thus weakening our alliance with the United States. Overall, the nations of the Western Alliance have lacked the courage to face up to practical facts.

It is an illusion, indeed illogical, to expect Russia to agree that a re-united Germany armed with nuclear weapons can be integrated into the Western Alliance—with nuclear launching sites on the Polish frontier.

Further illusions could be quoted—that the East German Government doesn't exist, or that events in Japan in June, 1960, were caused by a few communist agitators acting under external direction. Regarding Japan, I reckon the Japanese want to decide their own destiny, and do not wish to become an American satellite.

Probably the greatest illusion of all is for the United States to work on the assumption that the true government of China is in Formosa—refusing to give *de facto* recognition to the People's Republic of China with its government in Peking.

Then consider the problem of the likelihood of a third world war, an all-out nuclear war between East and West. During the years which followed the ending of Hitler's war in 1945 the world became split in twain by two conflicting ideological doctrines or moral codes; there is the Eastern bloc led by Russia, and the Western bloc led by the United States. At one time, say between 1947 and 1952, it was thought by many that the conflict between East and West might lead to war. The formation of NATO and the splendid work achieved by that organisation, together with the advent of a new key to military strategy—the nuclear deterrent—have ruled out the possibility of the Eastern bloc deliberately resorting to war to achieve its aims and objects. The Western bloc also will never initiate war; its rearming during the past years has been purely for defensive reasons and it will never attack the Eastern bloc except in self-defence—and, of course, it will never launch what is called "preventive war."

If only this basic truth could be accepted by the nations of the Western bloc, the way ahead would be all the easier to organise; furthermore, the possibility of drifting into war by miscalculation or accident would be greatly reduced. Agreement on this basic truth is the first move towards a reduction of the present tension existing between the two blocs—which, once reduced and finally removed, opens the road leading towards disarmament. But the West, under United States leadership, will not accept this fact.

Certain forces are on the move in Russia and in the Eastern world, and the West cannot afford to base its policies on illusions.

THE PROBLEM OF RUSSIA

The immediate problem facing Western leadership to-day is, of course, East-West relations—which can be boiled down to the key problem of Russia.

Russia has positive contributions to make to European civilisation and culture, e.g. music, the ballet.

There is one thing we do not want to see—Russia aligned with Asia against Europe; we want her to look West. But this will not be easy to bring about, since Russia is not one of the defeated nations of Hitler's war, as was Federal Germany; she is a triumphant nation, flushed with technical success and surrounded by satellites and allies. The Western Alliance was formed in a period of strains and tensions which began with the Russian blockade of West Berlin in 1948 and reached its climax with the outbreak of the Korean war in 1950. The alliance has existed and operated only for the agreed purpose of stopping Soviet expansion in Europe—and it has succeeded. Then in February, 1959, Mr. Macmillan went to Moscow; his visit was the beginning of a new personal relationship between the political leaders of the two blocs, and a de-frosting of the cold war took place—but unfortunately the whole thing crashed in ruins at the Summit Conference in Paris in May, 1960, as we have seen.

Can we regain the lost ground with Russia? I believe we can; but much will depend on how the situation is handled by the United States. We may have lost a few battles; but we haven't lost the campaign. The alliance is intact; the United States is still the most powerful nation in the world. Of course the West will need to be assured beyond any possibility of doubt that a settlement with Russia is sincere and solid; that she will not re-open the NATO front in Europe at some future date; that she will not attempt blackmail by threats of nuclear attack —in fact, that she will show a true readiness to meet the West at least half-way. But we might well go *more* than half-way to meet Russia; the difficulty here will be to get the United

States to face up to the changed conditions. What are these changed conditions?

I visited Moscow in April, 1959, and talked in the Kremlin for two days with Mr. Khrushchev, and with the Russian Minister of Defence and his Chiefs of Staff. Whereas the subject of a third world war is a topic of general conversation in the Western hemisphere, in Russia the subject is not mentioned; it is reckoned to be beyond the realm of possibility. When you visit Moscow you find relaxed friendship everywhere—in the Kremlin and in the streets.

The Russian people are hungry for consumer goods—for washing machines, refrigerators, television sets, and for all the luxuries of present-day civilisation. They are genuinely interested in the people of other nations, possibly for the first time in history; they lived in isolation for centuries, and the Iron Curtain was not invented entirely by Stalin. To-day the Russian people want to know and to see, and their curiosity is boundless. Khrushchev wants to cash in on this movement, to give the Russian people what they want, and to go down in history as the " man of peace," the man who brought prosperity and security to the people, as distinct from Lenin and Stalin—who did not.

But Khrushchev has two big difficulties. First, he must somehow bring about a relaxation of international tension so that he can pursue his internal policies in a peaceful climate; but he is under pressure from within Russia which is working against him. Secondly, he is not too sure about the attitude of the People's Republic of China.

Overall, it would seem only common sense that the West should show a sympathetic approach to the new spirit which is stirring in Khrushchev's Russia. If the NATO Powers could reach a settlement with the Government of the Soviet Union, one which will enable Russia and the Western Alliance to live peacefully together, we would benefit enormously as well as Russia.

If all this is true, and I believe it is, then the nations of the Western Alliance will need to re-think their policies—with regard to Russia as I have suggested, and also with regard to

China. The American policy of boycotting China has not succeeded in restraining and containing that nation, nor will it in the future.

THE NEW CHINA

In May, 1960, I decided to visit China to get to know the leaders of the People's Republic, to learn their views on what is going on in the world to-day, and to see something of the life of the people. I went as a private individual, with no authority except my own. An interesting reason for the visit was given me by a friend of mine who happened to hear two soldiers discussing the matter.

> First soldier: " What was the real reason Monty went to China ? "
> Second soldier: " Don't you know; it was a bit of skirt."

The two were London boys; the Cockney always has an answer for everything!

I will have something to say about the Chinese leaders and their aims in the next chapter; here it will be sufficient to indicate certain salient features about the new China which should be hoisted in by Western leaders.

China must have a long period of peace; Mao Tse-tung and Chou En-lai both agreed that it may well take fifty years to recover from the external aggression, the internal oppression, the long civil war, and generally all the troubles of the past—and to establish the economy of the country on a sound and firm basis.

The foreign policy of China is therefore based fundamentally on the domestic issue—the building up of the People's Republic to become a great and powerful nation, for which purpose peace is essential.

Western leaders should not think that Mao Tse-tung was the evil influence behind Khrushchev at the Summit Conference in Paris in May, 1960. China desperately needs peace, and it is not to her interests to persuade Russia to embark on a policy which would increase world tension and possibly lead to war;

my talks with the Chinese leaders produced no indications which might lead to a contrary view.

In twenty years' time China will be a nation of more than a thousand million people, with powerful forces armed with nuclear weapons, and with rapidly increasing economic strength. In fifty years' time this great and powerful nation will dominate Asia and be as strong as any nation in Europe—possibly even in the world. Western leaders should not suffer any illusions on this point.

Before we attempt to find the answer to the all-important problem of East-West relations, one further factor must be mentioned—the hatred of the Chinese for the United States and everything American. This hatred is not confined to the Chinese leaders; it extends to the man in the street and to the peasants in the Communes. Some may think this does not matter overmuch; but it does matter, very much. It is tragic that the leading nation of the Western Alliance should have incurred the hatred of the two greatest nations in the Eastern bloc—Russia and China—and particularly of China, the biggest nation in the world.

LEADERSHIP AND UNITY

What is the answer to all these troubles which beset us? When the West was in trouble in 1940 the way out was found to be leadership and unity; it is the same to-day. I have always been a firm believer in leadership; but there must be confidence in the leadership, and that is what is now lacking in the West. The first task of Western leadership is to plan a future strategy for the West; we need common policies based on realities, on facts—and not on illusions. The United States remains the leader of the Western Alliance, which is NATO; she must become firmly established in this leadership but she will need to do some re-thinking.

Clearly the first task of Western leadership must be to strengthen NATO politically, and to establish that true unity which it has always lacked—which lack has been primarily responsible for the situation in which we find ourselves to-day. But we in Europe must render the United States that help which she is entitled to expect—which is that Western Europe shall stand together and flourish as one united whole. In this respect we British must give a lead by putting our foot firmly into Europe. A major trouble is that Europe is divided in spirit. It is not too much to say that the political and military structures of NATO require drastic overhaul; only if this is done shall we get common strategic and political policies on a global scale —which we have never had yet.

THE BALLAD OF EAST AND WEST

In 1889 Rudyard Kipling wrote the following:

> " Oh, East is East, and West is West, and
> never the twain shall meet,
> Till Earth and Sky stand presently at
> God's great judgment seat;
> But there is neither East nor West, Border
> nor Breed, nor Birth,
> When two strong men stand face to face,
> though they come from the ends of the earth!"

That ballad is worth reading; it contains a lesson for us all. The time has come for East and West to meet, whatever Kipling may have written over seventy years ago.

The first essential in this particular matter will be some very clear thinking about the biggest nation in the East—China. The emotional forces bottled up in over six hundred and fifty million Chinese have been uncorked, and given an outlet in a way which is positive and constructive and which has excited their imagination. Great forces are on the move in the new China, and the Western world would be well advised to make friends with the People's Republic.

China is going to play an increasingly important part in world affairs as she grows stronger; at present it is a country about which many misconceptions exist. Whatever views any of us may hold individually about the policies of the Chinese Government, it is clearly to the benefit of everybody that the West should have some first-hand knowledge of the people and their leaders; it was for these reasons that I visited the country in May, 1960.

There are some who say that the West should have nothing to do with the communist world; it is not possible to believe anything they say; their written word cannot be trusted. This thinking can lead eventually only to war, to all-out nuclear war, with the destruction of Western civilisation as we know it to-day —and Eastern civilisation too. And in the intervening period the youth of our nation will grow up in a world split by controversy, with nations hurling threats of nuclear destruction at each other—a world, in fact, of peaceless co-existence. Is this what we want? God forbid!

For many years it has been clear to me that, in the long run, the key to the peace of the world lies in China. The rise of the new China to dominate Asia, which is inevitable, could be for the general benefit of mankind, and for that peaceful world which is so much desired by the common people of all countries. But a major factor in bringing this about is that the Western world should make an effort to understand the new China *now*, and especially that our leader, the United States, should cease to quarrel with her.

In fact, if we want our children to grow up to be good citizens in a peaceful world, which is what I personally most desire, East and West must meet and come to terms with each other as soon as possible, and not wait until we stand together at " God's great judgment seat."

THE PROBLEM FOR THE WEST

Briefly, the problem for the West is twofold, as follows:
First, to work for peace with the communist world. A way must be found by which States with different ideologies and

social systems can live side by side in peace without interfering with each other's way of life.

Secondly, and while doing this, to ensure that we safeguard our precious Christian heritage, and the freedom for which we fought and for which so many died, and do not cast away the good position we have reached during the weary years of cold war since 1946. *This must never be allowed to happen; it is fundamental to every step we take to end the present strife.*

I do not believe that these two tasks are incompatible, or that the problem cannot be solved. The leaders of the Western world face a period in which wisdom, steadiness and political courage are urgently needed. But they will have to break down barriers, and not listen to those people who want to erect them. If we take the population of the world to-day as about 2,800 million, it is obvious that in twenty years' time nearly half the peoples of the world will be communists—China over a thousand million, Russia over two hundred million, and smaller communities elsewhere. Unless our half of the world, the freedom-loving half, can find some way of co-existing with the communist half, the only alternative will be war between the two blocs—and that is as certain as is the fact that dawn follows the night.

THE FIRST MOVES

If the two blocs, East and West, are to live together, peaceably and without interfering with each other's affairs and way of life, it will be essential to break down the suspicion which now exists, and to replace it with mutual confidence and trust. Of course, the West should first put its own house in order in this respect. When you serve in the international set-up, as I did for ten years, you serve a group of nations unable to agree on fundamentals, and each refusing to make any sacrifice of sovereignty for the common good of all—because of intense nationalism. In fact, there is no true unity in the West; to get it means faith and confidence between Governments, and this is lacking. Therefore, unity in the West must come first, and this demands leadership. But there is no obvious acceptable leader in sight—if by leader we mean a man who is able and willing to give clear and sensible advice to the whole group, and in whom all the member nations will have absolute confidence. Besides possessing the qualities I have mentioned, the leader we need must be a man of decision and action; but in a fifteen-nation alliance of democracies it is difficult to decide anything; indeed, the leader rather has to try and persuade an infinity of unharmonious musicians to play in tune.

When discussing unity in the West, some will say that a United States of Europe—a Federated Europe—is the answer. I once discussed this with Winston Churchill, saying that in my view a Federated Europe was not possible. I added that nations with old civilisations, with roots deep in the past, will never submit to a Federal Parliament in Europe; we British certainly would not. Winston thought it could have been brought about soon after the end of Hitler's war if Stalin hadn't pinched the eastern half of Europe. On reflection, I think Federation is possible only with emergent nations who have recently won independence—not with the older nations.

Having established a degree of unity in our own ranks, we must aim to break down the barrier of suspicion about us in the Eastern bloc. I am sure that the best way to achieve this is for the armed forces of *both* blocs, East and West, to return to their own empires or territories and to end the military occupation of other people's countries in Europe and Asia. This would be a decision of policy and one which would take time to implement, five or ten years; but it could well be agreed now, in principle, as a measure towards which both blocs would work simultaneously—increasing the pace as confidence and mutual trust began to make themselves felt. The withdrawal of forces would have to be simultaneous on both sides, and reciprocal control and inspection would need to be organised. It seems to me nonsense to call this "disengagement" as some would argue; the NATO front in Europe could be guarded by the forces of the nations of continental Western Europe, whose populations total nearly two hundred million. The fact that these continental nations want the forces of overseas nations in their countries *in addition* to their own, merely goes to highlight the lack of confidence they feel. Also, if they can get other nations to help bar the front door, they needn't provide so many forces themselves! But if only the nations of Europe would understand that Russia hasn't the slightest intention of attacking the West, how much simpler it would all become!

In Asia, a similar withdrawal of United States forces should take place from the countries of other nations—from Japan, Formosa, and from the mainland of Asia. Such a withdrawal would also take time to negotiate and to organise, five and perhaps ten years, and no doubt certain safeguards would have to be written into the agreement. Both in Europe and in Asia the time lag would not matter overmuch; the agreement to withdraw is what will help.

Unless we can make these first moves—get unity within the Western Alliance, and get it agreed that all armed forces should be withdrawn to their own territories in due course, say by 1970 —no progress towards disarmament, or towards lasting and durable world peace, is possible. And we must work on the policy that the time has come for East and West to be friends.

The gist of the whole matter can be expressed shortly as follows.

The risk to-day is not that Russia will deliberately resort to war to achieve her aims more quickly; it is rather that some cold war issue may precipitate a head-on collision between East and West. This risk, a very grave one, will not be removed by the leaders on each side writing letters to each other—although the Macmillan letter to Khrushchev read to the House of Commons on the 19th July, 1960, was excellent. Earlier, Mr. Macmillan had tried to counter the risk by a visit to Moscow in February, 1959, but it did not succeed; the failure was not his fault but was due to American blunders.

The only real way to counter the risk is to remove the causes, and I have tried to suggest how a start can be made in that direction without weakening our own position in any way. The West should make the initial proposal; but the East would have to show sincerity in carrying it out.

We hear a great deal these days from political leaders the world over about peace, and the need for States with different ideologies and social systems being able " to live and let live " together. But after sixteen years of peace, or so-called peace—certainly a very uneasy peace—we are hardly any better off in the matter of peaceful living than when we began to try and make it work in 1945. Are we now to contemplate another sixteen years of *peaceless* co-existence?

Are the youth of the Western world to grow up in a world in which fear walks abroad—peace being kept only by a balance of nuclear terror? I trust not. But if we continue to base our policies on illusions, and refuse to face facts, the eventual end can only be war between East and West—as I have already said.

The cold war—the ideological tumult—will, of course, continue; that is very clear. But if we can remove the causes of suspicion and mistrust, perhaps not all at once but gradually on a master plan, the cold war may well become less turbulent and begin to subside. There, I submit, is where we will find the gleam of light. I am all for searching for that gleam, and having found it—as I believe we can—exploiting it. If we are successful we could then hand over a peaceful world to our children's children.

I'm all for trying.

WHERE IS THE LEADER?

But where is the leader who will handle all these things for us? Who will persuade the Western nations to face facts, to agree on common policies which are based on reality and not on wishful thinking, and to begin to remove the causes of East-West strife. There must be no vague illusions, no skirting round vital points, no verbal procrastinations. Everything petty and extraneous will have to be pushed aside, the vital factors exposed, and a solution reached which is based on solid foundations. And the generals will have to be dealt with; they will fight hard to preserve their empires.

Who is going to grasp this nettle? He will have a terrific job. A major problem will be to unravel the spider's web which has been so laboriously spun in the NATO Council in Paris by so many different types of spiders—all experts at putting up smoke-screens when items on the agenda do not suit them. What is needed in the NATO machinery is simplicity, common sense, and courage—and a thorough overhaul and spring cleaning.

As I have already indicated, leadership in a fifteen-nation alliance of democracies is difficult. But surely it is not impossible! The essentials are:

> Conviction
> Transparent honesty and sincerity
> Tenacity
> Political courage.

No leader can last for long without political courage.

These essentials rule out all dishonesty on the part of politicians—all angling for votes, all meaningless platitudes which at present come from both sides of the Atlantic. They demand that the people be told the truth, and that action be based on logical facts and not on wishful thinking nor on factors which will swing votes to a particular political party—but which are impracticable and untrue.

Where is this man? I know all the national leaders of the Western world. The man I would select as our leader for this great task is President de Gaulle of France. He has the wisdom, the conviction, the tenacity, and the courage to reach a decision. In fact, he is a leader—he is honest and sincere, and he doesn't indulge in political intrigue or in meaningless platitudes.

His first task will be to remove the fear and suspicion between East and West; until that is done there can be no progress towards disarmament. He will also have to make it clear that it is impossible to discuss world affairs, or disarmament, sensibly if we ignore the biggest nation in the world—China.

CHAPTER THIRTEEN

COMMUNIST LEADERSHIP

I MUST make it clear that this chapter is not a study of Communism; I am not equipped to make such a study, nor is there any place for it in this book. My purpose is rather to take those leaders of the communist world who are known to me, to discuss their characters, and to examine what they seem to be trying to achieve—and how their leadership affects the Western world.

Some may say that I am not qualified to express opinions on these subjects; but that can hardly be true. I have visited in their own countries and have talked with the following national leaders in the communist bloc: Stalin, Khrushchev, Tito, Mao Tse-tung and Chou En-lai, and with their Ministers of Defence and Chiefs of Staff. It is doubtful whether anybody else from the Western world has talked with all these five, and with their professional military advisers. I know and have talked with the political and military leaders of the Western world. And I have had a ringside seat at the game of international high politics since the end of Hitler's war.

The following pages express my views, and if anybody can make a better assessment of communist leadership and problems in the world to-day (1961)—good luck to him.

Stalin

I would like to begin with Stalin, since he was the leader of Russia when most people in Britain became interested in that country—which was when Hitler's forces attacked Russia in June, 1941, and that country became our first active ally in the German war. Before that time we had been conducting the war alone; it can therefore be understood that the people of Britain regarded Stalin as a most welcome ally, and his name soon became a household word throughout the country. But when the war ended he appeared in a very different light, and he gradually began to be hated as few men have been before.

I first met Stalin at the Potsdam Conference in July, 1945. But I had studied his policy and actions for some years before that, and had reached the conclusion that he was very able—but also very cunning. It will be recalled that in August, 1939, he signed a non-aggression pact with Hitler and then, while in association with Germany, showed his hand by seizing territory on his western flank—the three Baltic States (Estonia, Latvia, Lithuania), the eastern part of Poland, a portion of Finland, Bessarabia, Bucavina, and certain islands on the Danube. By entering into this pact with Hitler, Stalin allowed the Germans to unleash their military might westwards. But when, despite his efforts to pacify Hitler, the Germans turned eastwards in June, 1941, and assaulted Russia, it was Stalin who demanded, almost as a matter of right, that the Allies came to his help—whatever the consequences! The British and Americans were very wise not to attempt the cross-channel invasion of Normandy until the military risks were acceptable.

Looking at those days in retrospect it has always seemed to me that Roosevelt under-estimated Stalin. He reckoned that by patience and friendliness the Russians could be guided to our way of thinking, and that he (Roosevelt) could bring this about. Indeed, he liked at times to assume the role of a mediator between Stalin and Churchill when the argument became heated—as for instance over Poland. Even Churchill at times seemed to forget the cunning of the Russian leader. He agreed in the autumn of 1944 to the boundary between the zones of occupation in Germany allocated to the Russians and those assigned to the West; the agreed line ran well west of Berlin! It is clear from a message Churchill sent to Stalin in July, 1944, that he was urging the Russians on towards Berlin, and the message seemed to accept the fact that they would reach that city before the Western Allies!

After Stalin decided that Russia could survive the German assault, and could fight back, he worked to strengthen the Russian hold on all the territory he could manage. And when he found that his actions were not popular with Western leaders, the tone of his messages to Roosevelt and Churchill changed—from amiability, to reserve, to bluntness, and on occasions to downright rudeness.

It is curious how Roosevelt failed to grasp the cunning of Stalin. Herbert Feis, a distinguished American historian, considers that American thinking about Stalin was " blurred by the more intense glare of Hitler's evil light." Churchill was not deceived, but he failed to correct the American view. But from what we know of the history of Stalin's career, and his rise to power in Russia, it is clear that he was sly, malicious, very skilled in the graduation of pressures, and as Herbert Feis has said:

" a person about whose every statement his familiars were apt to ask—what skein is he going to wind around that bobbin?"

When I first met Stalin in Berlin in July, 1945, he invited me to visit him in Moscow—which I did in January, 1947. Of course to me he was an intensely interesting personality; he had an amazing strategic sense, and I cannot recall that he put a foot wrong in our discussions about the strategic conduct of the war which we had all been fighting against Hitler's Germany. He was a very good host, and had a keen sense of humour. But the impression I gained was that under the Stalin régime the Russian people were depressed and miserable; this was not just the war weariness of a tired nation; there was fear abroad, the secret police operated ruthlessly, and individuals dared not speak what was in their minds.

I remember a dinner party he gave for me on the 10th January, 1947, in the Kremlin. The guests, including myself and my staff, assembled in an ante-room and engaged in light-hearted discussion while cocktails were handed round. Suddenly there was utter and complete silence, one could have heard a pin drop, and all the Russians present shut up like oysters and looked askance at each other as if they were fearful they had been speaking disloyally and might be given away—Stalin had entered the room quietly, alone. I have never forgotten the impression created; it was sinister. The Russians present at the party were all very high-level people; but they were afraid.

Such was Stalin's Russia. The Soviet leader himself determined to fasten his grip firmly, and ever more firmly, on Eastern Europe; the people depressed and frightened, and little being done for them; food scarce; consumer goods difficult to get; housing conditions appalling. And overall, fear stalked through the land. When I left Russia after that visit I was inclined to put Stalin down as a monster—and a clever one. I never saw him again; he died in March, 1953, after some thirty years of repressive dictatorship. He must have caused hundreds of his political opponents to face the firing squad, and the world wondered what sort of people were those who survived the many purges.

Stalin was succeeded by Malenkov; I cannot recall that I met him when I was in Moscow in 1947; if I did he made no impression. He reversed Stalin's policy in that he aimed to relax the East-West tension and to allow the Russian people more consumer goods—all of which raised hopes in the West, and it was thought by some that Stalinism was on the decline.

But suddenly Malenkov was unseated, being replaced by Bulganin and Khrushchev—a sort of duality. The former was known to me; I had met and talked with him in Moscow in 1947, and had then considered him a somewhat sinister figure. These two did quite a bit of travelling—to Belgrade, Geneva, India and Burma in 1955, and London in May, 1956—where their reception was " chilly," probably because of the insulting remarks Khrushchev had made in India about us British.

In due course Khrushchev dismissed Bulganin, Molotov and Marshal Zhukov—all three being known to me, and Zhukov very well indeed—and was himself elected Prime Minister in the spring of 1958, remaining First Secretary of the Central Committee of the Communist Party.

Khrushchev then had in his own hands the direction of the Russian governmental machine.

Khrushchev

We now come to the present-day national leaders in the Eastern bloc, which for our purposes can be taken as Russia and China. When I withdrew from active employment in the British Army and in NATO in September, 1958, I decided to visit the leaders of the communist world. Judgment without contact seemed to me to be unwise. I asked myself: "What sort of man is Khrushchev?" And I thought the best way to find out was to go and see him. So I sent him a message in early 1959 asking if I might visit him in Moscow and discuss the world situation; he replied that I would be very welcome, and I arrived in Moscow on the 28th April, 1959. My main object was to discover his views on the tangled problem of European security, and to get to know him.

I found him to be a remarkable person. He has a quick and clear brain and you never have to say anything to him twice. He is definitely a realist, and he sticks to his point all the time. He seems to have an amazing knowledge of the facts of any subject you raise, and is never at a loss for an answer. I sat opposite him across the table in the Kremlin and talked with him for the best part of two days, and even after that it would have been difficult to describe his face; he has an infinity of expressions, which change rapidly. The Almighty fashioned us humans in clay; I reckon a modern sculptor would find it difficult to make a good bust of Khrushchev in sculpture! I would describe him as a brilliant political leader, with all the arguments at his finger-tips. You would have to get up very early in the morning to get the better of him in discussion. You couldn't frighten him, nor out-smart him. In fact, he is a pretty tough guy; but he can also be emotional, and one gets an occasional glimpse of a warmth of heart which one would not expect in such a ruthless character. His self-confidence is tremendous; and he can walk with kings and yet talk in a friendly way with ordinary people.

He is definitely a formidable personality in international politics.

He is the son of a coal miner and was born in 1894; that makes him 67 to-day (1961).

I intended while in Moscow to find out, particularly, Khrushchev's thinking on three subjects:

> *First*, was he prepared to embark on a major war to achieve his aims more quickly? A major war implies an all-out nuclear war.
>
> *Second*, what was his thinking about the Germans?
>
> *Third*, how did he view the rise of the People's Republic of China—the Peking Government?

All very important questions; and the answers would have a tremendous influence on Western policy—if they could be believed.

First question—war. Some years ago, about 1953, Khrushchev used to say that the Soviet Union would survive a nuclear war, and the West would not. During my talks with him in Moscow in April, 1959, he started by being somewhat bellicose; but he changed his attitude when I had explained to him at some length what the West could do with its nuclear armament if war came —which was to destroy the major cities of an aggressor nation, together with its people and industries. I had a feeling at the time that he had been studying the consequences of nuclear fall-out. At any rate, in his speeches the following year, in early 1960, he began to say that a nuclear war would be a calamity for all the peoples of the world, and that even local wars cannot be tolerated because they could grow into a world war. And he made a remarkable speech in Vienna in July, 1960, in which he compared life in the Ark with life in this world—finishing with the following sentence:

" If on this earth we are not able to live peacefully together as living things were able to live in Noah's Ark, and if we start a war to settle disputes between States—some dislike socialism, some dislike capitalism—we shall destroy our Noah's Ark, the earth."

As the result of my discussions in Moscow with Khrushchev and with the Russian Chiefs of Staff, and when I had seen the progress made in the country since the Stalin régime passed away, it was clear to me that Russia must have peace. War, a nuclear war, would destroy all the progress made since I had last been in Moscow in 1947; it would put the country back half a century. I am convinced that Khrushchev is against war—not necessarily because he thinks war is wrong or evil, but because he reckons that the Soviet Union will be destroyed in a future war, and the rest of the world also. I wouldn't put it beyond Khrushchev to change his viewpoint if the West began to embark on a policy of unilateral disarmament, and abandoned the nuclear deterrent! But that will not happen. The great point for us to hoist in is that war is ruled out by Khrushchev because he thinks it will no longer pay—and he is right.

This is a considerable advance on his part; and if we add to it the fact that he wants to go down in history as " the man of peace," who gave prosperity and security to the Russian people —as outlined in Chapter Twelve—it will be readily understood that the advance is something we should recognise, and should use to help us in solving the East-West problem.

But Khrushchev is under pressure in Russia, and this must be understood. My talks with political and military leaders in Moscow convinced me that they can be grouped in two categories—those who agree with Lenin's theory that war with the West is inevitable in the long run, and those who think that war can be avoided by reaching agreement with the West on a policy of " live and let live "—in fact, peaceful co-existence. The first category contains the old Marxist diehards. Khrushchev belongs to the second category, believing that Lenin's theory about the inevitability of war is out of date; to this group belong the younger generation.

If a struggle for power takes place between the two categories, as could well happen, we would, I hope, want Khrushchev to win. But a continuation by the Americans of spy-flights like the U-2 affair, or the flying of aircraft at any time over Soviet territory, or any measures which have an offensive gesture such as alerting nuclear bomber forces for no apparent reason —all such measures merely tend to increase suspicion and tension between East and West, and help the diehard category in Russia. When the problem is viewed in this light, it is easy to understand why Khrushchev reacts so violently, and rudely at times, to American efforts to obtain information about his country.

The lesson is that if the West is genuinely interested in finding a way to live at peace with the East, our leaders must avoid the military aspects of what is commonly called "brinkmanship." Stupidity in this direction could lead to awkward situations, and might conceivably be a spark which would set alight a major fire—a nuclear war. And, of course, there is the further point that when such intelligence activities are discovered they give ammunition to Khrushchev in his campaign to split the Western Alliance—which must never be allowed to happen. NATO is already a bit shaky, and any further disruption could frighten the smaller nations—especially those which are near Russian territory, e.g. Norway, Denmark, Turkey.

Everybody knows that all nations conduct secret service activities to collect information about the countries of potential enemies. But intelligence activities must be carried out intelligently, and without being found out. The proper political action before the Summit Conference in April, 1960, should have been not to upset the *détente*, which was going along smoothly. But a spy plane was sent over Russia by the Americans shortly before the conference—which was not very intelligent! And it was caught, which was worse!

Second question—Germany. When talking with Khrushchev I gained the impression that Russia was apprehensive about the revival of Germany, and about a possible revengeful spirit which might arise in that country. He made it clear that he was disturbed about the constant references to a united Germany. Politically, economically and geographically, the German Democratic Republic (East Germany) is Russia's most important satellite and she is continually investing capital there. She will not relinquish her grip on East Germany under present conditions; she will not agree to a re-unification of the two Germanys except under her own terms—which the West, of course, will not accept. In fact, a united Germany is impossible in the present circumstances and Khrushchev was very definite about that.

It followed, he added, that it was not possible to make any fundamental re-design of the Berlin situation until the European security problem had been untangled and sorted out to the complete satisfaction of both blocs—East and West—and that fact must be faced by the West.

I have always felt that everybody knows this. No nation wants a united Germany. In private conversation with me at various times, every Western political leader has agreed that it would be most unwise to unite the two Germanys; but none of them will say this in public for fear of offending the Western Germans—who, I reckon, also do not want it! We will just have to carry on in Germany with the *status quo*, and this includes the Berlin problem.

Third question—China. I found it very difficult to fathom Khrushchev's feelings about China. He repudiated any suggestion that China might become a problem for Russia in the future. I put it to him that, geographically, Russia was poised between two nations either of which could make things difficult for his country. He had admitted he was apprehensive about the Germans. What about the Chinese? Not being altogether satisfied with his answers, and being myself a bit suspicious that he wasn't being quite truthful, I suddenly shot a very direct question at him:

"Which are you most frightened of, the Germans or the Chinese?"

Now Khrushchev is very quick to reply to a question; he is

never at a loss for the answer. This time he paused for some seconds, and then said:

" For the moment, the Germans."

He was right. His answer implied that the future of that great nation in the Far East, which was moving ahead quickly, was wrapped in mystery; it was difficult to unravel that enigma. I was left with the impression that he was in some doubt about what might happen in China in the long run, as are many others; but the picture will become a little clearer when we come to examine the Chinese leaders. One thing was very clear—the Germans were his immediate fear, and he wasn't going to give an inch in that direction.

Before leaving Khrushchev I must make it clear, in case the reader should think otherwise, that I wouldn't go in the jungle with him. But Western leaders would do well to ponder over what might happen in Russia if he were unseated; somebody much worse might arise.

Tito

It will be convenient to discuss Tito next, and that will leave the way clear to deal with the Chinese leaders and the Far East. Tito's real name is Josip Broz, and he is 69—being born in 1892. I first got to know him in September, 1953, when he invited me to attend the manœuvres of the Yugoslav Army in the Zagreb area. I was then serving at SHAPE as Deputy Supreme Allied Commander Europe. The Americans were the only Western nation dealing with Yugoslavia, giving military equipment and economic aid, and my visit to Tito was resented in certain quarters; General Ridgway was Supreme Commander and he did his best to stop the visit. I appealed to the Foreign Office in London and received strong backing from that quarter, which saw in such a visit nothing but good. So I went.

I recognised in Tito a strong man, a leader of great character and personality. We became very friendly, and I wrote later and asked if I could visit him in Belgrade and get his views on the general world situation. He said I would be very welcome and my next visit was paid in September, 1954, and lasted a week. I visited an elementary and a secondary school, a private farm, a collective farm, a vineyard, several heavy industry works, went to Sarajevo, where the spark was lit which started the First World War, and saw several instructional centres of the Yugoslav Army. I made many friends, particularly the two officers who accompanied me on that visit and on all others—Major-General Milos Sumonja, and Lieut.-Colonel Bruno Vuletic, both of whom spoke English. I paid many visits to Tito after that, the last being on the 2nd September, 1958—when I went to say good-bye before leaving SHAPE on the 18th September and withdrawing from active employment in the British Army. It was the final farewell visit I paid; I felt I must go and see him as he had been so friendly over a period of years.

In conversation one day I asked Tito to tell me about his early life. By trade he was an electrician. He served in the ranks of the Austrian Army in the First World War, became a sergeant, and finally got captured by the Russians. He then spent seven years in Russia, during which time he became a communist. On his return to Yugoslavia he joined the workers' movement, and quickly became its leader; he then led a very hectic life and was more often in prison than not! He found it convenient at that time to have several names, thus making it more difficult for the police to keep contact with his movements. One of the names he used was Tito, and he finally adopted it permanently —he said he liked it and it was easier to pronounce than Broz! And "Tito" he has remained to this day.

When the Germans overran Yugoslavia in April, 1941, Tito organised a communist movement and harried the Germans with guerilla warfare. There was also a right wing force under a regular army officer called Mihajlovic, and the two factions at first combined against the Germans; but eventually the two groups came to blows, and Tito won. When the German war was over in 1945 he became Prime Minister, and later President.

He has done much for his country, without any doubt. His greatest service has been to unify the six republics into a united

Yugoslavia. It is a communist country, but as Tito himself once said to me they are not Moscow communists; they do not want to thrust their ideology down the throats of any other nation. Tito himself is against international Communism, which aims to communise the world. Indeed, so much did he disagree with Moscow that in 1948 he was denounced by the Cominform; he then left the Soviet camp and became a neutral country. He now wants to live in peace with all his neighbours, to be left alone to develop the resources of his country, and to improve the standard of living of the people—all of which he is doing very well. He is under no delusions about what could happen to his country if the conflict between East and West led to general war. He would remain neutral; but under his leadership the Yugoslavs would fight any enemy who attempted to invade their country—and I would be sorry for any military force which made the attempt.

I remember well a talk I had with Tito after Nasser had been to see him in Brioni in 1958. The two had had long talks together. He told me that Nasser had changed greatly since the days of the Suez affair in 1956, realising that he had many problems on his plate and must go slowly. Tito had advised him not to irritate too many people all at the same time, which was good advice! He considered Nasser was there for keeps, and the Western nations should try and help him in so far as they were prepared to do so without damaging their own vital interests or their prestige.

Apparently Nasser told Tito that he realised he must have friendly relations with the West as there lie his markets; and he wanted friendly relations with Abyssinia and the Sudan as those countries could interfere with his water supplies. His long-term aim was an Arab Confederation or Republic, comprising all the Arab nations of the Middle East and being completely neutral—trading with both East and West but joining neither bloc. He realised this aim would take time to achieve.

Tito had replied that he was working on the same lines for Yugoslavia. There were the two blocs, East and West; of the two he preferred the West and he advised Nasser to adopt the same philosophy.

Tito said he personally wasn't anxious any more about the Middle East situation; he thought the dangers lay in the Far East and in Africa. He hoped the Western world would be realistic about the Egyptian leader, accepting the inevitable and trying to guide him into achieving an Arab world which was neutral—trading with every nation, and looking Westwards in times of stress. He said that was what Nasser really wanted; he had been considerably impressed by him; he reckoned he was a leader who had a clear and definite object, who had courage, and who spoke to his followers in language they could understand—which, Tito said, many other political leaders often fail to do.

This conversation interested me enormously. Tito is a very shrewd judge of character, and in the talks we have had together he has always impressed me as a man of sound common sense. I never heard him say a harsh word about anybody, or against any nation. He is very realistic in his outlook on world problems. He wants his own country, Yugoslavia, to be left alone, not to be pushed about by international Communism or other external influences, and to have friendly relations with all her neighbours. Given fifteen to twenty years of peace, I reckon that Yugoslavia will be a thriving State of over twenty million people—a neutral State whose friendship will be worth having.

I put Tito in the top category of national leaders. He has conviction, tenacity, and political courage—all qualities of greatness. Indeed, put shortly, he is a great man.

Mao Tse-tung

We now move eastwards to the People's Republic of China, ruled over by Mao Tse-tung. What kind of man is he? I went to China in May, 1960, to get the answer, and to talk with him.

Mao is the son of a farm labourer. When he was a young boy his family was poor, and the only way he could educate himself was to gain admission to a school where he could receive not only free education but also free board and lodging—and this he did. Like all sons of the soil, he is a genuine democrat; I could detect no snobbishness, and if any does exist it is purely ideological. In his speech he is slow and deliberate, choosing his words carefully and speaking in short sentences. He can understand a few English words and occasionally used one, perhaps as a compliment to me; our talk was carried out through interpreters.

He is 68—being born in 1893. At first it seemed to me he showed his age, and one could hardly be surprised when one considers the hard life he led when young, and the trials of the long war against the Japanese which began in 1937, and then the civil war which ended in 1949 in the final overthrow of Nationalist forces under Chiang Kai-shek. But as our conversation progressed my opinion began to change; although he is heavily built and walks slowly, he appeared to be very fit; his chief form of exercise to-day is swimming.

He is highly intelligent, and intensely practical in his approach to a problem. He may be slow in speech but he is not slow in thought; he answers a question at once, leaving no room for doubt about what he thinks. And he is a very shrewd judge of people, as I quickly discovered; his views on certain political personalities in the Western world, all well known to me, were pretty accurate—at any rate in my opinion!

Mao has never been outside China except to visit Moscow; but his knowledge about what is going on in the world is amazing. He either reads a great deal or has the foreign news reported to him verbally every day. Like all Chinese, he has a great sense of humour. When we first met he said:

"I suppose you know you are talking to an aggressor. I have been branded as such in the United Nations. Do you mind talking with an aggressor?"

It was said with a twinkle in his eye. And when I remarked that certain nations in the Western world had in the past not been altogether blameless in this respect, he laughed heartily.

During our conversation we got on to the subject of revolutions; this was when, to my surprise, he mentioned something about Cromwell. I said that if it hadn't been for Cromwell the England we know to-day would be a very different place. I added that revolutions are not, in themselves, necessarily bad. For instance, the American revolution forced the United Empire Loyalists to go north and create the Canada we have to-day. Then the French revolution resulted in a better France. And finally the revolution in China, which he himself led, swept away internal feudal oppression, corruption, and external aggression. Mao listened to all this with tremendous interest, and silently. He then looked at me with a smile and said:

" You seem to be very enlightened."

I asked him why he was surprised that I appeared enlightened, and he finally admitted that he was wrong to have been surprised! All-in-all, Mao Tse-tung is a most interesting person to meet and talk with, and sincere in his statements—in my opinion. He is, of course, a dedicated communist. But he didn't give me any indication that he is planning to communise the whole world; China has far too much on her plate to want to take on that task.

If I had to go into the jungle with Mao Tse-tung *or* Khrushchev, and there was no other choice—I would prefer Mao.

Chou En-lai

We had better have a look at Chou before considering what is likely to happen in China in the years ahead. He is Prime Minister of the People's Republic of China, and is the executive agent who carries out the policy of the Central Committee of the Communist Party—of which Mao Tse-tung is the Chairman.

Chou En-lai is a very different person from Mao; he is highly born, being the son of a Mandarin. He is 63. One can see at once from his face that he is intellectual and clever; it did not take me long to discover that as far as brain-power is concerned he is brilliant. He is a quick and clear thinker, lucid in his speech, and with a most attractive personality and a nice sense of humour.

Altogether we talked for over seven hours, spread over two

days—alone except for two interpreters. Our conversation began with the situation facing a split world, with East and West growling at each other; then I got him to tell me about his own internal problems in China. He can understand English and spoke it to me at intervals; he can also speak French, which language I used once or twice when searching for exactly the right word to explain some point of view. But when we got down to real business, the problems of China and her place in world affairs, he used his own mother tongue—with two interpreters, both from his own staff and both speaking very good English. I took no interpreter with me from the British Mission; I have found it advisable to go alone to such meetings and to let my host provide what is necessary; this is essential if you want him to speak his true mind, without any suspicion that what he says will be at once reported to the Foreign Office in London. I did not tell the British Chargé d'Affaires what we talked about—which disappointed him no doubt, but I reckon he understood the reason.

I liked the use of two interpreters, one doing all the interpretation and the other intervening if a correction seemed necessary—which happened several times. For instance, the interpreter once used the word "war" when putting over something the Prime Minister had said. His assistant quickly intervened and said the words used by Chou En-lai meant "threat of war," and this intervention changed the whole meaning of the point we were discussing.

Our talks roamed over a wide range of subjects. I had already met the Minister for Foreign Affairs, Marshal Chen Yi, and had discussed foreign policy with him; but I was able to confirm with the Prime Minister the foreign policy of China, and then to direct the discussion on to home policy, and to Asian affairs generally. In all my talks with the Chinese leaders, I asked that we should be alone; this was agreed, provided we could have what they called a "gentleman's agreement"—which meant that we would not disclose to the Press *the details* of what had been discussed.

Both Mao Tse-tung and Chou En-lai were insistent that the status of the ordinary man in China must be raised up from its very low level under the régime of the Emperors and the "foreign devils"—the latter being the Western peoples! This question was raised by me when I asked Chou En-lai about rickshaws, which were drawn by men when I was last in China in 1934 and now had been replaced by pedicabs (drawn by men on bicycles)—and even these were now to go and be replaced by taxis. I had asked the question because in Hong Kong there are still man-drawn rickshaws, and the average life of those men was given me as twenty-eight years. Chou En-lai said that it was considered degrading for a man to run in the shafts of a rickshaw as if he were a horse; the communist régime had forbidden the practice.

Chou En-lai is not the second most powerful man in China. The first is, of course, Mao Tse-tung—Chairman of the Central Committee of the Communist Party of the People's Republic.

The second is Liu Shao-chi, Head of State, Commander-in-Chief of all the armed forces, and the first Vice-Chairman of the Central Committee of the Communist Party. He is 65. The second Vice-Chairman of the Central Committee is Chou En-lai. These three are the real rulers of China; they meet frequently and decide the policy—which is then implemented executively by Chou En-lai, the Prime Minister, and his State Council of Ministers. The order of succession to Mao Tse-tung has been laid down clearly—first Liu Shao-chi, second Chou En-lai.

There are sixteen Vice-Premiers in the State Council. This would correspond broadly to the Cabinet in Britain, and each of the Vice-Premiers has policy and planning functions corresponding approximately to those of Cabinet Ministers in England. But the difference is that "high policy" is laid down by the Central Committee of the Communist Party, and the Vice-Premiers (the Ministers) tend to have executive and administrative functions rather than policy-making—that is, high policy. The nearest equivalent to the Vice-Premiers would be the Permanent Under-Secretaries in British governmental departments. The Secretary-General of the State Council is Hsi Chung-hsun, equivalent to the Secretary of the Cabinet in Whitehall.

It will be evident that power, the real power, is centralised at the top in the Central Committee of the Communist Party—and, in fact, in the hands of the three I have mentioned. These three are the most powerful men in China, the real rulers of the country. If I had to name a fourth it would be Ko Ching-shi, of the Political Bureau of the Communist Party and Mayor of Shanghai; he is older, rising 70, I would guess; I met him in Shanghai and he was present at my four-hour talk with Mao Tse-tung.

Chou En-lai explained to me that this centralisation of policy at the top is essential for the new China, if it is to progress smoothly. In such a vast country, with a population of over six hundred and fifty million which is increasing at the rate of fifteen million a year, a very tight grip from the top became necessary when the People's Republic was proclaimed in 1949; without a tight control from the top, affairs could well get out of hand. This I can well believe. It was for this reason that, once the new régime got well started, Mao himself gave up his post as Head of State and became Chairman of the Central Committee of the Communist Party—where the real power lies, and where policy is formulated.

Such are the rulers of the People's Republic of China. Now let us discuss their policy in so far as I was able to determine it.

WHITHER CHINA?

Many people do not understand the change which has taken place in China since the revolution. For many years the old China suffered severely from two major troubles—external aggression in which perhaps we British were not altogether blameless, and internal oppression of a feudal nature. The country was poor and backward; foreigners exploited China for their own mercenary purposes and grew rich, the mass of the people remained very poor. The régime of the Emperors was corrupt and did nothing for the working classes; a revolution seemed inevitable, and it duly came—the leader being Mao Tse-tung. It swept away the Emperors, the war lords, the absentee landlords, the "foreign devils"—and a new China was born. Many suffered, and many died, in the birth pangs of the new-born China—possibly millions. But very many more millions have profited,—well over six hundred million. The great mass of the Chinese peasants and urban workers have been liberated from the oppression of the old régime; they now have to conform to the strict discipline of the communist régime, and they will have to decide in due course whether the change has been worth while. If asked that question to-day, their answer would be "Yes"; at least they have enough to eat, and feudal oppression has ceased. The new rulers of China are determined that out of evil good shall develop—if only slowly. They are also determined that the new China shall be master in her own lands, with freedom to plan her destiny in her own way—without any outside interference.

There are many misconceptions in the Western world about the new China, particularly in the United States. Of course, not everything in China is good, nor is it in the Western world—very far from it. But not everything is bad, as some think. It is definitely wrong to think that China is a nation of unhappy and depressed people, down-trodden, starved into submission, exploited by ruthless leaders, with fear abroad in the land. That was possibly a true picture of the old China; indeed, it would be the picture I saw in 1934. It is not a true picture of China to-day.

One thing is certain about the new China. Mao Tse-tung has created a unified and dedicated nation of over six hundred and fifty million people—with a sense of purpose. His word is law, absolute and final. The new rulers want to make China the most powerful nation in Asia, and maybe in the world. Of course the task which lies ahead in that respect is difficult, and the way is long—maybe fifty years. But China has certain assets. She has a huge and virile population who work hard; they are possibly the most industrious people in the world, all determined to work for the prosperity of China under their new rulers. Then the people have a definite ideology—Communism. They have strong and firm discipline; they have leaders they trust; they are prepared to accept the stern discipline of the communist régime preferring it to the oppression of the Emperors and warlords. And so long as a man does accept these things, and ninety per cent do, he has nothing to fear.

I knew the old China. I must frankly admit that, from what I have seen, I vastly prefer the new China to the old.

The two matters which we of the West need to understand about this new China are—first her immediate policy, and secondly her ultimate aim.

The immediate policy of the Chinese leaders is based fundamentally on the domestic issue. As I have said, the country is poor and backward. It faces tremendous problems of reconstruction, industrialisation, irrigation, housing, food supply, harnessing the great rivers for electrical power and to prevent disastrous floods. I suggested to Mao Tse-tung that to put all these things right may well take up to fifty years, although within possibly twenty years the nation will have put a good deal right and will be forging ahead rapidly. He agreed. During this period China must have peace; one has only to spend a few days in the country, and visit the major cities and country areas, to realise that another world war would be disastrous and would put the nation back fifty years or more—both Mao Tse-tung and Chou En-lai emphasised this point.

As part of her immediate policy, China is closely allied to Russia; it is not correct to think that the two nations are at loggerheads. China is dependent on the Soviet Union to a certain degree for capital equipment and technical know-how—but not so much as formerly and she is growing more independent every year. Russian experts come to China to teach the use of new equipment; but when the Chinese have learnt, which they do quickly, the Russians are sent home. In defence matters the two nations are tied-in closely; they would fight "back to back" in war, each looking after the other's rear areas.

I asked Chou En-lai if China would, in due course, have nuclear weapons. He said they would so long as other nations had them; but if it was generally agreed to ban all nuclear weapons, China would follow suit, and gladly. In this connection it should be understood that China has some very good scientists.

What is China's ultimate aim? I put the following question to Mao Tse-tung:

"In a given number of years, maybe twenty or possibly more, China will be on the way to becoming a great and powerful nation—with a population of well over a thousand million and with growing economic strength. What will happen then? In fact, what is the ultimate aim of the new China?"

He listened intently while this was put over by the interpreters, and then said:

"Ah! You obviously think China will then practise aggression outside her borders."

I replied that I didn't want to think thus. But the teaching of history was that when a nation became great and powerful it began to acquire territory outside its own frontiers; many instances could be given, and my own country might be included in the number who acted thus. He thought a little before replying. Then he said it was impossible to be precise about what might happen in China, indeed in the world, twenty or thirty years ahead; one could only guess. He himself, and all the present leaders of China would have passed away; new leaders would have arisen. So far as he was concerned, he would use his influence during the remaining years of his life to insist that China kept within her legal frontiers, using negotiation in all cases where those frontiers were disputed, and never practising military aggression beyond those frontiers. He added that China had suffered so much herself from foreign aggression, and from external exploitation, that the nation as he knew it to-day had no intention of inflicting such indignities on any other nation. China wanted to be left alone, to recover from the past aggression of other nations. But if attacked she would defend herself with all the means in her power, and was ready and prepared to do so.

In further conversation when discussing this particular problem with Marshal Chen Yi, the Foreign Minister, I raised the subject of China's legal frontiers. It became clear to me that included within these were Hong Kong, Tibet and Formosa. Hong Kong island is British owned; it was ceded to Britain by the Chinese in 1841. Of course the present People's Republic of China doesn't recognise the validity of any Treaty signed over a hundred years ago (The Treaty of Nanking) with a Manchu Emperor. The New Territories on the mainland, the Kowloon side, are a different case; these comprise some 350 square miles and were leased from China on a 99-year lease as from the 1st July, 1898. Again, the People's Republic doesn't recognise the lease. But Chinese policy is to be friendly to Britain and there will be no trouble about Hong Kong; of course it would be different if we became engaged in a war with China, or even ceased to recognise the People's Republic.

Tibet is now part of China and that argument is closed. Most authorities I have consulted agree that in past eras Tibet was a Chinese sphere of influence; now it has been absorbed into the Republic. I was interested to learn that in 1954 Nehru signed an agreement with Chou En-lai which recognised Tibet as part of China.

The case of Formosa is complicated. Some four hundred years ago, say in the sixteenth century, various nations tried to establish settlements on this island in the western Pacific—notably the Portuguese, Spaniards, and Dutch. Then the Manchus conquered China and became interested in the island; by the close of the seventeenth century Formosa was reckoned as part of the

Chinese Empire. In 1895 the island was ceded to Japan and was developed by that nation into an important military and naval base, and was used as such by the Japanese in World War II. At the Cairo Conference in November, 1943, at which Chiang Kai-shek was present, it was agreed that, on the final defeat of the Japanese, Formosa should be returned to China—and it was formally surrendered to Nationalist China in 1945. There was then *one* China, i.e. Nationalist China under Chiang Kai-shek.

But when the Japanese were defeated in 1945, the two factions in China, led respectively by Chiang Kai-shek and Mao Tse-tung (who had both combined against the Japanese invasion which can be said to have begun in earnest in 1937, although the Japanese had entered Manchuria in 1931)—these two factions turned against each other and the civil war raged furiously. The forces of Chiang Kai-shek used Formosa as a base for their operations on the mainland; when they were finally defeated by the communist forces under Mao, those who did not surrender withdrew to Formosa.

There then became *two* Chinas—the People's Republic with its government in Peking, controlling a population of over six hundred and fifty million on the mainland—and Nationalist China in Formosa, an island with a population of under ten million.

The problem then was—which of these two Chinas should have sovereignty over Formosa—the People's Republic, or Chiang Kai-shek and his set-up?

Here was a pretty how-de-do!

The British Government recognised the People's Republic and its Peking Government, and did *not* recognise the Formosa Government of Chiang Kai-shek—rightly, in my opinion.

The United States did the opposite; they recognised Chiang Kai-shek and refused to have any dealings with the People's Republic—wrongly, I believe.

Furthermore, as part of their Pacific strategy the United States have established a chain of military bases in the western Pacific, which the Chinese consider are intended for offensive

THE PATH TO LEADERSHIP

purposes against their country—which actually is not the case, but nothing will persuade them to think otherwise.

So there are the rulers of the People's Republic of China, and an outline of their policy.

It is my view that China does not want Formosa as a base for military operations farther afield, and she would not indulge in such action. She wants Formosa, and the off-shore islands, because she considers they legally belong to China—and I agree with her. But nothing is likely to happen in that direction until the United States can be made to see reason. And *that* is unlikely to happen until she is forced to change her policy by some external action, or by pressure in the United Nations.

Several questions must be asked. Will the communist régime in China, now under the leadership of Mao Tse-tung, last? Some may wonder whether the enthusiasm, and the terrific pace of work, can be sustained over the period necessary to achieve the aim. For the moment the country has been galvanised by the philosophy of the "great leap forward."

Another question. As the country develops, and to-day this is happening at an amazing pace, will Mao continue to be the leader it needs—particularly if the promised land never seems to come any closer, and, as education improves, an élite begins to emerge?

And one last question, but very important.

Can one believe all we are told about the new China?

These imponderables are anybody's guess. All one can say is that the conviction, the determination, the tenacity, the progress, all are there to-day (1961) to be seen, and cannot be laughed off.

SUMMARY—COMMUNIST LEADERSHIP

From what I have written about the communist leaders I have met, it will be clear that they have risen to power the hard way, and finally have seized power and imposed their will by force.

And on the way to the supreme power they have usually liquidated all other contenders for the post. They have not been elected in free elections. There is no alternative for the voter, no opposition in Parliament. In the Western world we consider that to have good government there must be a united and effective opposition, and that is one way in which we and the communists differ—indeed, it is a fundamental difference.

As Mao Tse-tung said to me, the philosophy of Communism is " everybody according to his ability and needs "; this involves a certain distribution of wealth. He would say, and did say, that China is not yet a communist state; it is a socialist state, moving towards Communism as it gets richer and stronger.

In a communist nation all power is concentrated in the state, and no other allegiance is possible. Hence the Christian religion cannot operate—since in that the first allegiance must be to God, and the state comes second.

I have always the feeling that in most Western countries about sixty per cent of the nation don't really care about democracy or Christianity; they care about themselves. About thirty per cent call themselves Christians, in order to keep up appearances and be considered respectable. And only the last ten per cent are genuine Christians, and believers in democracy.

But my travels in communist countries lead me to think that the percentages among their peoples are different—certainly in Russia, Yugoslavia and China. If this is true, the reason presumably is because of the stern discipline imposed by the leaders of the régime—who impose their will by force.

The hard core of communist leadership lies in Russia. There we see international Communism, and a wish, perhaps a determination, to communise the world. I have explained that Khrushchev has certain problems in Russia. He now considers that war will not pay—not because it is evil or wrong, but because it would destroy the Soviet Union; in this matter, and other related ones, he has to reckon with the Marxist diehards or determinists.

Khrushchev has some good cards. Will he overplay his hand?

Will he go too far with "brinkmanship" and fail—as he is bound to do if the West is united under steady and wise leadership?

All these are imponderables. Recent events lead me to think that Russia will continue to fish in troubled waters, unless and until the West can come to some sensible agreement with her in the near future—which I advocate strongly.

With regard to China, the situation appears to me to be somewhat different. That nation has its eyes fastened on Asia, not on the world—at any rate at present. China aims to remove all Western influence from the mainland of Asia, as she has already done from her own mainland. Her further aim appears to be to dominate Asia—not *to conquer* other countries by military operations, but to get them to look to Peking by means of ideological and political graduations of pressure. In this respect the reader will recall how Mao Tse-tung said to me that during his lifetime China will not commit *military* aggression beyond her legal frontiers. I believe him. It is just a matter of agreement about where those legal frontiers lie.

Perhaps a word of warning may not be out of place to those who scoff. I do not believe it is possible to judge a man correctly if you have not met him; nor can a nation be judged if you have not visited its country and seen the people. In fact, judgment without contact can be most unreliable—and that is why I visited the leaders of Russia and the People's Republic of China in their own countries.

This chapter is only an outline of a very big subject. I have tried to state briefly and simply, to boil down, what I believe to be the essence of the matter. I hope it will be sufficient to explain how the fundamentals of communist leadership, aims, and future action appear to me to be shaping.

CHAPTER FOURTEEN

A BACKWARD LOOK—
MOSES

BEFORE we try to draw some conclusions from the thoughts on leadership which I have expressed, let us have a look at Moses. I have often examined his career as a leader and found it a fascinating study. It can be read in the early books of the Old Testament—the Books of Moses. We will have to tackle his activities in a somewhat different way because the information and facts are not so clear as in the case of the other leaders we have discussed. Also, of course, I did not know Moses!

According to the historians, the children of Israel arrived in Egypt about B.C. 1720, and the date of the Exodus under Moses was about B.C. 1290. Between these two dates, a period of some 430 years, Israel lived in misery as slaves of the Egyptians, being dragooned into forced labour.

> "And the Egyptians made the children of Israel to serve with rigour; and they made their lives bitter with hard bondage in mortar and bricks, and in all manner of service in the field."

It has always seemed to me that Moses was given a most difficult task—to lead Israel, a shepherd people, out of Egypt and into the land of Canaan, which would be their new home.

I have never believed that once they had got clear of Egypt, they wandered aimlessly about in the Sinai desert for forty years—lost. I reckon Moses knew very well that he could not carry out the second part of his task, one which would almost certainly involve much fighting, until the old grumblers had died and a new generation had grown up—imbued with a fighting spirit and trained to war. He knew that a slave people cannot be turned into a fighting race in a few weeks or months; a new spirit has to be born; for this, time is needed; it would have been useless to embark on the invasion of Canaan without a sound plan and one which could be carried swiftly to a successful conclusion without any reverses. This latter point was important; defeats in battle might well cause a loss of confidence in his leadership.

The story takes us back over 3,000 years and it can be put together as follows:

Moses decided that he must first gain some information about this new country and he sent scouts ahead—one of whom was a young man called Joshua, who was later to succeed to the Supreme Command of the host of Israel.

> " And Moses sent them to spy out the land of Canaan, and said unto them, Get you up this way southward, and go up into the mountain and see the land, what it is; and the people that dwelleth therein, whether they be strong or weak, few or many."

This was pretty good for somebody who was not a soldier by profession. The scouts spent forty days on the task and brought back information about the opposition which was likely to be met—large populations, strong men, and fortified cities " great and walled up to Heaven."

Here was confirmation of his thinking on the task ahead. The immense and difficult problem which faced him was now clear—he knew for certain that he had to turn his nation into a fighting race and train them for battle. A further and disturbing factor was that the report of the scouts had a demoralising effect; morale, never high, became very low.

> " And all the congregation lifted up their voice and cried, and the people wept that night. And all the children of Israel

murmured against Moses. . . . Wherefore hath the Lord brought us into this land, to fall by the sword, that our wives and our children should be a prey? And they said one to another, Let us make a captain, and let us return into Egypt."

This was a pretty how-de-do! Not only low morale, but also almost a mutiny.

And food was scarce too. All they remembered was the good living in the delta of Egypt; they seemed to have forgotten the misery of the forced labour.

"Would to God we had died by the hand of the Lord in the land of Egypt, when we sat by the flesh pots, and when we did eat bread to the full."

"Who shall give us flesh to eat, for it was well with us in Egypt?"

That must have been a difficult period for Moses, knowing there was considerable unrest—particularly among the older people. Despite their new faith, the children of Israel were not yet welded into a disciplined community with a fighting spirit; also they were poorly armed, having only the most primitive weapons. He therefore decided to cancel his plan to march against Canaan from the south. Instead, he must keep them moving in the desert sufficiently long for them to develop into a tough national force, schooled to battle; this period must be long enough for a new generation to emerge, but how long was not yet clear. So he embarked on his task. In the end he had to keep them on the move for forty years; during this time a new generation sprang up, ready to carry out the invasion of the Promised Land. It is interesting to read how their skill in battle, and morale, became gradually built up. A new plan had been made, to invade Canaan from the east. This new route involved passing through the territories of certain rulers, whose permission was sought. One of the earliest was the kingdom of Edom.

" And Moses sent messengers from Kadesh unto the king of Edom. . . . Let us pass, I pray thee, through thy country . . . we will go by the king's highway."

Permission to pass through Edom was refused, and Moses decided not to risk battle but to make a wide deviation.

Later they came to the kingdom of the Amorites. Again they asked for permission to pass through. " along by the king's highway." Again permission was refused. Moses was now pretty sure of his forces and he decided to fight. The result was a great victory; morale was restored, the children of Israel became conscious of their strength, and they were not again defeated in battle until the task was completed.

Moses now had to hand over command; he was not allowed to enter the Promised Land. But he was allowed to see it from Mt. Nebo. I have seen that view from the top of Pisgah; I went there with my wife in 1931, when my regiment was stationed in Jerusalem. What Israel now needed was a good strategist, one who could wield effectively the weapon forged by Moses—and they found him in Joshua. Trained by Moses, he also sent out scouts—to reconnoitre Jericho, the strategic key to entry into Canaan from the east—and, indeed, the key to the conquest of all Canaan. The fact that the two scouts billeted themselves in the house of a harlot should not be allowed to detract from their scouting ability!

Joshua's battle for the city, his first, established his reputation —even if the tactics were somewhat unusual.

" And it came to pass, when the people heard the sound of the trumpet, and the people shouted with a great shout, that the wall fell down flat, so that the people went up into the city, and they took the city."

Probably it was an earthquake which shattered the city about B.C. 1250, since it lies in an earthquake zone. But whatever may have been the cause, when the walls did fall down Joshua quickly assumed credit for having produced such a tactical rabbit out of the hat—and took full advantage of it!

While everything and everybody in the city was destroyed by fire and the sword, Rahab the harlot who had sheltered the two scouts was rewarded with her life—and all her family too.

What can we say of Moses before we leave him? What was his contribution to leadership? He had been brought up by a princess and was highly educated. He may possibly have had something to do with the Egyptian Army. At any rate, he was a good judge of what was possible in war, and what was not possible with the resources available. He refused to launch Israel into battle until he was ready. He had the wisdom and the insight into human nature to realise that the best way to raise morale in an army is by victories in battle; soldiers will always follow a successful general. In the tactical sphere he understood that time spent in reconnaissance is usually justified—and in his case it certainly was.

His method of command in battle would hardly be suitable to-day. In the battle against Amalek he entrusted the tactical command to Joshua. He himself sat on a nearby hill, holding up his hands. So long as they remained up, Israel gained the advantage; when he became tired and his hands dropped, the enemy prevailed. Once this became apparent, Aaron and Hur took care to see that his hands did not fall—they held them up!

The point here is that, having done all he could, he prayed for his men as they fought. And I presume that his staff saw to it that the C.-in-C. was not disturbed by visitors, V.I.P. or otherwise! And when the battle had been won, Moses gave the victory a new name—" Jehovah Nissi," the Lord my banner.

I have always admired Moses for his leadership and insight into human nature. In my opinion he has a sure place among national leaders. And he was firmly convinced that " The Lord is a man of war "—which the pacifists might note.

I said in Chapter Seven that my first thought had been to include Moses and de Gaulle in the same chapter; but it would have been difficult to compare the two since they were very different personalities. Moses often despaired and could be accused of vacillation on occasions. De Gaulle can never be accused of either of these bad habits; he knows exactly what he wants to do, and does it—waving all opposition aside. But in both men we see sincerity and selflessness, and a total lack of anything mean or underhand—which surely are essential requirements in a national leader? We must note, however, that whereas Moses completed his task successfully, de Gaulle has not yet done so.

I sometimes ask myself the question:

"If de Gaulle had lived 3,000 years ago, with the same personality and make-up he has to-day, would he have been able to achieve what Moses did?"

My answer would be "No." Nor could Moses do what de Gaulle is doing to-day. Moses was exactly right for his own times—and in France de Gaulle is right for his.

In fact, man is the product of his age.

CHAPTER FIFTEEN

CONCLUSIONS

IF CHAPTER TWELVE (Leadership in the West) was difficult to write, this chapter will be more so. I delayed writing it for some time and even wondered if it could be omitted, since the title implies that I am only trying to point to the path which leads to efficient leadership. But without some conclusions it would be only half a book. I have spent some fifty years in a close study of the subject, and having given my thinking in previous chapters, I must now give some conclusions.

I said at the beginning of this book that leadership is a battle for the hearts and minds of men, and I hope the reader, having come to the end, will now agree with that statement. Leadership is a great human problem—a study of human nature—and this fact must be clearly understood by all those who aspire to lead. It is human beings, men and women, who are the factors of reality in the world in which we live; *once you can win the hearts, and the respect, of those who work for you, the greatest achievements become possible*. No greatness can be achieved without a clear realisation of this very simple fact.

The greatest leaders of all time were the founders of the three main religions, because they achieved something and their work has lasted—I refer to Christ, Mohammed, and Buddha. They were simple men, of humble origin—except Buddha, who was a prince. They gathered men to themselves; they understood human nature; and they had within themselves that " something " which appealed to men and persuaded them to follow.

True greatness cannot be achieved without moral virtues; once these are mixed with talents of a lesser kind, the latter become improved—perhaps inspired. A man can have moral virtues without being a Christian; good examples in the modern world would be Nehru of India, and Ben Gurion of Israel. But in a Western nation, with our long Christian tradition, I believe a leader would have little or no success unless he practised the Christian virtues.

Perhaps it is permissible to state here that I am not without experience in summing-up a man, although of course my experience in this respect has been greater in the military sphere than in the political; even so, my contacts with political and national leaders have been considerable—and still are to-day.

MILITARY LEADERS

I do not propose to dwell on great military leaders. It is stated in Chapter Two that Marlborough and Wellington were two of the finest soldiers produced by any nation, and there is no reason to change that opinion. If I was forced to name two soldiers of my own time for whom I have the highest admiration and regard, two great soldiers, they would be Bill Slim and John Harding. These two are not only qualified for a sure place in history by their technical ability in the conduct of war and the handling of men; they have also earned a sure place as proconsuls in peace, in Australia and Cyprus respectively. And to add to these qualifications, I would deem them both utterly incapable of intrigue and of anything mean or underhand; in addition they possess wisdom, a sure judgment, the ability of decision, and have always had in full measure the confidence and respect of those who served with and under them—knowing how to speak to men in language they can understand, and winning their hearts. If I had to name two more they would be Horrocks and Dick O'Connor, both sterling characters and grand soldiers. I have not mentioned Field-Marshal Alexander, for whom I have always had the very highest regard, because my tribute to him was paid in my *Memoirs*. I admire him enormously.

CONCLUSIONS

NATIONAL LEADERS

I do not think a man can be considered great, a genius, in the realm of national leadership unless he has achieved something for the good of his country and the nation he leads—something which lasts, which has a permanency. With this yardstick, who can go in my list?

As examples I take two from the past—King Alfred and Abraham Lincoln. These will go down to history as two of the great men of all time, both being in the front rank of national leaders, and in both cases their work has stood the test of time.

Then we come to twentieth-century leaders. In previous chapters the qualities to be looked for in a leader have been enumerated. In modern times it seems to me that ordinary men, men with minds trained mechanically, men who are docile, men who one might call "yes men" (everybody knows what that means!)—such men will generally triumph in peace-time over men of strong character possessing true insight and genius, and they will triumph because a political leader prefers such docile men in his team or as a Service chief advising the Cabinet. The true attributes of leadership can be boiled down to character, decision and action—which assets are not always popular with the political leader in quiet times. But when a crisis occurs, when the nation is in urgent need of leaders with initiative who can be relied upon to get on with the job *and do something*, taking risks if necessary—then matters are seen in a very different light. Just as the raging of the seas creates a swell which throws up things to the surface, so the man of character and vision comes to the surface in a crisis. He is needed, but he will most likely be discarded when he has done his stuff. All the world will cry out for men of character and decision when danger looms ahead, men who believe in themselves and are prepared to take full control of the emergency, men who are ready to launch great undertakings and who have the courage and determination to see-the thing through to the end. The best example I can give of such a man is Winston Churchill, who was discarded by our nation when he had done his stuff—and by doing it had saved not only Britain but also Western civilisation.

I once discussed this subject with General de Gaulle. His view was that a military leader, brought to the surface under such conditions, must be prepared to disobey when necessary; and he told me a story about the Battle of Jutland which I had not heard before. His story was that some considered that Admiral Jellicoe should have destroyed the German fleet at Jutland. One of these was Admiral Fisher, and when he was reading Jellicoe's despatch about the battle he exclaimed: " He has all Nelson's qualities but one—he doesn't know how to disobey."

Against this general background, who are the great national leaders of to-day (1961)? I will exclude Winston Churchill; he reached the pinnacle of fame but his day is past; he was well described by Sir James Grigg as " Triton among the minnows." In my opinion there is only one great national leader in the Western world to-day—General de Gaulle. He has vision, political courage, tenacity, and the ability of decision. He has achieved something, done something, for his country; of course we have yet to see whether his work for France will endure. One has only to read the three volumes of his *War Memoirs* to realise the problems and troubles which faced him during the years after France fell in 1940, and those volumes show how he overcame them and triumphed in the end. He didn't wait until he was discarded by the nation whose honour he had saved; he went into the wilderness of his own volition, and waited until France called on him again in her anguish—which she did in 1958. He is most certainly a Triton among a multitude of minnows in the Western world. I have a tremendous admiration for him. He is a great man.

The only other European I would place in the category of great national leaders is Marshal Tito, President of Yugoslavia. He also has political courage, tenacity and the power of decision. And he has most certainly done something; he has created a

CONCLUSIONS

unified nation and given it a sense of purpose. He has tremendous character and a very attractive personality. Definitely a great leader both in the military and national spheres, with outstanding political wisdom. From his earliest days up to the time when he became the political head of his country, he was faced with difficulties which would have daunted most men; but he triumphed over them all. A great man indeed.

In the Eastern world there are two men I place in the top category of national leaders—Nehru and Mao Tse-tung, each a great man in his own sphere, and each totally different from the other. I have devoted a whole chapter to Nehru and there is little more which can be said. He is the leader of a nation of four hundred million people who literally worship him; if he can solve his many internal problems, and his health lasts, he will be the man on whom will depend much of what happens in Asia in future years. He is not a Christian, but he bases his life on the Christian virtues. I admire him enormously. He is a great leader of an Asian people.

Mao Tse-tung is another great Asian leader. He has done something for his country without a doubt, fighting foreign aggression and internal oppression and corruption. And in the end he triumphed; and he is to-day the leader of a united and dedicated nation of six hundred and fifty million people. He is now engaged in putting right much that was bad in China, and so much was bad that it will take him a long time. But he has courage, tenacity, and can decide—all qualities of greatness. When one meets him one cannot help liking him. He is, of course, a communist. But he also is a great man.

I would like to see a friendship develop between Nehru and Mao Tse-tung. In point of fact the two have much in common, particularly in their devotion to the welfare of the mass of the people—the peasants. In each country, India and China, the revolution was based on the peasantry. If such a friendship could be brought about, without either attempting to change the ideology or way of life of the other, peace would be assured in Asia—and that would be a major factor in securing world peace.

I have named as great national or political leaders in the world to-day only four men, two in Europe and two in Asia. I can see no other great leaders in any nation. It will be interesting to learn if my list is challenged; perhaps somebody will produce a different list, giving, I hope, the reasons for greatness in each case.

Of my four, only one is a Christian—de Gaulle. Two are communists. Does this mean that the communist world produces better leaders than we do? I hope not. But it is difficult to exercise leadership in the democratic world, as I have pointed out in Chapter Twelve. In the communist world, government is imposed by force; there is no alternative, no free choice, and therefore it is easier to lead since the people have to obey.

I would ask the reader to note that all those I have named as great leaders rose to their positions from humble positions; all were very poor men—with one exception, Nehru.

Slim and Harding were the product of grammar schools; Slim then became a teacher in a secondary school, and Harding a clerk in the Post Office. Neither had any money, except what they earned themselves.

De Gaulle was the son of a poor colonel in the French Army. Tito was an ordinary soldier in the ranks of the Austrian Army. Mao Tse-tung was the son of a farm labourer. And yet all these men rose from their humble beginnings to become great. It would seem to prove the statement made by me in Chapter Eleven that most of the best men come from the poorest homes; they had to struggle when young and this toughened their characters. But they all realised that education was essential, and all took steps to acquire that education. They all dedicated themselves to their profession, and worked unceasingly for the good of others—eschewing distracting influences and social activities. They were all able to dominate, and finally to master, the events which encompassed them—which is the great and final test of a leader.

All of these men whom I have named as great leaders in their respective spheres are known to me—Alexander, Slim, Harding,

Horrocks and O'Connor very well, of course. I have visited in their own countries the four named as great national leaders—de Gaulle, Tito, Nehru and Mao Tse-tung. It may surprise some to hear the latter described as a great man, but his achievements speak for themselves. Look what he has done! If only we can now persuade him that the best interests of China lie in being friendly to India and to the West—then indeed the Western world will be able to give a sigh of relief. I shall do *my* best to bring this about.

What conclusion can be drawn from the illustrations given? The conclusion is that if we in the Western world are to hold our own with the communist world in the matter of leadership, we will have to change our thinking on the subject and educate our boys, our young men, to lead.

EDUCATION FOR LEADERSHIP

It is regrettable, but true, that the Western world is suffering to-day from a lack of courageous leadership, and that opinion will be obvious from what I have been saying. How is this defect best tackled?

We must realise at the outset that the whole idea of " leadership " is regarded with deep suspicion by certain influential sections of Western social opinion. This attitude of mind arises partly from hatred of the debasement of the leadership-principle in the twentieth-century dictatorships, partly from a genuine desire to ensure equality of opportunity for all children, and partly from muddled thinking about the equality of man and the classless society. It follows that little can be done until Western opinion is re-educated to appreciate the crucial necessity of devoted and able leadership in all aspects of democratic life. But this will be difficult unless we can think rightly about " equality."

It is stated in the American Declaration of Independence, dated 4th July, 1776, that:

" all men are created equal."

But nobody can seriously believe that the many thousands of boys in the schools of Britain (or the U.S.A.) were all created with equal possibilities as regards their brain-power. The mark of a machine is "sameness," but of nature and life it is "difference."

Of course every human being is a soul of equal value in the eyes of God. But this does not mean that all men are born with equal talents. The hard fact is that all men are *not* created equal in ability to each other, and as they grow up this difference in ability becomes increasingly evident.

Equality means equal access to the law and an equal right to justice under it. In the free world we all enjoy equality before the law in about as perfect a degree as is consistent with this imperfect world. Then we have the form of equality under which every man is as entitled as any other to determine the form and complexion of the Government by which his affairs, and the affairs of everybody else, are to be regulated. This broadly means one man one vote and one woman one vote, and *that* we have certainly achieved. All we are asked to give in return for having a voice in how our affairs are to be regulated is a modest contribution in the form of taxation!

Then we come to equality of opportunity. Perfect equality of opportunity is impossible. However hard we may try, greater inequalities of capacity and therefore of opportunity will develop as children grow into men. For this reason it is harder to give equal opportunities to those who in early life disclose no marked bent or aptitude.

Because of muddled thinking about equality, many sections of Western democratic society are suspicious of the whole idea of the necessity for leadership, and of the need for any special training in order to produce a sufficiency of leaders.

But we must train heads as well as count them. There will always be heads and tails; there can never be a ship without a captain or a good team without a leader; it is captaincy that counts. The whole concept of leadership needs re-defining and re-stating.

CONCLUSIONS

What did Don Alhambra say?
" When everyone is somebodee,
Then no one's anybody."

It will be unusual to find combined in any one individual all the qualities needed for successful leadership; however, much can be done to inculcate and develop the necessary qualities by training. But we shall make a great mistake if in trying to cast our net as widely as possible for leaders, we lavish our limited resources for leadership-training on those who (through no fault of their own) will always be among the *led*: to the detriment of the potential leaders. Leaders are a small class and must be taught in small classes.

It is obvious that a nation cannot produce a sufficient number of men with these essential qualities of leadership unless the education of its boys is organised on sound lines, and this is the crux of the whole matter. In any educational system certain essential principles must be followed.

First and foremost is the right type of teacher. Generally, secondary school teachers are underpaid. An underpaid teacher usually means a narrow teacher, fatally restricted in his contacts and life; it is hard for such a man to communicate to his pupils what he has not himself got. The masters in our schools must be first class and must be paid accordingly. Given a good educational system and good teachers, there must be a proper organisation for religious instruction in the school, worked out in co-operation with the Churches.

In general, schools must provide the right kind of education which will enable leaders, when they leave school, to approach the problems of the world from the right point of view. Some may say that this is a training of intelligence and brains; but it is something rather more than that. Fifty or a hundred years ago, a boy was trained almost entirely on the discipline of classics and mathematics, with slight beginnings of modern languages and science. But too few schools made any attempt to teach modern history, or to introduce boys to the world in which they have to take their place. I am sure, therefore, that part of the duty of a school is to train boys to understand the general context of the world in which leadership is to be exercised. Let me give an example.

The continent of Africa is in a troubled state. One kind of leadership is to take troops to Africa and fight, and suppress, the Mau Mau organisation or other disturbers of peace. But there is another and quite different kind of leadership, and the only really creative one, which goes out and sees what is in the African mind and civilisation, such as it is, and which understands the longings of the Africans to be in the end their own masters —leadership which will keep them from running before they can walk, and at the same time will encourage them and help them to fit themselves for the goal they want to reach.

Therefore, any school has a great and necessary task to see that its boys who, by virtue of their character, or their brains, or their natural leadership, will inevitably exercise strong influence in the future—that these boys will understand the complex problem of human relations, and will know where these problems are presenting themselves in the world and how they are to be met and solved.

The ultimate test will be the standing and influence of a boy twenty or thirty years ahead. We must produce " stayers " who will last the course, and not just " sprinters " who will fall out of the race.

In fact, the education and character-training that we must give our boys is, by itself, not the most important matter. The vital point is what they *do* with that education: what use they make of it in the years ahead. And a definite part of that education and training must be to inculcate the qualities that are an inseparable element of good leadership; this must be developed by good example on the part of the very best masters who can be provided.

There must then be a desire on the part of the boy to emulate that example. To illustrate my meaning I would quote some words by John Drinkwater in his play, *Abraham Lincoln*:

CONCLUSIONS

> "When the high heart we magnify,
> And the sure vision celebrate,
> And worship greatness passing by,
> Ourselves are great."

EAST-WEST RELATIONS

This is the great problem facing a troubled world. Each group of nations, each bloc, is labouring under the impression that the other is organising for military aggression—for attack. Nothing could be further from the truth; but because of this delusion each bloc spends vast sums organising for defence, and each is ever more suspicious of the other. One hears no talk of war in Russia, or in the East; but in the Western hemisphere it is a general subject of conversation, and nowhere more so than in the United States.

It is essential to solve this problem; if we fail the arms race will continue, and ultimately the arms will be used. We must move towards some degree of disarmament; but we will not do that by discussions at Geneva, or by national leaders writing letters to each other. *The causes of the suspicion must first be removed.* That can best be done by the nations of both blocs demonstrating their good faith by withdrawing their armed forces back to their own territories.

For example, if the United States would withdraw her forces from Japan and Formosa, the lessening of suspicion in the Far East would be immediate. Similarly in Europe—if the forces of Russia, America, Britain and Canada were withdrawn. These moves would take time to carry out; but the two blocs could agree to begin at once, moves to be completed by, say, 1970.

In any case, whether this plan is agreed or not, the Western Alliance needs a new strategy. The NATO strategy was designed to resist military aggression from the East; once we can reduce *the suspicion* between East and West, that threat disappears. The remaining threat will be ideological, political, and economic; this is a global threat, and not one which can be confined to the

NATO area. It is not a threat to be defeated by military weapons. Hence the need for new thinking in NATO, and a new strategy.

The new strategy must be to establish friendships without asking the nations concerned to be our military allies. It should aim to bring about gradually, and with all military precautions, the withdrawal of Russian armed forces back to the territories of the Soviet Union. My talks with Khrushchev lead me to think that while there are definite difficulties for him in carrying out such a withdrawal, there will be greater difficulties for him in the long run if Russian forces remain in Eastern Europe—because of the rise of nationalism in those lands, where I do not believe the Russians are liked. Western strategy, for obvious reasons, should plan to cash in on this trend, withdrawing our own armed forces from Western Europe simultaneously. In short, we should plan to end the military occupation of the continent of Europe—gradually, and with all necessary inspection and control by the United Nations. That military occupation has gone on now for sixteen years—which is far too long, and involves an expenditure of money which can be better spent on education, housing, reduction of taxation, etc.

There must be a second pillar to the new Western strategy. That pillar should be to combat and defeat the communist challenge for the leadership of Asia and Africa. A glance at the map will show that the corner-stone of this pillar is the sub-continent of India and Pakistan; if those two nations will become firm friends, and if the United States and her allies will give them both massive economic aid (not military weapons), that is the best way to meet the communist challenge in Asia. Having met and held the challenge in Asia, it will be much easier to defeat it in Africa. The reverse procedure, to tackle Africa first and neglect Asia, will not produce success.

The lead in all these matters must be given by the United States, but that nation will need to re-think its policies. In the late 1940s and early 1950s there were only two great powers in the world—the United States and Russia—and the only thing which counted in the struggle for power between East and West was the military strength of those two nations. But to-day other things count; one is the rise in wealth and economic strength of Western Europe. In the immediate post-war years the United States was the leader of an alliance of tired nations, worn out by over five years of struggle against Hitler's Germany. To-day the United States heads up a different alliance—a group of rich nations which have regained their economic prosperity and which are, in consequence, more difficult to lead. Former American policies are now out of date; it is not now so much a matter of " leading," and of " thumping the table " occasionally, but more one of trying to influence a community of rich and independent nations—a very different matter. It will be interesting to see if the United States can produce the leadership and the wisdom necessary to understand the new shape of things to-day, and can bring itself to give up its old policies and think out a new strategy.

If that great nation cannot adapt itself to the changed conditions, then the outlook is grim. I think Winston Churchill once called Hitler's war " the unnecessary war." A third world war is most certainly unnecessary; it can be prevented by wisdom and courageous leadership in the West.

It is unpleasant to realise that the youth of to-day is the first generation of the twentieth century not to be decimated by war. When we take part in memorial services, or wander through our war cemeteries, we must realise that those men gave their lives in order to ensure that the great traditions of our country, our Empire, and indeed of the whole free world, should be delivered safely into our hands—and they were. We have now got to ask ourselves whether we are taking the right steps, and making the right effort, to be worthy of our great inheritance, and whether we are planning to hand it over *intact* to our successors—who are the youth of the 1960s. We do not want them to be decimated by war, as two previous generations have been, if it can possibly be avoided with honour.

SOME FINAL REFLECTIONS

It is interesting to reflect how the selection of national leaders has changed throughout history. I suppose the oldest system of all was the hereditary one; in the wandering tribes of antiquity the eldest son succeeded his father, and this method is still in force in countries with a monarchal system. That method applies to-day in business concerns, but not so much as formerly; most firms take steps to limit the power which might come to sons unfit to succeed.

I once had an interesting talk with Marshal Tito of Yugoslavia on this subject. He explained that Nasser was against having in the Arab world kings who succeeded each other on the throne merely because they were descended from the Prophet, irrespective of whether they were fit to govern. Tito considered that heads of State, and of Governments, should be elected by the people—and he said Nasser agreed with him, which I can well imagine!

To-day we have in the free world a system of democratic election; in our country the nation selects the political party which is to govern, and the party chooses the leader. We have free elections and a constitutional system, the Sovereign governing by advice.

The qualities which make for leadership cannot be discovered by examination. What examinations can do is to discover whether there is sufficient education to enable a young man to be worthy of training in leadership—it being stated in Chapter One that leadership can be developed by training and that, generally speaking, leaders are " made " and not born.

There is, of course, little to be said for choosing leaders by seniority. The system in the British Army is to consider officers in order of seniority, with rejection of the unfit.

It is interesting to note how political leaders do not like to name their successors—perhaps " indicate " is a better way of expressing what I mean. We have examples in Churchill, Nehru,

CONCLUSIONS

Khrushchev, de Gaulle, Adenauer, and Dr. Salazar of Portugal. But Mao Tse-tung has named his successor—he is Liu Shao-chi, the first Vice-Chairman of the Communist Party, aged 55.

I have sometimes wondered whether a political leader, observing one of his team as being a bit too keen on the succession and possibly intriguing, does not put him in a post where he is bound to " muck it up "—and that finishes him!

It will be recalled that Cromwell named his son Richard as his successor, but he didn't last long—less than a year.

There is a need, I reckon, for any leader, military or political, to have a brilliant and devoted chief of staff who will sift all the relevant information, seek out the facts, and relieve his boss of all irrelevant detail. This will enable the leader, the chief, to survey the whole field of endeavour and to keep his finger on the pulse of those things which matter. A man who is always immersed in details is unfit to be a leader in any walk of life. The Chief of Staff must be anonymous and must never attempt to take unto himself the powers of his leader; on the other hand, he must be prepared to give decisions on all matters of detail. He must, therefore, be completely in the mind of his boss, nothing being hidden from him, and being trusted absolutely. A good Chief of Staff is a pearl of very great price. My impression is that political leaders don't like them! But in the highest level in the military world, a Chief of Staff is essential; without one a Commander-in-Chief would become hopelessly entangled in detail, as do so many political leaders. Perhaps it will not be considered unseemly to compare the two types in our nation— the soldier and the politician.

Both are British, but with this difference—military training imposes a certain pattern of behaviour on the soldier and he becomes disciplined; this leads to comradeship, and the ability to endure hardship with his comrades and to triumph over disaster; it makes him easy to lead, and he responds to leadership. Steadiness and tenacity are the hall-marks of the British soldier; he possesses self-reliance and resourcefulness. He is intensely loyal to his comrade; he will never desert him, nor intrigue against him, nor leave him in the lurch. In the midst of the most appalling situations the British soldier stands calm and resolute, dominating all around him by his quiet courage and cheerfulness, his unflinching acceptance of the situation. In fact, he is unconquerable; and it is just as well he is, for without his exertions over many years none of us would be here to-day.

How does the politician compare with this assessment? Not too well. It would be interesting to learn how many know what went on in high political circles at the time of the Suez problem in 1956—how, when the crisis burst and developed in ever-increasing fury, Anthony Eden was deserted by certain of his comrades who previously had backed him. Again, the true story of the departure of Antony Head from the Ministry of Defence in January, 1957, has yet to be told. The discipline which has moulded the soldier and given him his pattern of behaviour, his obedience, his loyalty to his officers, seems to be lacking in political life—which is a pretty rough affair, with quite a bit of dishonesty.

At a dinner party in London one night a few of us were discussing the integrity or otherwise of politicians. I pointed to Derick Heathcoat-Amory, Chancellor of the Exchequer, who was present, and said to my neighbour: " There is one of the few honest politicians in England." He replied: " Yes, but he's not a politician!"

Of course there are notable exceptions; one such is Antony Head, whose integrity and sincerity are absolute.

It is for consideration whether our British form of government is suitable for the mid-twentieth century. Personally I don't think it is, and it will be less so in the twenty-first century. There was a terrific hullabaloo when Mr. Macmillan put his Foreign Secretary in the House of Lords. In point of fact it was most sensible, since the House of Lords meets only three days a week and the Foreign Secretary need not be in constant attendance as he had to be in the Commons, particularly at question time; he will thus have more time to attend to foreign affairs.

CONCLUSIONS

In the United States the Chief Executive is not a member of Congress, nor is his Secretary of State, nor are any of his cabinet; in consequence they can all get on with their jobs. It is not suggested that we should adopt the American system in the United Kingdom, but it has its points. We might well adopt some middle line, one which combines the best points in the American system and our own. For instance, why should not Ministers who sit in the House of Lords be allowed to address the House of Commons and be cross-examined when the lower House so requests, and the Prime Minister agrees? There can be no sensible reason against such a procedure.

My final reflection is that we have just got to find a way of living peacefully with the Russians; we need leadership which will persist until the way is found with honour to both sides—which, in my view, is possible.

If we have to admit that there is no way, then the final end will be war between East and West, which we would not win, nor would they; both sides would lose, and civilisation would be put back for a hundred years, or more. This is the great and immediate problem, and Western civilisation waits anxiously for the answer—particularly the mothers of the present generation of our boys.

After that will come the problem of China. But there is no world threat from that nation at present; indeed no nation wants peace more than the Chinese. But in the interim we need leadership which will be friendly to that great nation, and will try to get her leaders to understand the context of the world in which their newly arisen nation has to live.

ADVICE TO A LEADER

What advice can be offered to a leader? He must discipline himself and lead a carefully regulated and ordered life. He must allow a certain amount of time for quiet thought and reflection; the best times are in the early morning, and in the evening. The quality, good or bad, of any action which is to be taken will vary directly with the time spent in thinking; against this, he must not be rigid; his decisions and plans must be adaptable to changing situations. A certain ruthlessness is essential, particularly with inefficiency and also with those who would waste his time. People will accept this, provided the leader is ruthless with himself.

Then he must have a dogged perseverance; perhaps tenacity is a better word. Having decided on his policy, his objective, he must not be led off his target by the faint-hearted; he will do well to discard the faint-hearted once they are discovered. There are always those men who are dissatisfied, not so much with their own littleness as with the bigness of other people; such men are incapable of trying to better their own positions except by the relative method of dragging down their more fortunate comrades—planning to pull down rather than build up. Most leaders will find there is so much to do and so little time to do it; that was my experience in the military sphere. My answer to that is not to worry; what is needed is a quiet contemplation of all aspects of the problem, followed by a decision —and it is fatal to worry afterwards.

Abstemiousness is vital—in food, in drink, in smoking, in social activities. So is need for regular sleep. My life has been one of unceasing work; when young my outside interests were games; as I got older I took to work, and ever more work. But I always made it a rule to go to bed early, and I refused to be disturbed by anybody after 9.30 p.m.—even during a tough battle. I remember an incident in May, 1940, when a staff officer at my Divisional H.Q. woke me up at midnight and told me the Germans had fought their way into Louvain. I told him to tell the Brigadier to turn them out and not to bother me—and went to sleep again.

General de Gaulle retires to his private apartments in the *Elysée* in Paris at 9 p.m., and nobody is allowed to disturb him —because he is thinking. He knows very well that a leader must first " understand," then make a decision, and finally order action to be taken. The right action will not be taken unless the

CONCLUSIONS

leader has been able to weigh in his mind the various factors bearing on the problem—and this requires quiet thought. The analogy of the doctor will apply—first diagnosis, then decision as to the cure.

It is a good thing to read in bed before going to sleep—and the book should have nothing to do with one's work or profession. The Bible is very good reading; so is poetry, or a good novel.

It is interesting to note the extent to which great men can be helped by their wives; I think all those I have mentioned in this book who are now living, would admit this—including Mao Tse-tung, who made quite a point of it. There are cases where the marriages of public men have ended in failure, and it has seemed to me they have not understood that they must devote a certain number of hours a day to their wives and families—whatever the calls of business or work. When the wife is very pretty, and young, the number of hours may have to be increased—if not the worst might happen, and I could give several examples!

When I wrote the Introduction to this book I said my purpose was to seek to discover what it is which makes a man capable of exercising his position at the head of affairs for the good of his fellows. It will be clear to the reader from what I have written that "what it is" is the possession of certain qualities of which the following are some of the more important—deep conviction, decision, courage and tenacity, sincerity, the ability to dominate and finally to master the events which encompass him, and a thorough understanding of human nature, with all that that implies.

There must also be a clear-cut understanding of situations as they arise, forthrightness in saying what is needed to be done, and the avoidance of all emotional complications. When in doubt about honesty, trustfulness, and other moral qualities, a good test is to say to oneself, "Would I go in the jungle with that man?"

I consider that the four men I have mentioned in this chapter as great national leaders possess these qualities—de Gaulle, Tito, Nehru, and Mao Tse-tung. And applying my final test, I would willingly go in the jungle with any of them, and trust him. If I had to boil down the whole matter of leadership into one sentence, it would be this:

> *It is "captaincy" which counts, or leadership in the higher sense, together with the power of decision and an understanding of human nature; in fact, a leader must first understand, and then decide, and act. And he must be articulate; he must be able to express himself in clear and simple language.*

Some may accuse me of saying in this book many things which I have said before, and that would be correct. Winston Churchill once said to me that there is no harm in saying the same thing over and over again, provided it is right; "constant reiteration" he called it. This reminds me of the story about the negro preacher who had been converted to Christianity and had, in his turn, been converting many others of his race. He was asked to what he attributed his success. He replied:

> "I tells 'em de good tidings, then I tells 'em what I's told 'em, then I asks 'em if they can tell me what I's told 'em, and then I tells 'em again, to make sure dat they knows what it was I told 'em."

This is the end of my thoughts and conclusions on the subject of leadership. One more chapter remains—the Epilogue.

CHAPTER SIXTEEN

THE EPILOGUE—
IN MY GARDEN

THE BOOK, my thoughts on leadership, was finished. There would be, of course, a need to read the chapters carefully for errors and repetitions; but in the main the task was completed and my thoughts committed to paper. There remained this last chapter, the Epilogue, and I went out to my garden one hot summer afternoon to ponder on how to write it—hoping that silent musings would show me the way, as has so often happened in the past.

I love my garden; it is entirely my own creation, and has grown from a wet meadow full of weeds to its present state of beauty—with its carefully planned coloured foliage and flowering shrubs, the river, and mill stream.

The afternoon sun was hot and it was difficult to keep awake. I thought of my father and of the wise counsel he had given me, and I wished for his advice now about how to write this Epilogue. Suddenly I saw him. Yes, it was he—standing by the beds of red and white *spiraea* on the bank of the mill stream. When I was a boy all my youthful affection and love was given to my father; if ever there was a saint on this earth it was him, and there he was in my garden. I rose and crossed the lawn towards him, hoping eagerly for some conversation. Would he speak to me?

There was a look of great peace on his face. He was dressed in the clothes he always wore when tramping the hills in Donegal or fishing the mountain streams—a grey norfolk jacket and trousers and carrying a shepherd's staff or crook. He saw me and smiled; I did not approach closer, it was holy ground. Then he spoke:

"You have a lovely garden; it is different from ours in the old Irish home, better kept and tidier. But you were always neat and tidy in your habits and in your thinking, and that has helped you in your military life. I have watched your career as a soldier. I did once hope you would join me in the Church, but I have no regrets; you chose well and you reached the top of your profession. Have you always been happy?"

"Yes, Father, very happy. But at times it has not been easy. I have learned that he who achieves a degree of military fame is often misunderstood; but he must put up with it all, even when it is hard to bear. I have tried to do my duty and have never been afraid to say what I believe to be right, and to stand firm in that belief—but it has often got me into trouble."

"I know, my son. There have been moments when I wondered if you would surmount all the difficulties which beset you—but you did, helped by your Christian faith. I am proud of you; and, you, I know, are proud of your son, which gives me great pleasure. Your grandchildren in their turn will, I hope, keep up the family tradition of service and duty."

The old man looked as if he was about to move on, and I moved a step closer to him.

"Father," I said, "stay with me a while and give me some words of wisdom from your world to strengthen me in my remaining years in this world."

He turned towards me.

"My son, I am not permitted to stay long. I would say this to you. There is much talk the world over about freedoms. But there is only one positive freedom—the freedom to choose between good and evil. And the best definition of that little understood word is:

'whose service is perfect freedom.'

After two thousand years, He lives. For many years the Romans tried to stamp out His memory; it was of no avail; He cannot be killed. For myself, when I was with you I used to feel I was a weak vessel in His strong hands.

"When I survey your world to-day I am sometimes anxious about the younger generation; they have temptations you and I didn't have. They seem to mature earlier, but do so in an insecure world; they tend to place a high value on material things and to neglect spiritual values. They must continually remember that life is an education mainly that it may also be a service—to others. For them, too, life is a struggle; the great problems, the great trials, the great temptations, go on continuously, and a young man has to be well armed in the spiritual sense if he is not to be swept downstream.

"I was watching you once when you said that true freedom is having the liberty to do what you ought, and not what you want; that is very true. The great problem which faces a boy is reconciling what he wants to do with what he knows in his heart he ought to do; his choice is free, only he can decide, but he needs help—by daily prayer, and from others like yourself. It rejoices me to see how much of your life is spent in helping young people; continue in that way because they need it in your world to-day."

The old man paused and looked towards the house.

"You have a nice home. May I go inside and see the family portraits? I must leave you now and will go alone. God bless you, my son."

I wanted desperately to ask one more question.

"Father, just tell me this—my Betty, is she in the garden?"

He smiled and moved down the path, past the lavender bushes and the pigeon cote towards the front door, and he disappeared from view behind a pyrus tree.

Then something seemed to happen in the garden and I longed to see what it could be. There was a slight breeze, and a stir, too, among the shrubs—not like the whispering of leaves in the wind but more human, as though they murmured in their own language. And I thought I saw figures of people, shadowy figures which I could not see clearly.

Was my wife, my darling Betty, in the garden? I hurried down the grass paths between the beds, along the river bank, through the orchard, but could not see her—and I knew that I must wait yet awhile.

And then a great stillness fell, a silence to be felt; but there was nothing to be seen except the beds and shrubs. At first I was unhappy. But I soon became content; for I knew that for us here in this life it must be, it ought to be, a life of faith—with just now and then an uplifting message by a word, a dream, a look, an event.

And I awoke, and lo! I had been dreaming. But I was happy, and I hoped that such a dream, mingled with memories of the father I had so worshipped in his lifetime, might give me strength for the remaining years of my life.

And I went indoors to my study and wrote it all down—as the Epilogue.

THE END

COLLIER LIBRARY
FLORENCE STATE COLLEGE
FLORENCE, ALABAMA

DATE DUE			
DEC 5			
GAYLORD			PRINTED IN U.S.A.